D0582021

By the same author

Tintin: 60 Years of Adventure

as translator
Tintin and the World of Hergé
Hergé and Tintin, Reporters

To Eileen and Len,
     Remembering happy
Days in Bonn and now
   in Cheltenham
       With very best wishes,
     and love
Michael Farr
       Michael   8.9.93

VANISHING BORDERS

The Rediscovery of Eastern Germany, Poland and Bohemia

VIKING

VIKING

Published by the Penguin Group
Penguin Books Ltd, 27 Wrights Lane, London W8 5TZ, England
Penguin Books USA Inc., 375 Hudson Street, New York, New York 10014, USA
Penguin Books Australia Ltd, Ringwood, Victoria, Australia
Penguin Books Canada Ltd, 10 Alcorn Avenue, Toronto, Ontario, Canada M4V 3B2
Penguin Books (NZ) Ltd, 182–190 Wairau Road, Auckland 10, New Zealand

Penguin Books Ltd, Registered Offices: Harmondsworth, Middlesex, England

First published 1991
1 3 5 7 9 10 8 6 4 2

Copyright © Michael Farr, 1991
The moral right of the author has been asserted

All rights reserved.
Without limiting the rights under copyright
reserved above, no part of this publication may be
reproduced, stored in or introduced into a retrieval system,
or transmitted, in any form or by any means (electronic, mechanical,
photocopying, recording or otherwise), without the prior
written permission of both the copyright owner and
the above publisher of this book

Printed in England by Clays Ltd, St Ives plc
Set in 11/13½ pt Lasercomp Sabon

A CIP catalogue record for this book is available from the British Library

ISBN 0–670–83522–6

For Anna
and
Emma-Victoria

Contents

Contents

List of Illustrations

Acknowledgements

This book could hardly have been written without the strategic backing of the newspapers for which I was privileged to report during a decade of historic change in Germany and its eastern neighbours, Poland and Czechoslovakia. Certain individuals played decisive roles at particular times. William Readman, former foreign news editor of *The Daily Telegraph*, alone among Fleet Street deskmen saw the broader significance of the landmark Güstrow meeting between Helmut Schmidt and Erich Honecker. He ensured as the paper was 'going to bed' on a Sunday night reverberating from the declaration of martial law in Poland that the news of the frosty German encounter was given its proper prominence. Similarly, just over three years later another *Telegraph* stalwart, former deputy foreign editor John Dudman, sensed the reader interest in the return to Colditz forty years on of its former inmates and kept a precarious telephone line to Leipzig open on a Sunday morning – as well as half a page in the paper.

I would also like to thank Paul Webster, foreign editor of *The Guardian*, and Martin Woollacott, a distinguished predecessor, for encouraging more recent travels in eastern Germany.

Touring Colditz with that redoubtable band of men who had tried everything to escape its cold confines and ceaselessly and courageously harassed their Nazi guards was for me very near to the fulfilment of a childhood dream. Like many other schoolboys I had numbered Pat Reid and his fellow officers among my heroes. And as a journalist I can think of no story that I enjoyed reporting more than their boisterous return to Colditz. I am grateful to Pat Reid and his comrades in arms

Acknowledgements

for their recollections on that cold April day. I asked him then about further 'team visits' and he shook his head and spoke of mortality. Five years later, on the very afternoon I was finishing this book's chapter on Colditz, news came of his death, aged seventy-nine. Mortal they may be, but the exploits of the men of Colditz have become legendary.

As long as the Iron Curtain remained, forays in Eastern Europe were, however fascinating, always arduous. The key to success, quite apart from enjoyment, would rest with one's travelling companion. In this very special respect I would like to pay tribute to David Smeeton of the BBC, with whom I would confidently travel through hell and high water – and enjoy it. Richard Bassett has a surer feel of Eastern Europe than any contemporary writer and I can think of no better or more inspiring companion. John Nicholson, now looking after concert artists across Europe, was solidly dependable – unless distracted by a Bohemian discothèque – Stephen Baxter always eager and enthusiastic. The greatest encouragement and support inevitably came from my wife, who, as Anna Tomforde, has been *The Guardian*'s correspondent in Germany since 1982 and who before, on and after the momentous night the Berlin Wall was breached reported the decline and collapse of communism in the East.

I would also like to give special thanks to the oldest of family friends, Olga Jelínková, for the many insights she has given me into her beloved Prague, truly the 'Golden City'. No one helped me on research more willingly or tirelessly than Stefanie Jordan, with the benefit of her unique and varied library. Finally, I am indebted to Christoph Jaschke for his invaluable assistance in preparing the manuscript, and to Roger Wilde for his photography.

Michael Farr
Bonn, 1991

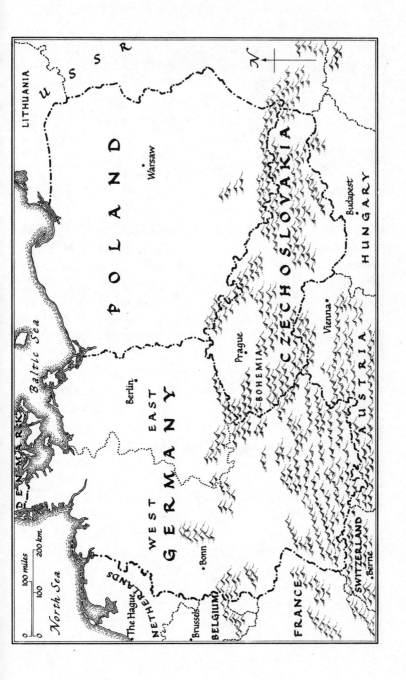

Introduction

In the venerable episcopal city of Trier, on Germany's western frontier with Luxembourg and France, is the house where Karl Marx was born in 1818. At a time when his ideas were more in vogue, it was transformed into a museum charting the life of one of communism's founding fathers, a place of pilgrimage for Marxists. When finally after much political procrastination Erich Honecker, the erstwhile East German leader, visited capitalist West Germany in September 1987, he included the Marx house in his itinerary and confidently declared, 'A world without Marx is inconceivable.' Exactly two years and one month later Honecker was toppled and communism's rapid demise was under way in Eastern Europe: a 'domino theory' in reverse. In March 1990, the month of East Germany's first free elections, which so conclusively rejected communism, a visitor from the eastern city of Erfurt wrote in the Marx house's visitors' book: 'Luckily you didn't have to experience forty years of East German socialism.'

The forty-year-long chapter of communist rule in eastern Germany had begun with a Stalinist purge that among its excesses included the execution of political prisoners in Dresden gaol using the same guillotine employed by the Nazis. Several of Hitler's notorious concentration camps were re-opened to accommodate those considered by the communists to be politically suspect. Many were never to be seen again. Their bleached skulls and bones were discovered after the revolution in mass graves in Brandenburg's woodland.

The communist state was built on an extraordinarily thorough and very German secret police network, where every citizen was expected to spy and report on neighbours or colleagues, where even church confessionals were bugged for indiscretions. The dreaded Stasi (Staatssicherheitsdienst, or State Security Service) learned from the example of the Gestapo and, though at the other ideological extreme, could be quite as evil. German totalitarianism had for the unfortunate people of East Germany merely taken on a different complexion. It meant, in effect, that they had to live through dictatorships lasting from 1933 to 1990, something their compatriots in the prosperous west of Germany, whose experience was limited to twelve years of fascism, often found hard to comprehend.

Compared with the West, East Germans were backward: economically some twenty-five years behind, according to studies, with their economy corresponding at best to West Germany's in the mid-1960s. The country's infrastructure was often even more dated, having been left unchanged and uncared for since the 1930s. War damage remained widespread, as in Dresden or Berlin, and cobwebs of utter neglect shrouded the provinces. Communist funds were narrowly and ideologically allocated towards environmentally destructive open-cast mining and heavy industry, leaving whole cities and regions to fall into decay. Paint and plaster last applied before the war were allowed to curl, flake and crack on many old houses and historic buildings which nevertheless were fortunate to be left standing. Private investment and an urgent desire for swift progress married to profit had not always been so tolerant in the West. The listing of historic buildings frequently came too late. In the East gigantic grey concrete complexes of uniform, anonymous workers' flats became the unloved, soulless socialist housing norm.

The priority given to basic industries and the productivity targets of the five-year plans had no regard for the environment, which suffered chronically and often tragically here as elsewhere in Eastern Europe. During the revolution in

Wittenberg, where Luther had preached reformation and nailed his ninety-five theses to the door of the castle church, an off-duty railway worker clutched a bottle of beer from which he quenched his thirst at regular intervals and told how pollution was 'one of our main worries'. He related how 'the city's coat of arms includes a fish, but the river Elbe is now so polluted that no fish can survive'. The incidence of cancers and heart disease was well above the western average. The very young and old were particularly at risk, and it came as no surprise to learn after the revolution that West Germans could expect to live two years longer than East Germans.

Backwardness could extend to medicine. There was Otto Baudisch with his turn of the century dental surgery in the northern East German city of Schwerin. One of only 460 private practitioners among the communist state's 12,000 dentists, he boasted that he still charged 'only 5 marks for a repair, 15 marks to replace a tooth and 120 marks for a complete set of dentures – rates unchanged since the guidelines published by the Prussian state in 1924'. The almost eighty-year-old Baudisch, Schwerin's last private dentist to practise under communism, though hardly rich on the proceeds, could bank on more than enough patients because of the often month-long waiting lists for treatment at state clinics – and this despite the fact that he was no believer in painkillers, which had led, he admitted, to his being known as 'gruesome Otto'.

And then there were the numerous barbers and hairdressing parlours, an East German peculiarity. In Güstrow, a town of only 36,500 inhabitants still locked in its sixteenth- and seventeenth-century past, some fifteen such establishments could be counted in its centre, offering cuts, washes and perms for only a mark or two. A worker from the local Nordkristall sugar factory and his wife explained that because of a lack of hot water and other facilities, it would be most unusual to do one's hair at home. 'And with prices so low, why bother? It is part of our life.' But it was a life, an old-fashioned one, which the vast majority of East Germans chose to leave behind when they opted for unification, capitalism and free competition. The barbers soon began to be turned into boutiques, the needlework shops into banks.

As in a Perrault fairy tale, eastern Germany, along with its East European neighbours, Poland and Czechoslovakia, was waking from a long dream which had been a nightmare for many. It was time, the people believed, for the cobwebs and dust to be brushed aside and for good to take the place of evil. While those in the East craved for western freedom of choice, to those in the West a long-forgotten cultural inheritance was suddenly revealed east of the Elbe. The cradle of German history and culture was waiting to be rediscovered in what had been Prussia, Brandenburg, Saxony and Thuringia. While the pace of revolution was being forced by the mass exodus of East Germans westwards via Hungary, Czecho-slovakia and Poland, a wag hung a sign on the famous double statue of Goethe and Schiller outside the National Theatre in Weimar. 'Wir bleiben hier!' (We're staying here!) it said simply.

Borders started vanishing: the cruel divide between the two Germanys, which for years had been marked by guard towers, searchlights, trip-wires, dogs and minefields, was torn down with glee, leaving a barren scar as a memory. The Cold War was over, the oppressive Iron Curtain had been lifted. The most poignant symbol of Europe's division – the Berlin Wall – was cut and chipped away to be auctioned and sold as art work.

In January 1991 Polish border guards took away the un-crowned eagle of communism from frontier markers, only to replace it a few days later with the properly crowned national emblem. In newly democratic Czechoslovakia, the popular playwright–president Václav Havel declared that it was 'heraldic nonsense' for the Czech lion to have a communist star above its head and it was just a matter of time before Bohemia's heraldic beast had its majesty restored.

Meanwhile, always enterprising Poles found a way of making money out of Marx. With only a few strokes of the brush, artists managed to convert unsaleable portraits of Karl Marx into depictions of St Joseph, the patron saint of workers – and in time for his feast day on 19 March. In another initiative that successfully matched capitalism with religion, unwanted volumes of the complete works of Marx, Engels and Lenin were bought in bulk at knock-down prices and their quality bindings reused profitably for hymn- and prayer-book covers. The Polish people's solid faith in religion – Marx's 'opium for the masses' – was clearly more durable than any transitory belief in Marxist theory.

East Germans could also respond quickly to the rapid gear change from communism to capitalism. In the northern port of Rostock the fleet of Volvo limousines which had made up the Stasi car pool used by Erich Honecker and other members of the communist leadership soon became available for private functions and weddings at fifty marks per hour. Similarly, the luxuriously and specially furnished government train which was built in 1960 and had its own cinema, conference and dance carriages, quite apart from sleeping and restaurant cars, became available for hire – 'Travel like the Red Prussians' ran the advertisement.

Perhaps the most remarkable transition was made by a previously secret East Berlin factory which had been making sophisticated listening devices for the secret police. A few months after the revolution it adapted its production line to the manufacture of deaf-aids. 'You can be sure our hearing-aids will be a success,' joked one worker; 'you will be able to pick up what someone is saying in another block!'

Introduction

One lesson learned during ten years as a foreign correspond-ent based in Germany with the always fascinating opportunity of regular travel eastwards was the historical incongruity of the communist experiment in the longer term. Its sudden end during the amazing autumn of 1989 came sooner than the boldest would have dared guess: a tribute to the people of Eastern Europe, their courage and their long, common past, but also to Soviet realism. Cultural and historical links tradi-tionally bridged borders in Central Europe and once again they had free play. How absurd it was for the communists to have hijacked the chief protagonists of German history and art and claimed them for their own. How could Goethe, born in Frankfurt-on-Main, a student in Leipzig before becoming Weimar's most distinguished courtier and a *habitué* of the Bohemian spas, be fitted into a communist context? Or Frederick the Great? By anyone's account he was a cultured despot whose expansionist policies and invention of the blitzkrieg altered the map of eighteenth-century Europe, yet he was rehabilitated by the communists in 1980. Or Augustus the Strong of Saxony? A warrior too, but also an incorrigible womanizer, collector and connoisseur who after converting to Catholicism took the crown of Poland and, transforming Dresden into the 'Florence of the Elbe', sought to emulate France's 'Sun King', Louis XIV. The communists' adoption of Luther, for whom the Politburo declared 1983, the 500th anniversary of his birth, 'Luther Year' and struck commemorative coins and Meissen medallions, was espe-cially ridiculous. He would have railed as much at the corruption of the communist hierarchy as against Roman indulgences.

Yet the cultural and historic heart of Germany had always beat in the East, whether with Saxony's formidable elector, with Frederick the Great in Berlin and Potsdam, Goethe in Weimar or earlier, with Luther's relentless preaching of reform in Wittenberg and Johann Sebastian Bach's colossal musical achievement in Leipzig.

In the following chapters I have tried to portray the rich fabric of the past against which the revolutions in eastern Germany and its East European neighbours were set but which may have been glossed over in the initial euphoria. Drawing on personal experiences and encounters, I have endeavoured to present a picture of people and places before, during and after the overthrow of communist rule. I have looked east of the Oder–Neisse since German history is also Europe's and over centuries has affected none more than Poland and Bohemia. Before the excesses of this century, Augustus the Strong ascended the Polish throne, Frederick the Great ravaged Silesia and Goethe sought reinvigoration in the Bohemian spas. I have included a chapter on Colditz, a name which is today better known in Britain than in Germany, as a reminder of a dark yet inspiring episode in modern German history and the indomitable Allied spirit, which the chilling castle so signally failed to suppress.

Finally, I would like to add the reassuring if hardly startling finding of Günther Drosdowski, editor of the standard Duden dictionary, that after more than forty years of division East and West Germans still shared broadly the same vocabulary and spoke the language of Luther and Goethe. 'After forty years of division, the German language is almost the same here and over there,' he told a Munich Press conference with the utmost seriousness. There was then really no remaining hurdle to the rediscovery of the East.

Part 1

THE WORKERS' AND PEASANTS' STATE

1 Hunting at the Werbellinsee, the Other Berlin and Güstrow in the Dark Days

Hidden deep in the forests north-east of Berlin is a small castle or hunting lodge, Schloss Hubertusstock. Appropriately named after the patron saint of hunting – St Hubert, who, cornering his quarry one day long ago, saw a vision of the crucified Christ between the stag's antlers – it has long been a favourite retreat of German leaders. The hauntingly beautiful Werbellinsee lake, once replete with fish and framed by pine forests rich in deer, already attracted the attention of the early electors of Brandenburg. The later Hohenzollerns built Hubertusstock as a modest residence, filling it with heavy country furniture and covering the walls with antlers and trophies preserved by their best taxidermists.

Theodor Fontane in his *Wanderungen durch die Mark Brandenburg* likened the tally of game here to 'a military parade'. The Hohenzollerns brought their guests to Werbellin on gala days to show just how good the hunting was in the Mark Brandenburg. According to Fontane, the Werbellin forests contained some three thousand deer, the largest concentration in one area anywhere in the world. And in the rutting season, between the middle of September and mid-October, a thousand more 'wandering stags' would come a hundred miles from far-flung corners of the Prussian domain – from Pomerania, Silesia, East Prussia and Poland. Starved of female deer in their north-eastern forests, the stags trekked the long journey westwards to the banks of the Werbellinsee. Local people would speak of the 'Konvivium' lakeside rendezvous; only the fittest beasts made it and then, battling heroically among each other – Pole against East Prussian, Silesian versus Pomeranian – would all too often let the local stags secure the female prize.

The cool, clear waters of the Werbellinsee, full of fat Moray eels, considered a delicacy by the Romans, were especially good for fishing. In 1565 Elector Joachim wrote to the governor (Magistrat) of Neustadt-Eberswalde instructing him 'to catch as many Moray eels and carp, such as can only be found at Werbellin, and bring them to the elector's kitchens with two horses and a wagon'. Almost three hundred years later, however, the arrival via the Baltic coast of cormorants, birds that originated in Japan and China, was to put an end to these delicious-tasting fish. Soon, Fontane relates, 'there were as many cormorants as flies in a farmer's living-room'. Foresters suffered too as some trees were weighed down by up to ten cormorant nests. Action had to be taken, so foresters and gamekeepers from all around the region, as well as the best sharpshooters from a Guards battalion based in Potsdam, came to blast the birds away. This they did with notable success and the cormorant did not return, but nor, alas, did the Moray eels.

East Germans today are avid anglers and while hunting remained the preserve of the privileged classes – even under communism – the less exalted would continue to test the waters of the Werbellinsee for carp, pike and perch. Angling was the ordinary man's pleasure, an escape from the obligatory group activities of communism, an opportunity for the individual to maintain some contact with nature in a heavily industrialized and organized society.

During that darkest of German chapters, the twelve years of

Nazi rule, Hermann Goering, the vain and high-living Luftwaffe commander, loved to come to the Werbellinsee to shoot deer on an absurdly immodest scale. So richly stocked were the woods here that hunting was never a sport. But then for all his pretensions, Goering could hardly pass as a true sportsman.

One of the perhaps surprising weaknesses of the brood of communist leaders that emerged in the years following the Second World War was their common partiality for hardly 'egalitarian' blood sports. Russia's Brezhnev, Yugoslavia's Tito, Romania's Ceauşescu and East Germany's Honecker loved shooting, and used every opportunity to invite each other to hunting parties where affairs of state could be discussed. During the 1970s and 1980s a form of 'hunt diplomacy' developed among those leaders of Eastern Europe who were still on speaking terms. Soon after East Germany's 1989 revolution and Honecker's overthrow, astounded citizens found among the guns and trophies stored at Honecker's several hunting retreats a portrait of the bespectacled miner's son painted on a stretched boar's hide – a gift from 'a fraternal leader'. Western statesmen had been careful to cultivate a different image, at least ever since 13 August 1961 when the Berlin Wall suddenly went up and Harold Macmillan, the British premier, was out of contact on a grouse moor and the American president, John F. Kennedy, was out of port, sailing on his dinghy.

In December 1981 the then West German chancellor, Helmut Schmidt, arrived at Schloss Hubertusstock for the first inter-German summit meeting for more than ten years; he was not especially impressed by its hunting possibilities or Erich Honecker's much vaunted prowess with a gun. Schmidt was a man of very different interests, preferring to play Bach, Mozart and Brahms on the piano (more than competently, as demonstrated by two commercial recordings) and to gaze at the works of German expressionists with which he decorated his Chancellery. He would punctuate his conversation by – rather ostentatiously – taking regular pinches of snuff, a habit acquired to curb his previous chain-smoking of cigarettes. Honecker, a more austere figure, had been a hardened communist since his boyhood and had spent the Nazi years in prison. Schmidt had a good war, rising to the rank of lieutenant. The two men could only have been brought together by matters of state.

And so as outside the snow fell steadily, they talked, occasionally drinking fruit juice, constantly surrounded by Schloss Hubertusstock's array of hunting trophies. Honecker's authoritarian grip on his country was at its firmest. Moscow's most loyal ally was economically the most successful of the Comecon trading group, exchanging high-quality machinery and technology for Soviet oil and raw materials. It had a comprehensive secret service, the Stasi, and a well trained and equipped army and, through a diplomatic offensive supported by undisputed superiority in sport and the arts, was striving desperately to gain the full international recognition it had always been denied.

Schmidt's task was that of every recent West German chancellor: to try to wring concessions that would improve the lot of East Germans, so artificially separated from the West, and that would increase contacts between Germans on either side of the border. In return, he could offer the one thing West Germany had plenty of – money. By bridging differences between the two Germanys, he could also try to reduce broader East–West tension, which had mounted considerably since the 1979–80 Soviet invasion of Afghanistan and the western decision to press ahead with a new generation of missiles to offset the growing Russian medium-range rocket arsenal.

But other storm clouds were massing that were to bring fundamental change eight years later. The unofficial trade union Solidarity, born in the shipyards of Gdańsk, had caught Poland's imagination and was proving a very real opposition movement. Fears of Russian intervention grew daily; a 'Warsaw 1981' was widely expected to follow the precedent of 'Prague 1968' when Soviet tanks had last crushed a departure from Moscow-dictated communist orthodoxy in Eastern Europe. Honecker himself was intensely worried that the progressive and independent thinking displayed by Solidarity in Poland could spill over the border and infect his own people. Possession of a Solidarity badge or sticker was pounced on by the Stasi and considered sufficient grounds for arrest and conviction for 'anti-state activity'.

On the very day that Honecker and Schmidt wound up their talks at the Werbellinsee and the first stage of their summit, 'Warsaw 1981' happened. But it was Polish not Russian tanks that rumbled through the streets of the principal cities. General Jaruzelski, a stiff, corseted cavalry officer, had decided to introduce martial law himself and clamp down on Solidarity before the Russians did. This time, unlike in Prague in August 1968, Warsaw Pact allies were not called in. East Germany's crack regiments, ready 'to defend socialism', remained in barracks.

Clearly Honecker had known of Jaruzelski's impending move and equally obviously Schmidt and western intelligence were caught by surprise that Saturday night. It was a tense ending to their first round of talks and the press conference given by Schmidt in the local town hall the following morning was, not surprisingly, preoccupied with Poland rather than any inter-German breakthrough, which anyway had not materialized. The Cold War was as frosty as the weather outside and, in the back of Honecker's Volvo limousine, the two leaders endeavoured uneasily to maintain a dialogue all the way north to the city of Güstrow and the final stage of their summit.

*

A horde of hundreds of journalists from East and West had descended on East Berlin two or three days before, to an unusually hospitable welcome. This was one of those few official occasions when most western journalists were readily given visas, presumably in the hope – in practice unlikely – that they would generate some positive publicity. Most of us were put up in the Metropol Hotel, near the Friedrichstrasse station, which was then East Berlin's most modern hard-currency hotel. Indeed one distinct advantage for the hard-currency hungry authorities was that the journalists who came on such occasions brought plenty of dollars and marks to pay for their rooms, highly priced telephone calls, meals and gifts to take home. The first floor of the hotel had a fine display of Meissen porcelain for sale, of course only for hard currency. There were also books and a good choice of classical music recordings. The restaurant, decorated with a compelling wall-painting showing scenes from Berlin night-life in the 1920s (sadly since replaced by more modern black and chrome screens), offered unusually good food for East Berlin at predictably high, hard-currency prices.

The Metropol also gave a sinister insight into how the Stasi monitored foreign guests. Every corridor had an eye, a camera aperture which watched day and night. Each room was bugged around the clock. 'Hostesses', over dressed and made-up, but certainly not unattractive, lingered at the first-floor bar for their prey. As in every similar hotel in Eastern Europe and Russia, these were prostitutes trained and employed by the secret service to compromise westerners. A few drinks and a promise of fifty marks would be enough for acceptance of an invitation upstairs, quickly and damagingly followed by the Stasi photographers. Each floor had a room reserved for a Stasi 'operative' who maintained a constant vigil. Finally in January 1990, three months after the peaceful October revolution that toppled Erich Honecker, East Berlin's main hotels closed for three days for them to be 'debugged' and for Stasi rooms to be reconverted for normal use.

There was no doubt that East Germany's 130,000 full-time Stasi agents kept their eyes and ears open as effectively as Hitler's dreaded Gestapo had during the Nazi years.

David Smeeton had been the BBC's Bonn correspondent for just over nine months and was making one of his first trips to East Berlin to cover the Schmidt–Honecker summit meeting. Unfortunately, outside the Metropol, as we were about to board the Press bus that was to take us to the Werbellinsee, he slipped on the snow-covered pavement and fell heavily, banging his Uher tape recorder hard on the ground. Worried that it might have been damaged, he decided to test a tape there and then and to the astonishment of the passing Christmas shoppers played back a statement by the West German chancellor. A crowd quickly gathered and only a couple of minutes passed before David was hustled on to the bus by two Stasi men in black leather coats who had taken him for a troublemaker.

Two months earlier I had been denied a work visa to cross to East Berlin to report the annual 7 October parade marking the founding of the communist German state, but decided to try to go over on a day tourist visa. I took a taxi to Checkpoint Charlie, one of the most poignant symbols of the Cold War. An East German border guard peering through a pair of binoculars watched as I paid the taxi driver and disembarked to cross the last few yards on foot, past the sign 'You are now leaving the American sector', into the chillier East. Entering one of the Nissen-type sheds, I joined a queue of tourists waiting to be vetted and approved by unsmiling border officials sitting behind glass panes in cramped cubicles. Several youths with long hair and studded leather jackets were turned back without understanding why. The queue moved up a few places and a sallow-faced young officer took the next passport, studied the photograph minutely and then glared at the subject, front and, using the mirror hanging behind, back. 'Why do you want to visit the capital of the GDR? You know today is a special day,' the pale-green-shirted guard asked me. I confirmed that I knew it was and that I wanted to visit a couple of museums, look around and perhaps go to the classical music shop on the Alexanderplatz. There was a pause as he glanced at a list and then picked up the telephone. A border guard captain then poked his head through the side of the cubicle. More consultation.

'But you are a journalist?' I was then asked.

'Yes, I would like to visit East Berlin for the day.'

'But you will not be working?'

'No, I will not be working.'

The interrogation ended satisfactorily with my being asked for five marks for the day visa. The door buzzed, sprang open and I moved on to the next hurdle, the customs. It was like a game, I thought, like snakes and ladders. Will I throw the right number to move forward, or will I slide back again? Next I had to go through the compulsory exchange of twenty-five Deutsche Marks for the same number of Ostmarks, worth only a quarter as much. That was painless, but the customs procedure was less of a formality. 'Do you have any western newspapers? Any books? Are you bringing any gifts?' I was asked to empty my wallet to see if its contents tallied with the currency statement I had filled in. On a later occasion a particularly aggressive official found one unaccounted Ostmark in one of my jacket pockets and ordered me into a small room to undress. After I had taken most of my clothes off, he insisted that I should also remove my socks. His disappointment at not uncovering a currency smuggler did not make him any more agreeable.

Communism in East Germany was an unyielding blend of German order and thoroughness. Diplomats used to say that it would be the last of the East European communist systems to be swept away. But only eight years later it was in the vanguard of the East European revolutions, a victim of its own rigidity.

Leaving the labyrinth of Checkpoint Charlie, I breathed a sigh of relief as I walked to the Leipzigerstrasse and waited for the men depicted on the pedestrian light to turn from red to green – only in East Berlin do they wear Homburg hats. The lignite-laden air had the distinctive smell of Eastern Europe. Blindfolded, one could be deposited anywhere in Eastern Europe and identify it immediately from this smell, I thought. A few hundred yards away, across the Berlin Wall in the West, this cloying odour no longer existed.

I had only gone a short distance down the Friedrichstrasse when I sensed something else which was then peculiar to Eastern Europe: the feeling of being followed. I continued on my way, noting the red flags and banners with their slogans in praise of socialism hanging from the windows, the portraits of the three mentors of German communism: Marx, Engels and Lenin.

Turning right into what was still Berlin's finest street, the lime-tree lined Unter den Linden, I walked towards the central Alexanderplatz: past the university, elegantly housed in the Prinz Heinrich Palais, which was built for a brother of Frederick the Great, then Schinkel's perfectly composed Neue Wache with a pair of jackbooted, steel-helmeted sentries on guard outside, and the stately opera house opposite built by Knobelsdorff for the music-loving Frederick. Both Knobelsdorff and Schinkel variously had a hand in the mighty Arsenal building (Zeughaus), best known for the series of sculpted medallions of dying warriors by Andreas Schlüter which adorn the courtyard. This was now the Museum of German History, offering a strongly Marxist interpretation from prehistoric times to the present. If I was being followed, and in view of my declared intention of visiting a museum or two, this was the ideal opportunity.

Before the war the Arsenal had suitably contained a collection of uniforms and weapons; there were still some of both, but its character was now social rather than military. The oppression and struggle of the proletariat were vividly described, through the Middle Ages, the Reformation and the Thirty Years War to the so-called Age of Enlightenment, the years of bourgeois prosperity, industrial growth, war and world revolution. The horrors of Nazi rule were graphically portrayed, the emphasis being more on the violence directed against communists and socialists, and neighbouring 'socialist' countries, than on the systematic extermination of the Jews. The final section was devoted to the brief history of East Germany, portrayed as constantly under threat from the capitalist West but staunchly protected by its Soviet ally, to which it was indebted for its liberation from fascism. Most curious and interesting were the explanations for the sudden erection of the Berlin Wall in August 1961 as 'an anti-fascist barrier'. This extraordinary operation was masterminded by Erich Honecker, who was then the Politburo member responsible for security under state and party leader Walter Ulbricht.

I came away with a slightly improved understanding of the East German communist mentality, and the feeling of being followed had definitely diminished.

Crossing the Marx-Engels-Brücke, previously known as the Schlossbrücke since it had led to the royal palace, I arrived by the Lustgarten. On the left was Schinkel's great masterpiece, the severely classical Altes Museum with its imposing Ionic colonnade, and opposite lay the bombastic turn of the century cathedral, a vulgar Wilhelmine attempt at creating London's St Paul's or Rome's St Peter's in the heart of Berlin. A more modest but elegant cathedral, which Schinkel had reworked in the 1820s, had sadly been demolished for its sake.

But the communists, who later with some justification boasted of their painstaking restoration of some of East Berlin's finest historic buildings, could also be architectural vandals. They did not hesitate before razing the bomb-damaged royal palace on the other side of the road. As a symbol of oppression by the ruling classes, it had no place in the newly founded socialist society; only a portal and the balcony above, from which Karl Liebknecht preached revolution in November 1918, were saved and later reincorporated in the nearby Staatsrat building, an unusually harmonious modern structure dating from 1962. On the site of the royal residence a new palace was raised, the Palace of the Republic, a vast cube notable for its generous use of brown reflective glass, which as well as having a huge auditorium for cultural and sporting events housed the Volkskammer, communism's rubber-stamp parliament.

Progressing on, I passed the site by the river Spree where building of a new luxury hotel, the Palast, was well advanced. This too was to overindulge in reflective glass, mirroring the heavy dome of the cathedral at various angles. The Palast was to supersede the Metropol as East Berlin's premier, hard-currency earning hotel, only to lose this particular distinction at the end of the decade with the opening of the more traditional Grand Hotel. The Grand alone could make any claim to be some sort of a successor to the fabled Adlon, which before its wartime destruction ruled supreme among Berlin hotels from its splendid situation on Unter den Linden near the Brandenburg Gate.

At last I had reached the Alexanderplatz, which, under communism, had become the unattractive concrete heart of the city. Big brother was symbolized by the soaring television tower built on a former cemetery. On a sunny day, Berliners loved to relate, the light formed a cross on the great shiny ball of the tower, proving God's superiority to atheist man. Meant to be daringly modern in the 1960s and 1970s, the block-like grey and glass buildings, relieved only by brightly coloured socialist slogans and signs, had quickly dated. Among this Lego-land of bad taste, only the Marienkirche, a fine Gothic church – Berlin's second oldest – with a tasteful eighteenth-century tower by Langhans, better known as the creator of the Brandenburg Gate, stood for more enduring architectural values.

The Karl-Marx-Allee, previously the Grosse Frankfurter-strasse, cut across and it was here that the podium was raised for Erich Honecker and the die-hards of the communist leadership to salute the passing troops and ranks of uniformed 'factory militia' that afternoon. The 7 October march past violated the city's demilitarized status under the Four Power regulations laid down by the wartime Allies, which allowed only their troops to be visible in Berlin, and every year the British, American and French commandants issued a joint note of protest that was studiously ignored. Post-war Berlin was a complex place with strange rites.

Scarlet banners and East German flags, with a hammer and divider superimposed on the red, black and gold, hung in abundance from the windows of the box-like flats, whose construction for party functionaries sparked the June 1953 workers' uprising, the first of the East European revolts to be bloodily suppressed by Russian tanks.

Turning back, I passed the record shop on the corner of the Alexanderplatz, which was to become a favourite haunt of mine, but found it closed for the holiday. Full of good-quality classical recordings costing a uniform 12.10 Ostmarks, I used to bank on buying two records to use up the 25 marks which could not be taken back to the West. Instead I decided to wait for a place in a subterranean beer restaurant on the Alexander-platz. There for 8.10 marks I could lunch on a piece of pork with red cabbage and potatoes, accompanied by a glass of beer for another mark. As was invariably the rule, I was placed at a table by a taciturn waitress and eyed discreetly by the other guests. Conversation was impossible, for contact with a westerner was sure to be misunderstood by the ever watchful Stasi and was not to be risked.

Lunch cannot last long under such circumstances and I was soon on my way, returning along Unter den Linden with a stop at Stüler's conventionally neo-classical National Gallery building, dating from the 1860s, tucked away behind the greater perfection of Schinkel's Altes Museum. The suavely worked white Carrara marble of the neo-classical statues in the hall pleased me, and I was heartened by the warmth of the old lady attendants who seemed as content in and as proud of their elegant environment as the avid connoisseurs and collectors who originally commissioned the works.

Leaving East Berlin at Checkpoint Charlie was also a more cheering experience. The border guards were waiting for me and had clearly had a satisfactory report from my invisible minder. I had not strayed from the harmless programme I had declared. Once satisfied that I was not taking any unspent East German money with me and had not disposed illegally of any of the West German currency I was carrying, I was allowed through. My brief odyssey into East Berlin was over. I could return to my West Berlin office, watch the afternoon's parade on East German television and offer a detailed report to my newspaper.

It was going to be a race to get to the northern city of Güstrow in time after Chancellor Schmidt had concluded his Werbellin press conference. The steadily falling snow and icy conditions would not help. The overnight declaration of martial law in Poland added drama to the proceedings and the moment the press conference came to an end there was a rush for the door and a scramble for the cars parked outside. I was travelling with John Vinocur of *The New York Times* and Michael

Getler of the *Washington Post* in a powerful Mercedes. We got off to a good start. It was motorway, the same laid down by Hitler forty-five years earlier as part of his comprehensive Autobahn network, for most of the route. But the snow, driven hard by a relentless wind, slowed progress, reducing visibility to little more than twenty yards. Vinocur tried to maintain a steady speed, peering hard through the screen and stopping every so often to scrape the ice away. To pass time, we attempted to analyse the situation in Poland and its wider implications. We hardly foresaw how it was indirectly to lead to the liberation of Eastern Europe less than eight years on.

Vinocur, who was later to become editor of the *International Herald Tribune*, would have made a good rally driver; after one and a half hours it seemed we would reach Güstrow in good time. But just as the pressure lessened, we saw a police car across the road and were abruptly waved into a lay-by. The Volkspolizei had been given orders to close the road until further notice. The display of our accreditation made no difference. We returned to our discussion of Poland and compared our notes from the Schmidt Press conference.

Suddenly there was a wailing of sirens and a series of flashing lights as the official convoy accompanying the two German leaders swept by on the empty road. Another ten minutes passed and we were allowed to resume the race to Güstrow.

The city itself was sealed off and when, after a drive of three hours, we reached its outskirts, we had to park the car and transfer to a Press bus that would take us to the centre. By now it was mid-afternoon and frustratingly we had to wait longer until more journalists arrived to fill the bus.

When eventually the bus set out, we were offered a remarkable sight. Güstrow was a city preserved from the twentieth century; there were no modern buildings to be seen, just street after street of gabled houses, many from the sixteenth and seventeenth centuries in north German red brick, more from the eighteenth and nineteenth, but none from our own. The absence of modern buildings was matched by the empty streets. Under a thick blanket of snow Güstrow was more like a stage set, suitable for the reawakening scene from *The Sleeping Beauty*. There was even a fairy-tale turreted Renaissance castle, the seat until 1695 of the dukes of Mecklenburg. Blow away the cobwebs and you have a city exactly as it was a hundred years ago or more. Güstrow had been ravaged by fire and war in earlier times, but not recently. In 1945, when so much of Germany was laid waste, Russian troops took the city without a fight.

The bus parked near the post office and we disembarked to walk the short distance to the cathedral square, where Schmidt and Honecker were to emerge before going into the imposing red brick church. As we turned the corner the streets were suddenly filled with a mostly male crowd aged between about fifteen and fifty, four rows deep. They too, it transpired, had been brought in by bus from surrounding areas and were to a man Communist Party loyalists. While waiting, and to keep moving in the cold, we worked our way from one group to another, asking what they thought the significance of the inter-German summit was. Parrot-fashion they replied, 'to ensure world peace'. When we asked why they had come, they responded, 'to support comrade Honecker in his peace efforts'. But when questioned where they came from, not one admitted to being from Güstrow. In fact the local people had been excluded from the occasion. In 1970 the then chancellor, Willy Brandt, travelled to the East German city of Erfurt for the first inter-German summit and received a tumultuous welcome in the main square, which echoed to shouts of 'Willy! Willy!' The Stasi were in Güstrow to ensure there was not a repeat performance. This time when Schmidt, jauntily wearing his north German Prinz Heinrich cap, and Honecker, in an extravagant red fox-fur hat, left the Stadt Güstrow Hotel for the cathedral, three cheers went up, but not for the West German chancellor. 'Erich! Hoch! Hoch! Hoch!' the crowd bellowed loyally, and Honecker responded with a beaming smile and a confident wave.

The two diminutive men entered the great Gothic cathedral, completed in the fourteenth century, to be shown its sights. One of the reasons Güstrow had been selected for the second stage of the summit was its strong association with a favourite sculptor of Schmidt, Ernst Barlach, who lived there from 1910 until his death in 1938. Here in the cathedral Schmidt could admire a memorial to the dead of the First World War which Barlach had created in 1927 and which ten years later the Nazis branded as 'decadent art', took away and melted down to make guns. In 1952, from a second casting in Cologne, it was moulded anew and returned to Güstrow, an early example of cooperation between the divided Germanys. During his brief stop in the city Schmidt had also visited the small fifteenth-century Gertrudenkapelle, which in 1953 was converted into a memorial to the sculptor, displaying his works both inside the former funerary chapel and outside in the cemetery.

Schmidt's programme drew to a close with a short recital by the cathedral organist, a welcome chance to meditate. His party then moved on in haste to the railway station where the first inter-German summit for nearly eleven years ended with a platform farewell. The smiles did not reflect the reality. Buffeted about outside with the journalists, Klaus Bölling, Schmidt's representative in East Berlin who had accompanied the chancellor throughout, said the encounter had been fraught with tension, especially the drive to Güstrow.

Almost exactly eight years later, in the wake of the East German revolution, Schmidt returned to Güstrow on a private visit, which, he noted, 'would not this time be under the auspices of the Stasi'. A few days afterwards a display of black and white pictures appeared in the window of Kraschewski's photography shop near the cathedral. They showed the crowd of Güstrowers who came out to greet Schmidt now that they were free to do so. They held up placards that declared, 'This time the people of Güstrow welcome Helmut Schmidt' and 'Welcome former Chancellor Schmidt. On 13.12.1981 we were not allowed to stand here. Now we can finally walk again through all of Germany.'

2 *Leipzig and Torgau: The Acceptable Anniversary*

In April 1985 Leipzig was still politically a dormant volcano. The omnipresent Stasi were in total control in their ugly concrete pile in the Grosse Fleischergasse. The grey concrete building, shutters down, bristling with short-circuit cameras and antennae, remained the city's most feared address. Young men and women, particularly those involved in the church activities which amounted to East Germany's unofficial opposition, would disappear in the night. They could spend days in the cells of the Stasi headquarters being interrogated under bright lights, brainwashed, forced to admit 'anti-state activities'.

Leipzig was not Berlin. It was not, except during the annual spring and autumn trade fairs, under any international focus. It could remain one of Europe's most industrially polluted cities with impunity. In the greyest of surroundings the people were expected to get on with their lives. For their consolation they had arguably East Germany's finest orchestra, the Gewandhaus, under a chief conductor of the highest integrity, Kurt Masur; they lived in the knowledge that this was Johann Sebastian Bach's city, that the great composer was buried in the Thomaskirche (St Thomas's) and that they could visit a fine zoo.

They could also, if they were so inclined, take pride in having Europe's biggest railway station, in terms of platforms. I remember a year or so earlier interviewing Frankfurt's chief stationmaster, the top railway post of its kind in West

Germany. 'When I was a young boy I used to dream of getting the Leipzig job,' Wilhelm Schäfer confessed. 'Here the biggest and best job is Frankfurt and I am very proud to have it.' His counterpart in Leipzig, rejoicing under the old German title of Reichsbahnrat, enjoyed complete authority over twenty-six platforms and a cathedral-like construction dating from the start of the twentieth century which itself had played a role in modern German history. In the huge hall is a plaque paying tribute to 'the revolution of soldiers and sailors of 8.11.1918 which precipitated the Armistice'. Almost seventy-one years later, however, Dresden's smaller station was to steal a march over Leipzig in East Germany's bloodless revolution. 'Freedom trains' bearing thousands of East German refugees, who had sought asylum in West Germany's palatial embassy in Prague, passed through Dresden on their long journey to the West, and riot police battled to prevent the people from surging on to the platforms and track from the appropriately named Pragerstrasse.

Waiting one morning in Leipzig aboard a train bound for Dresden, I was surprised how a station so large could be so eerily empty, almost dead at 9 a.m. There were more pigeons than passengers. Perhaps after all, I thought, the Frankfurt stationmaster had the better job.

Twice a year, in the spring and autumn, the communist authorities made a great fuss over the international trade fairs for which Leipzig was famous. It was their opportunity to show that East Germany was the top industrial nation in Comecon, the East Bloc trade group. While the people of East Germany laboured for little, their country rose to eleventh place among the nations of the industrialized world. Leipzig, strategically well placed for commerce between East and West, had been holding trade fairs for more than eight hundred years. But from being one of Europe's principal centres for the fur trade and for publishing, it had become heavily industrial.

My first night in the towering Merkur Hotel, reserved for foreigners, offered a remarkable, almost beautiful view from the seventh floor. As far as the eye could see the night sky was brightly illuminated, in reds, oranges and greens, by the lights of factory chimneys from which trailed, like from giant cigars, great spirals of smoke. It outdid even Moscow's industrial illuminations at night, which may be equally well viewed from an upper room in the Intourist Hotel behind Red Square.

It was not the trade fair which had gained me a visa and brought me to East Germany's second city, but the approaching fortieth anniversary of the April 1945 link-up at Torgau, on the river Elbe, between the advancing American and Soviet armies. There was an urgent need for 'the spirit of Torgau' to be revived since East–West tension was running high over rearmament and American–Soviet relations had been severely strained in recent days by the shooting dead of an American officer, Major Arthur Nicholson, by a Soviet soldier in East Germany. Nicholson, who was attached to one of the Allied military missions based in Potsdam, had taken photographs of a Soviet military installation while on patrol. The Americans argued that he was carrying out legitimate duties, the Russians said he was spying.

It was a chance to explore Leipzig, which though no longer an attractive city, having taken its share of punishment at the end of the war and subsequently suffered from gross neglect, is, like so many of the cities of eastern Germany, particularly rich in history.

The first stop in Leipzig should be the Thomaskirche with its tall octagonal tower. A statue to the church's most famous cantor stands outside in the shade of a lime tree. Inside, lightened by its long windows, the Gothic building seems to soar like one of Bach's toccatas and to be as solid as one of his fugues. A simple stone in front of the altar marks the final resting-place of J. S. Bach, inscribed in bronze lettering. That day half a dozen red carnations lay spread carelessly on the ground. A group of bespectacled Japanese were chattering away in the corner, having just been filming.

Eating in Leipzig can be a complicated performance. As one approaches from the grandiose station, a small side street, the Kleine Fleischergasse, runs off the right-hand corner of the largely seventeenth-century market square. Less than a hundred yards on, an iron sign and a fine old stone gateway, presided over by a fat, turbaned Turk carved in relief counting his coffee beans, mark the entrance to the Kaffeebaum. This has long been a favourite haunt of Leipzigers, inspiring J. S. Bach's Coffee Cantata – he came to consume the then costly beverage, as did the young Goethe and Schumann later – and is generally impossibly full. It is not that the food is particularly good, nor the beer better, but the surroundings are unusually congenial. This time I was lucky and we were shown to a couple of places left on a table occupied by two students. It would be difficult to avoid conversation, despite awareness of the ubiquitous Stasi. We ordered a plateful of Hungarian salami, the safest alternative to the unappetizing variations of greasy pork with which East German menus are overladen. The small slices of dark red salami from Hungary are in fact an underestimated delicacy, one of the epicurean delights of Eastern Europe.

After ten minutes of being sized up, conversation opened with 'Guten Appetit' on the arrival of the salami. It began cautiously: where were we from, small talk, what were we doing. But it soon developed in a way that would have been unlikely among strangers in an East Berlin restaurant at the time. The two young men expressed their concern at the number of Soviet troops stationed in their country, exactly as West German students questioned the American military presence. They complained about obligatory military service. More beers were ordered; the frustrations of living in such a strictly regimented society began to be aired freely. One of the men, cherub faced and wearing a dirty blue-checked shirt, said what he missed most was the range of electronic goods cheaply available in the West. By working part-time as a garage mechanic, saving, grafting, swapping and tinkering about with parts, he had managed to put together 'a respectable hi-fi system, but not like the ones you can get in the West,' he said with a gleam in his eye. Perhaps not surprisingly, his military service had been spent as a radio operator. His companion, taller with a narrow pallid face, dark short hair and thin stubble on his chin, talked less but was a listener, especially interested in the progress of the Green Party in West Germany and how it had raised awareness of environmental issues. He offered to take us around Leipzig, left his telephone number on a scrap of envelope and arranged a rendezvous outside our hotel for that evening. The Kaffeebaum was emptying and it was time to move on.

The Nikolaikirche (St Nicholas's) is Leipzig's second church. In 1985 one would have hardly guessed that it was to be a hotbed of the 1989 revolution. But with the benefit of hindsight, there was a clue. At the back of the church, which has a bright, white-painted interior and elaborate, late baroque foliated capitals, were screens and notice-boards highlighting not only the originally Gothic building's history but also the activities of a fledgling church-based environmental movement. These were not encouraged or condoned by the state, which preferred meeting at any environmental cost the industrial targets it had set itself. There was no compromise; outdated industrial plant, like an old engine being driven hard, was forced on at full steam, uncontrolled and unchecked. The sky above Leipzig and other major industrial cities was thick with noxious chemicals and gases; small children and older people suffered from respiratory illnesses; the cancer rates were double those in the cleaner West. Leipzig's air had sulphur dioxide readings twenty times higher than the western city of Hanover. The communist state, which short-sightedly prided itself on the welfare it offered its people, was in fact guilty of criminal negligence. The rise of the Greens in West Germany and later in other West European countries had heightened awareness of environmental considerations. Western governments gradually responded, realizing that votes were ultimately at stake, but in Eastern Europe the people's concern was ignored.

It was to prove a grave political miscalculation, for the citizens of Leipzig, or those of the nearby chemicals producing town of Bitterfeld, shrouded daily in acrid smogs of its own making, could not escape the consequences. They breathed them in daily and saw how their homes and city were blackened. Unlike their leaders, they could not seek refuge in pleasant country 'dachas' or fill their lungs with fresh air at holiday homes on the Baltic or at their pine-fringed hunting lodges. Unable to express their fears normally, let alone vote freely, many turned to the church, and Leipzigers to the Nikolaikirche. Prayers for peace, a better environment and against oppression came to be said here on Monday evenings, and soon the church attracted more people than it could hold. The upstairs galleries were filled, the aisles packed, and in that momentous autumn of 1989 the people spilled out into the streets to demonstrate for what they had prayed.

The only merit of the Merkur Hotel was its capacity. The colossal tower block – completed under Japanese supervision in 1981 – was able to accommodate a maximum number of foreign businessmen during the trade fairs. Each room was individually bugged, not only by the Stasi but by an army of cockroaches which ran riot down the long corridors. Returning briefly that evening before taking up our rendezvous with the less talkative of the Kaffeebaum students, we passed by the Merkur's first-floor bar. There, apparently beyond warning, a colleague from a rival London newspaper seemed perilously near succumbing to the far from discreet charms of one of the Stasi's female militia. Our forthcoming outing would be much safer.

He was waiting, rather too obviously I thought, outside the Merkur's huge plate-glass lobby windows. He was not as shy as one might have expected. He could, of course, himself have been a Stasi part-time informer. There were several hundred thousand of them, it emerged after the revolution. I was suspicious, but if one was careful, there could hardly be much risk; the same could not be said of an entanglement with the Mata Hari at the Merkur bar. He was pleasant enough and I could perhaps learn more about Leipzig from him.

'What is it like in the Merkur? Is it really as splendid as people say? Marble in the bathrooms?' he fired away immediately. Like most other Leipzigers, he had only ever peered into the great black empty space of the lobby, relieved by brash chrome lights and a colour television surrounded by some sofas in a corner.

I told him I found it cold, characterless and depressing. He could not quite understand me.

'Isn't it like your hotels in the West?'

'Some,' I replied.

'Where do you want to go?' he asked as we moved on.

I was keen to see Auerbachs Keller, the legendary watering-hole where the young Goethe drank as a student.

We took the underground pedestrian crossing under the busy ring road and headed towards the market place. There in the bowels of the Mädlerpassage, a heavy Jugendstil arcade completed in 1913, amidst much wrought iron and dark oak panelling is what remains of the inn established in 1530 by Heinrich Stromer, a professor of medicine and town councillor. In 1766, as a seventeen-year-old attending Leipzig's fashionable university, Goethe first came here for refreshment. The unspoiled beauty of some of the local girls, which is still in evidence, may have provided the young poet with his inspiration for Gretchen. He was to labour on his first Faust ideas during the 1770s until *Faust, Part One*, was finally published in 1808. Ever since, Auerbachs Keller has been closely associated with the legend, its walls being covered with paintings depicting episodes from *Faust, Part One*, in 1867. I remember once reading a very curious Victorian volume of anecdotes which claimed that Goethe drank a bottle of wine with every meal during his adult life and then proceeded to calculate how many bottles this amounted to by the time he died in 1832, aged well over eighty-two.

In communist East Germany wine was generally rather less tempting, masquerading under colourful names that cloaked sweet, cloying concoctions. On a later occasion in Auerbachs Keller a colleague who was also something of an authority on fine cooking was forced to settle for tinned sardines on toast, accompanied by a rich, sweet Bulgarian red wine, the best the once venerable cellar could offer. It was an unhappy experience. This time we settled for something much safer, the locally brewed Sachsenbräu beer, which is excellent. But before we reached that stage we had to complete an old German ritual which still persists in eastern Germany.

On arriving at any restaurant, before even knowing whether a table is free, one is expected and asked to leave one's coat at the cloakroom. Stage two involves waiting at the door to be shown to a place by a waiter or waitress. Here a wait is *de rigueur* even if the restaurant is empty. Any attempt at eye-catching or attracting the attention of the waiter or waitress only prolongs the procedure. But if the rules are observed and patience shown, a table will materialize.

It did in our case, and we got off to a good start with the beer. On the basis that eggs are always good in Eastern Europe, I ordered some fried with ham, also generally reliable.

But I was then introduced to another curious restaurant ritual involving the pepper-pot. This did not keep the salt company on the table and had to be asked for. The waitress would bring it and then, at the earliest opportunity, take it away and return it to a central side table where it remained, along with many other pepper-pots, under her supervision. The origins of this performance must date from an earlier age, for good pepper was readily available and reasonably priced in East Germany.

Our conversation continued along the lines laid out at lunchtime: East–West German comparisons, in daily life and politics. Except in the so-called Valley of the Ignorant around Dresden, where because of the lie of the land reception had long been problematic, East Germans were able to tune in to West German television easily. This offered them a complete insight into life in the West, if not the experience of it. Rents, gas, electricity, food and public transport prices were all low in the communist German state, having been held unrealistically at post-war levels by subsidies. The shops were generally well stocked and there were none of the shortages which had become proverbial in other East Bloc countries. But there was a poverty of choice by western standards, and East Germans had been awakened to what was on offer in the West by its television advertising. Worse for young East Germans was the fact that they could not travel freely; they felt imprisoned in a far from golden cage. When we talked of the parts of the world I had visited and how normal and easy this was in the West, our companion was mesmerized. For him it was really a dream. 'If only I could see Paris! Walk along its streets,' he sighed.

We left the cavernous cellar with its memories of Faust and began a nocturnal tour of Leipzig. Behind the old town hall – an attractive Renaissance building begun in 1556, with a very fine off-centre octagonal tower, extended in 1672, rebuilt in

36

1909 and restored after considerable war damage in 1950 – is hidden one of the city's architectural jewels. The old Bourse in the Naschmarkt is Leipzig's prize example of early baroque, its elegant exterior carefully restored after the building was gutted by fire in the same 1943 air raid in which the town hall suffered. In front, in such pleasant surroundings and so near to Auerbachs Keller, stands appropriately a statue of the young Goethe.

Our next stop was the Karl-Marx-Platz, a modern hotch-potch of socialist city planning that replaced the once stately Augustusplatz, which was much damaged in the war. Most horrendous is the university complex, completed in 1975 and comprising a massive six-storey central building and a sky-scraper 142 metres high. Renamed after Karl Marx and with a bronze relief above the main entrance portraying 'Marxism', one would not think that it was one of Germany's most ancient universities, founded in 1409, or that it previously occupied fine premises completed in 1836 to plans by Schinkel, Germany's most inspired architect. It was established following the expulsion of two thousand German academics from Prague. Our companion was rightly proud of his distinguished univer-sity.

To the left and the right of it are two architecturally more successful creations, both concerned with music: the extremely austere, massive opera house, built between 1956 and 1960, but more typical of some of the pre-war architecture favoured by the Nazis, and the glassy New Gewandhaus concert hall, completed only in 1981. The opera offers outstanding visi-bility, with not a restricted-view seat in the house, while the Gewandhaus, which can accommodate almost two thousand seated around the orchestra, boasts superb acoustics. The Gewandhaus building is a fitting setting for one of Germany's great orchestras. Its airy foyers are full of paintings and sculptures which, because of the façade's transparency, may also be seen from outside. There further relief is provided by a flamboyant fountain installed in the nineteenth century, the Mendebrunnen, where Tritons, sea horses and naiads disport themselves beneath an obelisk and among the jets of water, all of which is reflected again in the Gewandhaus glass. From Johann Sebastian Bach, cantor at the Thomaskirche from 1723 to 1750, onwards, Leipzig has had a special place in the history of music. It was the birthplace in 1813 of Richard Wagner, the home between 1830 and 1844 of Robert Schumann, and was confirmed as one of Europe's principal centres of music by Felix Mendelssohn-Bartholdy, who directed the Gewandhaus orchestra and its famous concerts from 1835 to 1841, in 1842 and then again from 1846 to 1847. The Gewandhaus tradition was continued with distinction in this century by Arthur Nikisch, Wilhelm Furtwängler, Hermann Abendroth, Franz Konwitschny and latterly Kurt Masur, whose natural authority and bold intervention prevented blood from being spilled on the streets of his beloved Leipzig at the height of the East German revolution. But it was not just composers, conductors and a fine orchestra that gave Leipzig its reputation for music. It was also famous for its manufacture of pianofortes and for music publishing.

Ignoring the forbidding main post office and the dreadful Am Ring Hotel, which complete the square, we backtracked two streets to return down the Nikolaistrasse, past the Nikolaikirche. This narrow street is remarkable for its number of furriers, almost one after another, a reminder of the city's past pre-eminence in the fur trade and especially the handling of Russian furs. On a later visit to one of the furriers I was struck by how well frequented it was, proof perhaps that Leipzig more naturally forms part of Eastern than Western Europe. A steady stream of women arrived bringing fur coats for repair, garments which were not status symbols but items of daily winter wear.

Emerging from the bottom of the Nikolaistrasse towards the ring road, we noticed a huddle of young people waiting outside a dilapidated doorway. It was only surprising because the streets had otherwise been so empty. Most Leipzigers, having to get up early for work, spent their evenings quietly at home watching West German television. But this was an exception, one of the city's few discothèques, where young East Germans could get away from home and dance to blaring music, be dazzled by brightly flashing strobe lights and knock back glasses of sweet cola. It was the wildest thing then on offer in East Germany's second city.

Our tour had completed a rough circle. Midnight was approaching and we were nearing the Merkur. We thanked our student friend and said we would give him a call if it was possible to meet up again, but tomorrow it was Torgau, the official reason for our visit. He shook hands and wandered back to pick up a tram to his home in the bleak city outskirts. My doubts about him had been dispelled; he was too harmless to have anything to do with the Stasi, too ideologically uninterested. He was just genuinely curious to meet and talk to westerners and was not overconcerned at the risk involved.

One intriguing question remained unanswered. Curiosity over the evening's outstanding risk was sufficient for me to make a short detour and return to my room via the Merkur's first-floor bar. Our Fleet Street colleague and the alluring Stasi hostess had vanished. The barman smiled as he finished drying a row of glasses.

Early the next morning the Hungarian-built 'Icarus' buses were waiting outside to take us to Torgau, where in 1760 Frederick the Great won a famous victory over the Austrians and where on 25 April 1945 the American and Russian armies linked up to split the Third Reich in two. Reporting this fortieth anniversary was of special interest to me since my father, Walter 'Jack' Farr, a *Daily Mail* war correspondent attached to General Hodges's 1st US Army, was one of the few journalists to have witnessed the historic meeting on the Elbe. The encounter between the two allies after a long, hard war, with Nazi Germany now at last on the brink of defeat, made a deep impact on those present. It was a well-earned opportunity for emotional release and for several days there was much drinking, dancing and general good humour. My father used to regale me as a child with tales of driving around in a Russian jeep, endless parties and friendships struck. Unfortunately, he would not be among the veterans returning for the anniversary, or even be able to follow it from afar, having died almost exactly a year earlier. But a good collection of old soldiers, both American and Russian, were brought back for the occasion, which the East Germans sponsored as 'a peace initiative'.

As the buses arrived in the ancient town, dominated by the imposing Hartenfels Castle built in the sixteenth century and guarded by handsome black Russian bears roaming about its empty moat, it immediately became apparent that the East Germans were staging a major propaganda event. 'The meeting by the river Elbe – an expression of the people's desire for peace,' declared one banner. 'For successful disarmament negotiations between the Soviet Union and the USA in Geneva' or 'We support the peace proposals of Gorbachev' and 'We want no space weapons,' added others.

However, a huge banner stretched across the castle itself did refer to the past rather than present: 'Torgau welcomes the fighters of the anti-Hitler coalition and the anti-fascist resistance fighters.' The narrow cobbled streets by the castle and the gabled seventeenth-century houses were bedecked with red flags. Schoolchildren had been given the day off and their classrooms turned into a Press centre. On the river bank itself the memorial to the historic meeting bore an inscription to 'the glory of the Soviet people'.

Soon more buses arrived bearing the returning soldiers. Americans, less circumspect than forty years before when they had to watch for sniper fire but also slowed down by the advancing years, disembarked, many wearing peaked caps marked with the motto of their infantry division, the 'Fighting 69th'. They congregated in front of the dour Russian war memorial in the icy drizzle. Next came the twenty-five Russian veterans, grey-suited, medalled and flashing their gold teeth in broad smiles. They seemed burlier, more stocky, older and more dignified than their American comrades. Meanwhile, blue-shirted, yellow-scarved members of the Freie Deutsche Jugend, the Communist Youth League, which was so un-settlingly reminiscent of the Hitler Youth in its discipline and indoctrination, took on a policing role, holding back the crowd and Press with an aggressive degree of efficiency.

The speeches began. 'Greetings from all us Sixty-Niners. Gentlemen of the 69th, please raise your hands. There are sixty of us present,' said William Beswick. 'We have come here to commemorate our link-up, when we met units of the 58th Guards Division of the 1st Ukrainian Army – that is forty short years ago.

'One of our prime purposes is to place a wreath at this historic monument ... to those that lost their lives in the Torgau and Elbe campaign. And to renew friendships with some of our Soviet friends we met forty years ago.'

A message was read out from Mikhail Gorbachev, the newly appointed Soviet leader, which described the meeting as 'a symbol of hope for peace and friendship'. Similar sentiments were expressed in greetings from former American presidents Carter and Nixon.

But it was no day to stand outside listening to boring speeches, shivering in the cold, and there was general relief when the formal proceedings came to an end and it was time to adjourn to the town hall for a buffet lunch that had been laid on, with Soviet champagne and vodka in plentiful supply, courtesy of the Red Army as it had been forty years earlier, helping to spur reminiscences and jog memories.

Charles Forrester from South Carolina, who was then a 26-year-old private first class, remembered 25 April 1945 as a 'happy day, we knew that the war was almost over'.

The first encounter was between an American patrol of the 69th Infantry Division, led by Lieutenant Albert Kotzebue, and the Red Army's 58th Guards Division at Strehlm, near Torgau. Two hours later Lieutenant William Robertson led a patrol further east into Torgau itself and the meeting that became history.

'LINK-UP,' trumpeted the *News Chronicle* headline when the story broke. 'Secret is out: Americans and Russians met at Torgau on Elbe at 4.20 p.m. Wednesday.

'They have linked up. These words flashed round the world last night, announced the conclusion of two of the greatest military marches in modern history.

'From the banks of the Volga the Red Army has battled 1,400 miles to the west; from the beaches of Normandy the Americans have fought 700 miles to the east, and at Torgau on the Elbe, in the heart of the Reich, they have at last met.'

The Daily Express pronounced: 'The Third Reich of Adolf Hitler is dead. It died in its thirteenth year at four o'clock on Wednesday afternoon, when General Courtney Hodges' 1st US Army linked up with Marshal Koniev's 1st Ukrainian Army and cut Germany into two parts, north and south.

'Two junior officers – Lieutenant William Robertson, of California, and Lieutenant Alexander Silvachko, the Russian, shook hands on a twisted girder of the wrecked Torgau railway bridge over the Elbe and arranged details for the meetings between the regimental and divisional commanders on both sides.'

Both Robertson and Silvachko were back for the anniversary, shaking hands again, laughing, joking and enjoying the Russian champagne. Holding on to his glass, Robertson, a Los Angeles brain surgeon, described to me that day forty years ago: 'I was part of a four-man patrol from Wurzen. We were told the Russians were on the other side of the river bank. We could see the Russians moving in the woods.'

He related how he crouched on the castle parapet overlooking the Elbe, waving a makeshift flag and trying to ward off Russian rifle fire.

'I made a flag out of a bedsheet after breaking into a pharmacy and finding red and blue paint for a kind of Stars and Stripes, and climbed up the castle tower. I waved the flag and got shot at from five hundred yards. I was shouting, "Comrade" – "Tovarich" – in Russian, but it didn't work. So I sent a driver back to the prison where we found a Russian prisoner of war who then shouted to the Soviet side.

'The firing stopped and we went down to the remains of the bridge. I climbed across and met a Russian soldier halfway. We embraced over the middle of the Elbe. You just didn't need words. They were happy to see us and we to see them. We traded cap ornaments and I swapped my wristwatch for a Russian's wedding ring.'

Robertson then went across to the Russian side of the Elbe, where he met a Soviet major and other officers. 'We had a bottle of wine, a can of sardines, chocolates and some biscuits. We drank a lot of toasts, and they filled my water bottle with schnapps.

'Kotzebue stayed where he was and we got the credit for the link-up, though he actually made the first contact. The fraternization lasted several days.'

Relays of American and Russian troops joined the festivities. Wine was brought up from the cellars of Torgau and quaffed in beer mugs; music was provided by accordions 'liberated' from the Wehrmacht storehouse in the almost deserted town. 'We talked about peace and friendship,' recalled Robertson, who, though balding and bespectacled, had aged well. In a crumpled light corduroy jacket, adorned with the odd badge and medal, he was a picture of informality compared with his Russian comrades.

Silvachko, who had become a history and geography teacher at a secondary school near Minsk, was a bear of a man with an iron handshake. He certainly did not look as if he would tolerate any classroom nonsense. 'The times are such that we must join together and today is an historic day. We have not forgotten April 1945. Robertson also works for peace, Robertson is a good man,' he told me.

Alexei Gorlinsky, a thirty-year-old artillery major at the time, recollected that day forty years earlier. 'We were expecting the Americans, they were in front of us there on the Elbe,' he said as he pointed. 'But we nearly killed Mr Robertson at 2 p.m. on the 25th.'

He explained the confusion: 'In a nearby building we saw two soldiers but they were not Americans, though they should have been. They were German soldiers who might have changed uniforms.'

The reception was becoming lively. In a corner of the dining-room stood a group of serving Russian officers who had progressed from champagne to vodka. The large, bulky figure in the middle, well decorated with gold braid and medals, was General Mikhail Zaitsev, commander-in-chief of Soviet forces in Germany. As a young captain, Zaitsev had been present at the historic link-up.

A man who normally kept well away from western reporters, he was this time glad to have additional company and at once instructed his ADC to find more glasses and vodka. First things first: no conversation could begin until the Stolichnaya had arrived. The general filled our glasses himself, looked us in the eye, proposed a toast and then in one practised gulp emptied his glass. Rather less expertly we did the same, whereupon he called for the bottle again. The procedure was repeated several times before we could attempt questions and it was astounding how clear and well thought out his responses were.

'Major Nicholson was on a military reconnaissance mission in a restricted zone and was a spy,' Zaitsev said emphatically. 'He drove his car to the object and took the picture.'

The American officer was understood to have tried to photograph the contents of a tank shed north-west of Berlin. We asked the general what evidence the Russians had to back their allegations.

'Yes, we have a film and it has been developed. There is evidence of a spying mission which had nothing to do with his role.

'It is an unfortunate incident, but the fault lay with Major Nicholson. He should have followed the orders.'

For a moment Zaitsev looked uncomfortable when asked what had become of the Russian sentry and whether he had been disciplined for overreacting.

'No fault lies with the Soviet soldier,' he said. 'We cannot punish him.'

The whole episode illustrated how completely the Cold War had eclipsed the bonds created at Torgau. Fortified by so much vodka and with a burgeoning feeling of well-being, I left the discussion of current tensions for the far more compelling talk of the past.

An animated Elijah Sams from North Carolina was remembering how as a 21-year-old private he had 'stayed overnight with the Russians ... they gave us plenty of vodka and there was loads of dancing and playing of accordions'.

And Sam Lewis, a former first lieutenant from Houston, Texas, was talking about getting back to Leipzig 'to look for eight bullet holes I put in a fence . . . I got real mad when we took casualties and a couple of members of the platoon got killed.'

East Germany, I thought, would be one of the very few places where he could expect to find those forty-year-old bullet holes as he had left them.

3 Return to Colditz

The name Colditz is derived from the Serbian for 'dark forest' and stems from a mid-sixth-century invasion of the region by Slavs. To the British and their wartime allies, however, Colditz has a more immediate ring. For it was here, to the forbidding castle that surmounts a craggy hill, that the Nazis brought the most troublesome Allied officers they held prisoner. Goering deemed Colditz 'escape proof' and on arrival prisoners of war were greeted by their captors with the demoralizing words, 'Here you bite on granite.' But the apparent impossibility of escape from this daunting fortress was a challenge to the ingenuity and daring of the Colditz inmates, and enough managed to get away to render Goering's boast as idle as a good many others he made.

Sweeping eastwards, the American 9th Armoured Division liberated Colditz Castle on 16 April 1945, freeing its 1,400 inmates, 271 of whom were Allied officers. To mark the occasion forty years on, a busload of the original trouble-makers, who ran so many circles round their Nazi captors, returned to the camp to reminisce. For all but Major Pat Reid, the chronicler of Colditz and one of its select band of successful escapers, it was their first return to a place that most had solemnly vowed never to set eyes on again when they finally left its dark walls.

David Smeeton and I stayed on in Leipzig after the elaborate Torgau celebrations to meet the former POWs at Colditz, which was to be more of a private visit than a public occasion. Because of the 'anti-fascist' nature of the Colditz gathering, it had readily received the blessing of the communist authorities, as had our reporting of the event. The route from Leipzig soon took us on to small country roads, which remarkably frequently bisected huge Soviet military complexes. Nearly all the traffic was military. Russian troops regarded our blue Audi saloon with its Bonn number-plates quizzically as we sped by. This was not a road we would have been allowed to travel far on if our cause had not been officially sanctioned at a suitably high level.

Arriving at Colditz was once again a typical East German experience. The town was frozen in time. The sloping central market square with its grey uneven cobblestones, the few small shops, the beamed seventeenth-century houses and the narrow, winding streets could not have altered since they were last seen by the prisoners of war incarcerated in the castle. The buildings clearly had not had a lick of paint or a fresh layer of plaster for the best part of fifty years. Since Augustus the Strong, elector of Saxony and king of Poland, had built strategically more significant strongholds in the early eighteenth century, Colditz had become a backwater. Under communism the stagnation was extreme. The castle itself had reverted to its pre-war use as a psychiatric asylum, though for the duration of our visit the 350 patients were conveniently moved away. From the bottom of the massive rock on which it was built the sixteenth-century castle formed a dark, gloomy silhouette. It was certainly not a cheerful place.

But that day as over forty years before, spirits which refused to be suppressed returned with the group of former POWs. The late April chill and lifelessness of the town gave way to their boisterous exclamations as they stepped out of their bus and marched up the hill and through the castle's stone gateway, emblazoned with the arms of the electors of Saxony and the royal house of Denmark. The twenty-four officers from Britain, Canada, South Africa, Australia, New Zealand and France were still rebellious. They shouted, 'Achtung!', 'Raus!' and

'Appell!' when they entered the high-walled courtyard, where twice daily and after every escape attempt they had had to stand and be counted.

This time their East German hosts wished them a 'very pleasant stay and happy memories'. None of the castle guards were on hand, but two locals closely connected with the camp were there for the occasion. One was Frau Erna Kretschmar, who had worked in the canteen from 1941 to 1945, for which the former prisoners were hardly grateful. 'Dreadful food, thin soup made from kohlrabi, the most miserable of vegetables,' complained one. 'My most enduring memory is always being hungry,' added 'Peter' Allan, one of Colditz's British 'founder members'. The other German was certainly back by popular request. A tremendous cheer went up for 83-year-old Herr Willi Pöhnert, the camp electrician, who had always been a figure of fun to the prisoners. 'They were nice prisoners,' he said after overcoming his initial embarrassment. 'I hope that my nice prisoners won't forget me while I am alive.'

The moment the former inmates were back inside Oflag IVC, as Colditz was officially termed, they dashed about exploring every corner of the castle they had grown to know too well during the long years of imprisonment. 'Home, sweet home!' they shouted, stopping to take photographs. 'This is the way we came in and that's where Pat Reid got out.'

'Donaldson, get going, I'm not anxious to get back.'

'To think we lived in this bloody place.'

A light aircraft buzzed overhead, prompting: 'Look out, a Fiesler Storch! It's after us!'

Another shout went up: 'Mittagessen! Kohlrabi Suppe!'

'Those were the punishment cells. See the ledge,' said Tom Elliott, pointing; he had been a lieutenant in the Royal Northumberland Fusiliers. 'Two Poles went. They wanted me to go with them but I was ill that day.

'They were caught in the tree. The Goons shouted, "Hands

up!" as they were dangling in the tree. They were hanging by their fingertips.

'I came in on my birthday, 2 December 1940, and had five birthdays, five Christmases and five New Years here!'

Charles Hargreaves, a captain in the Hussars who had a shorter stay, arriving at Colditz only at the end of June 1944, said pure curiosity had brought him back. 'The day I left I said, "I never want to see this place again."'

Mike Moran, a Royal Navy lieutenant, agreed. 'I never had any ambition to come back. Only because a bunch of chums was coming, not otherwise.'

The East German officials were calling us to order, trying not to be too reminiscent of the former gaolers. We were to go to the Festsaal, the castle's old music room, which had been used for the camp theatre, for the formal part of the proceedings.

The Festsaal, on the third floor off a spiral staircase in the corner of the courtyard nearest the entrance gate, was a fine room, well suited for music-making. It had a raised stage at one end, which the prisoners used for such theatrical extravaganzas as *Ballet Nonsense*, and as a cover for one of the earliest and most famous escapes. Looking upwards, a series of stucco medallions of well-known German composers and writers stood out against the rather anaemic duck-egg green of the walls and ceiling. But, oddly, the one next to Richard Wagner, adulated by the Nazis, had been chiselled away. The missing musician was Felix Mendelssohn, so closely associated with nearby Leipzig and its famous Gewandhaus orchestra, who because he was a Jew the Nazis eradicated even from a music room.

Rather reluctantly, like schoolboys on an outing, the former POWs sat down for the speeches. 'Your visit is taking place at a time when we are concerned about peace. The international situation has become very complicated in the light of the number of nuclear warheads. The existence of mankind is in jeopardy,' droned on the local Communist Party official in his introduction.

'Get on with it,' mumbled one of the visitors.

A little more patience was shown for Herr Fritz Hase, an 82-year-old communist who had been cooped up in Colditz before the war when it was used as a concentration camp for those politically opposed to the Nazis. Less is known about this episode, but Hase remembered how it had been one of the first concentration camps to be set up in Saxony and how political prisoners were brought here from Leipzig and Chemnitz.

'There were on average six to eight hundred prisoners here. This courtyard was a piece of terror for us. The prisoners were brought by the police into the courtyard and had to get out of the trucks and line up in rows of two. After formalities, the storm troopers herded us into the far corner – where the spiral staircase was – to have our hair shorn. For many this round of hardship began in Colditz and ended in Buchenwald.'

His words were followed by respectful applause and then came the moment richest in irony. The twenty-four POWs were asked to come forward and sign the Colditz Castle guest book. They were also each given a medal of Colditz 'as a reminder'.

The formalities over, it was once again a free-for-all. Theatrical, musical and other goings-on were topical. 'The Frenchman playing the piano was posted away and I played the piano in the camp dance band . . .'

'I was the chap who played the tenor sax. I learned how to play that,' chipped in Jimmy Yule, who had been a Royal Corps of Signals captain. 'I wrote and orchestrated music. It was a splendid escape. If one couldn't escape physically one had to mentally.'

Airey Neave, then a Royal Artillery lieutenant, in January

1942 made the first British 'home run' from an escape route opened up by Pat Reid that began underneath the stage floor. His escape with Tony Luteijn, a Dutch lieutenant, was a tremendous fillip to the prisoners left behind. 'He was like the dove released from the Ark which had found land,' Reid later wrote. In 1979 Neave, by then a prominent Conservative MP, was killed in an IRA bomb attack in the House of Commons car park.

'I was a ballet girl and lost my lighter because the two of them needed it to light the way,' recalled Jim Rogers, a bulky South African who had been a Royal Engineers captain and adept both as a tunneller and radio operator. 'I was on a tunnel under the stores into the sewage system. But I was too big – it was only for little chaps.'

Turning to Jimmy Yule, he added, 'We were the radio operators. Right up at the top. They rescued all our stuff and somebody has the notebook.'

'We inherited the equipment from the French, who had installed it. They had got the radio sent from France. We could pick up the BBC,' Yule explained.

Together we sought out the bell tower, at the very top of the castle at the further end. While Rogers drew a diagram in my notebook of where the radio apparatus was tucked away in the attic under the eaves, Yule, despite his sixty-eight years, slipped down with considerable agility between two beams and rediscovered his old 'radio hide'. On his knees he started rummaging about. 'The French officers took the radio back,' he interjected, short of breath. 'Here we hid fake German uniforms and other escape equipment.'

'Were you with me when the two Goons came here and had a cigarette for half an hour and we had to lie absolutely still in the rafters?' asked Rogers.

Once Yule had extricated himself from his 'hide', we continued on our tour of the upper floors of the dilapidated castle.

'This is where the "Prominenten" had their cells. Giles Romilly, Churchill's nephew, was one. He would never eat margarine nor smoke anything but Turkish cigarettes,' Rogers recollected. 'We used to distil the jam into liquor,' he went on, but according to Kenneth Lockwood, another of the Colditz 'founder members', it left much to be desired.

'Bush Parker had a session on it and was speechless for three days.

'And here we made our ropes from Red Cross string. To make ink we melted down the jelly sent in the Red Cross parcels. We then ate the jelly.'

'We were geared to escaping,' Lockwood explained. 'The object was to get someone out, if not oneself.' A captain in the Queen's Royal Regiment, Lockwood was one of those caught in the unsuccessful canteen tunnel break-out in May 1941.

The ingenuity of the camp's inmates was later to be seen in the town's museum, where much of the home-made equipment, confiscated by the Germans after escape attempts, is on display. It includes an extraordinary wooden sewing machine, a turning lathe and moulds for making German buttons and insignia, as well as pot-still pipes later sacrificed for more serious purposes.

But sadly the most remarkable would-be exhibit no longer exists. The glider which was built and hidden in the attic workshop, but never tested because the end of the war came too soon, was destroyed by the Russians in August 1945 when they used the castle as a hospital. Explaining how it worked, one of its builders, Geoffrey Wardle, a Royal Navy lieutenant at the time, said a bath filled with water would have been dropped as a weight, launching the glider from the castle roof. 'We would have had half an hour's start on the old Kraut,' he was sure. An expert at picking locks, Wardle made several attempts to get out of Colditz for which he was given a total of 212 days in solitary confinement.

Having explored the castle's interior fairly thoroughly, we clattered down the worn stone steps of another spiral staircase back to the courtyard and went out through the gate to the park which was used for exercise. The group stopped to look at the spot where Lieutenant Mike Sinclair was shot and killed on 25 September 1944 in a desperate seventh and final escape attempt. 'Mike just jumped over the wire and ran.'

'That's the wall where they brought the first RAF chaps in November 1940 – a German joke.' The three flying officers, all Canadians, had arrived at Colditz at night and were told they would probably be shot. They were taken down to the high granite wall at dawn and told to exercise themselves for half an hour. 'Keith Milne had saved up enough cigarettes to keep him going for a week and wouldn't leave any ... He smoked like mad, finished them and when he found he was not going to be shot, he was furious with the Germans!'

Wardle led us next to the park manhole through which four Dutch officers had escaped during exercise periods in August and September 1941. On 22 November Wardle and a Polish lieutenant, Jerzy Wojciechowski, were less fortunate. An observant sentry had seen the two men enter the manhole during recreation and they were caught inside. The Germans subsequently sealed it off with concrete.

In September of the following year Wardle was involved in another attempt by a group of six prisoners, three British and three Dutch officers. This time the route began in the office of Oberstabsfeldwebel (Warrant Officer) Gephard, from under his desk. A key was made to open the office's difficult cruciform lock, the floor was carefully ripped up and a wall pierced leading to a storeroom below. From there, after unlocking the door, the escapers would emerge on to a path surrounding the castle. It had been noticed that the Germans occasionally came to the storeroom early in the morning with Polish POWs from the town of Colditz. Accordingly, one of the

Dutchmen, Lieutenant van Doorninck, a fluent German speaker, was disguised as a senior German NCO, another as a German private and the other four as Polish orderlies.

Wardle completed the story. 'We unlocked the doors, walked down and got to the gate. The Goon sentry was standing there and the Dutchman gave him such a hell of a rocket that he got the keys and let us out! Those of us dressed as Polish orderlies were carrying specially fabricated boxes of stores. The Dutch officer dressed as a German private brought up the rear.'

But triumph proved short-lived for four of the escapers. Wardle and Donkers, a Dutch lieutenant, were soon picked up after being spotted in a nearby village by a mayor who grew suspicious about the strangers. Captain 'Lulu' Lawton and Ted Beets, another of the Dutchmen, were arrested later that day at Döbeln railway station. But Flight Lieutenant Bill Fowler became the second British officer to complete a 'home run' directly from Colditz, reaching Switzerland with Lieutenant van Doorninck.

As for Wardle, 'I got another twenty-eight days in solitary. The standard drill.'

'Peter' Allan, a second lieutenant in the Cameron Highlanders, was, together with Pat Reid and Kenneth Lockwood, one of the three surviving original British 'founder members' who arrived in Colditz on 7 November 1940 after being caught escaping from the camp at Laufen near Salzburg. His moment came in May 1941 when some French troops held prisoner in the town came to take mattresses away. Being small and a good German speaker, he was hastily stuffed into one of the prisoners' straw palliasses, which was put on to a Frenchman's shoulder and thrown on to a lorry. 'The most difficult thing,' Allan remembered, 'was not to sneeze with all the straw.' Dumped in a deserted house somewhere in the town, he extricated himself from the mattress, slipped into the garden and found a road. He managed to make his way to Stuttgart and then Vienna where finally, exhausted, he was found out and, after an absence of twenty-three days, returned to the castle.

Following a tour of the town's museum with all the bizarre escape artefacts and paraphernalia confiscated by the Germans – provoking at least one disclaimer, 'I never lost a thing on a single search' – the former POWs were at last able to do the one thing that had proved impossible before. They adjourned to the inn at the bottom of the hill to savour the excellent Colditz beer they had never tasted during their imprisonment. The blue beer mats bearing the legend 'Colditzer Bier' proved almost as popular as the amber liquid itself. Handfuls were picked up from the bar and passed around as signatures were added. A still rather dashing French cavalry officer, Jean-Claude Tiné, who had been a lieutenant in the extravagantly uniformed 1re Spahis Algérien – with their reputation for setting many a female heart throbbing – tried all his Gallic charm on the inn's landlady in the hope that she might part with the end of a beer barrel, engraved with the words 'Colditzer Bier', that hung on the bar wall. But she would not give in, either to his smile or to the offer of a large wad of western notes. Three-quarters of an hour later she seemed highly relieved to see the last of one of the rowdiest bands of former prisoners she was ever likely to have entertained.

Tiné, serving with the Free French, was severely wounded in a tank battle in Tunisia in December 1942. He escaped from hospital, was recaptured and flown to Germany where he was sent to the concentration camp at Sachsenhausen before being transferred to Colditz early in 1944. Forty years on, he remained convinced he had joined one of the most exclusive of clubs. 'The spirit was so high. It was so very sporty,' he said, clutching his beer mats.

It was back to the bus for the return trip to Leipzig. A

rather special outing by a most remarkable group of men was coming to an end. Pat Reid stood up in the coach and counted to see if all the former POWs were safely on board. The numbers did not quite tally. 'Is anyone missing?' he called and counted again. Surely there hadn't been an escape?

'Aha, I am missing!' he concluded.

There seemed to be a sense of relief that they were all together and, without risk of recapture, leaving the gloomy castle and heading home. For all their intended hospitality, the East Germans, with their repeated attempts at political indoctrination, orders and instructions, were sometimes too similar to the camp guards.

'It's a really depressing place.' Kenneth Lockwood remained as convinced as ever.

Mike Moran offered his view: 'If it has changed, it has changed for the worse. What a hell of a dreary, stinking, nasty place it was.'

But Colditz had a positive side – the bonds of friendship that were forged in adversity. Moran waved his arm at the strangely youthful group of men approaching or just past seventy: 'All these chaps. These are the chaps we knew in 1945. The years between have just disappeared.'

As the bus moved off, Pat Reid invited me to sit next to him; it was time I heard his story from the horse's mouth. It was a tale which in the first of his books had thrilled me as a schoolboy.

Reid, a captain in the Royal Army Service Corps, was with the British Expeditionary Force's 2nd Division when on 27 May 1940 he was captured south of Dunkirk. 'We had organized the transport, trying to complete the Maginot line.

'I wouldn't be a prisoner of the Germans for ten minutes if I could help it – that was the feeling I had. I was taken to the camp at Laufen and I was out in September (initially dressed as a woman): six of us escaped by tunnel in two sets of three.

It was a concealed tunnel which was not discovered for a month afterwards. Yet nobody tried to get out, no one else tried to use it – a depressing note.

'We were all recaptured and later arrived together on 7 November in Colditz, the first British group after Flight Lieutenant Hank Wardle and the two other Canadian flying officers who had come on 5 November – the chaps who were taken out "to be shot". There were already over a hundred Poles here.

'When I first saw the castle I thought the chances of escape must be almost nil.

'By Christmas there were about twenty of us here and then the numbers just grew.'

Apart from the Poles and the British, over two hundred French officers were dispatched to Colditz, giving it an international character that was broadened in July 1941 with the arrival of a contingent of sixty-eight Dutch officers. Reid called them 'the famous sixty-eight'. He explained, 'These were the men who refused to sign the Declaration (not to take up arms against Germany). They were the truest, loyalest Dutch.'

Belgians had arrived and later a smaller American group, adding further to Colditz's diversity.

The Germans were sending their most difficult prisoners to the camp. It became an 'escape university' where a previous qualification was needed for admission. 'Any failed escaper or anyone who seemed to be a troublemaker,' as Reid put it. As a result a tremendous wealth of escaping experience was gathered under one roof.

Additionally, it was decided at the highest level in Berlin that particularly well-connected prisoners, such as Giles Romilly, Viscount Lascelles, Earl Haig, son of the late field marshal, and later John Winant, son of the American ambassador in London, should be held under Colditz's maximum security conditions in case there should be any attempt to free them. They also had some value as hostages. The 'Promi-nenten' had their own set of cells in the castle.

As 1941 slipped by the prospects of breaking out seemed poor indeed. 'There was escape attempt after escape attempt. But only failure, failure, failure,' Reid sighed. Then in April and May the French chalked up the first two successful escapes. 'It was summer by then and our canteen tunnel was an enormous failure – twelve of us were caught in the tunnel. We tried to bribe a guard and it didn't work.'

Two more French escapes followed in July. Then in August a pair of Dutch officers managed to get out through the park manhole, followed by two more using the same route in September. A Polish officer used a visit to the hospital in Königswartha as an opportunity to get away. Another French officer escaped first from hospital then from prison in Düsseldorf. Returning from hospital in October, two more Frenchmen got away, and another three in December on their way back from the town dentist. Colditz was proving far from escape proof, but the British, however hard they were trying, had so far had no luck.

'Then,' said Reid with a smile breaking across his tightly controlled face, 'in 1942 the British began to come into their own.' Already at the end of 1941 what was to be the first successful British escape was at an advanced state of preparation – four men, two British and two Dutch, were to get away from under the stage of the camp theatre and out of the guardhouse. On 5 January Lieutenants Airey Neave and Tony Luteijn, dressed as German officers, made a 'perfect exit' and reached Switzerland. The following night the next pair, Lieutenants Hyde-Thompson and Donkers, repeated the performance though their luck ran out and they were arrested at Ulm railway station. But for the British the ice had at last been broken and before the year was out they were to achieve further triumphs.

As the bus wound along the country roads to Leipzig, Reid continued his account of 1942, the escapers' *annus mirabilis*. 'There was the business under Gephard's desk in September. This time there were three British and three Dutch officers: one of each was successful.'

Reid himself had made two attempts in August: from the delousing shed and digging from a cell. 'The idea was we had to try everything.

'We went into the German Kommandatur, cutting bars and all kinds of other nonsense. But we found a way out through the kitchen and four of us volunteered. We prepared for weeks and then after evening Appell on 14 October 1942 we came out of the kitchen. We had to pass the sentries and the arc lights. We had arranged it that Douglas Bader, who was rehearsing the orchestra in the theatre and had a view of our passage as well as of the sentry, would stop playing when the coast was clear. We made it to a chimney leading down to a cess-pit. By stripping naked we could just squeeze through. We emerged stinking from the cess-pit and then had to dress again. We had collected or made up civilian clothing and carried specially fabricated suitcases – which though cumbersome were important, for anyone who travelled light across Germany automatically aroused suspicions. Our papers identified us as Flemish workmen working for the Germans.

'Soon after 5 a.m. we were finally over the boundary wall. Our long journey began and ended on foot. About 30 miles from Colditz, at Penig, we got on a train and then it was 350 miles of rail travel. Hank Wardle and I reached Switzerland after four and a half days. I remember the total darkness when we got to the Swiss border, the vague outlines, and how very cold it was. The others – Billie Stephens and Ronnie Littledale, who was to be killed by a landmine in Normandy – arrived the following evening. The escape had been a 100 per cent success.

'Two more got out and arrived in Switzerland after us,

Royal Navy petty officers Wally Hammond and Tubby Lister, submariner survivors of *Swordfish* and *Shark*, two real Colditz types who had joined us as officers.

'They were then totally organized for escape, learning all the tricks of the trade, before the senior British officer complained to the Kommandant: "We are an officers' camp and object to mingling with non-commissioned officers."' They were accordingly transferred to the less rigidly guarded troops' camp at Lamsdorf, from which they slipped out with the greatest of ease. 'They crossed safely to Switzerland in time for Christmas.' It had been a remarkable year for escapes from Colditz.

Although there were to be more, the height of the season had been reached. 'There were some brilliant escapes, but regrettably our officers seemed to get the idea that the Colditz route was sealed.' Certainly escaping did not become any easier.

The final score is nevertheless impressive. During the four and a half years the castle was used to hold up to 500 Allied officers at a time, nearly all with escape records, over 300 attempts were made and 31 prisoners got away, 11 of them British.

'Colditz was a minor yet major episode in the Second World War. It was the peak of how you can fight a battle as a prisoner. We continued the fight in Colditz. We were the besiegers within and we were holding down a large number of troops outside. It was an endless battle and we did not give in. It was a psychological battle of tremendous importance, an episode in World War II of historical significance,' Reid said with intense pride.

We were nearing Leipzig, Major Reid had told his story, but there was still something to say about the personal meaning of this unique return to Colditz. 'When you come back many years later and see the roof falling in, the plaster coming off, dereliction everywhere, lunatic faces all about, you think what was it all about. Our meeting is about loyalties that were forged in deprivation that will last until the end of our lives. It is as if we met yesterday. That's the strength and joy of it.'

Less than five years later East Germany's revolution swept through even the small neglected town of Colditz. The big city nearby, Leipzig, had led the people's revolt. At last Colditz was set to change and to be brought belatedly into the final decade of the twentieth century. Having few assets apart from its castle, this was at once put forward as a suitable investment opportunity. The psychiatric patients should be moved elsewhere, part of the castle could be turned into an hotel, another section into a museum of escapes. No doubt it will become a 'theme park' in a modern, united Germany. At the same time it will lose some of its most direct contact with history, its most immediate witnesses will, as soldiers do, just fade away. But their dogged determination and will to resist, their example, have given this small town in eastern Germany a reputation more compelling than any it had previously achieved in its long history.

For a country returning to democracy after an extended interval, there should be something specially significant in the words Pat Reid chose for the dedication of his final book: 'To the men of Colditz who tried but did not succeed, yet generously helped those few who did; to all prisoners of tyranny, wherever in the world they may be cruelly confined; and to the young people of the world that they may be vigilant in the pursuit of Freedom and guard it with tenacity and courage.'

4 East Berlin, the Jewel in the Socialist Crown

When the Wall finally came down in November 1989 after twenty-eight years and three months of dividing a people, prosperous West Berliners rediscovered the eastern half of the city. They found it grey, drab, shoddy and hopelessly old-fashioned. It was rather like the West Berlin they remembered from the 1950s and 1960s, even the prices were the same. It was still being reconstructed from the rubble of war, a process long completed in the West. Its backwardness had curiosity value and offered considerable scope for the shrewd investor and sharp businessman, but little else. It may have been rich in history and nostalgia; it was chronically short of glamour.

Yet for the visitor from Leipzig or Dresden, Nordhausen or Brandenburg, let alone from Warsaw or Bucharest, East Berlin was one of communist Eastern Europe's most modern and prosperous centres. It was, as the East German authorities proclaimed at every opportunity – and in contravention to post-war Allied agreements on the city's status – the 'Hauptstadt der DDR' (capital of the German Democratic Republic). There were therefore sound political reasons for transforming East Berlin into a socialist shop window. It was East Germany's most accessible and visible city, as well as being the seat of central government.

By East European standards, shops were extremely well stocked. Bread, meat, dairy products and basic vegetables were in plentiful supply at extremely reasonable prices. Fresh fish, rare in the provinces, was available in the city's few fishmongers'. Herring, mackerel and plaice, brought from the Baltic, lay piled deep on the slab of the Alexanderplatz fishmonger. Apart from apples and pears, fresh fruit was scarcer, with East Germans depending on tired and battered-looking Cuban oranges and lemons for their vitamin C. There were also the 'Delikat' shops, where luxury items such as tea and coffee, cakes, biscuits and preserves, some imported from the West, could be obtained more expensively. Unlike in neighbouring Poland, or Russia, the shelves were never bare, the queues never impossible, the prices never exorbitant. The range may have seemed limited compared with the excess of the West, but it was impressive to the family who had come up for the day from the country, the visiting Pole or the Russian troops stationed in East Germany.

Even for the affluent westerner there were pickings: Romeo and Juliet, Upmann and Partagas were just some of the premier brands of Cuban cigars available at absurdly low prices. There was also every calibre of Joya de Nicaragua cigar, in the opinion of some connoisseurs a smoke equal to the finest Cuban. For the real aficionado there were even untipped Montecristo and Ligeros – 'extra suaves', according to their description – cigarettes from Havana. And the VEB Vereinigte Zigarettenfabriken Dresden still made pleasingly aromatic 'Exquisit Orient' cigarettes from a 'mixture of outstanding quality tobaccos from Macedonia and the Orient'.

But such obviously capitalist tastes were undeveloped, even unknown among East Germans more used to socialist austerity and unadventurous by nature. The few cigar-smoking East Germans I ever met preferred cruder locally manufactured dark-leafed Brazil tobaccos. As for cigarette smokers – and East Germans smoke heavily – they chose the Virginia-type tobacco blends of poorly packaged local brands, at least until western cigarettes became available after the revolution.

High-grade rums from Cuba and Nicaragua, which East

Germans would waste on hot grogs rather than Planter's Punch, were stocked on the shelves of the liquor shops. The choice of Nicaraguan rums was especially wide, with different degrees of darkness and age from a light three-year-old to a dark oak brown, richly mature seven-year-old rejoicing in the name Ron, an unintentional tribute to the American president whose policies drove Nicaraguan products on to the unfamiliar markets of communist Eastern Europe.

I used to think that East Berlin must be a paradise for an opera-loving, theatre-going, museum-visiting, cigar-smoking, rum-sipping aesthete. Unfortunately for them, few East Berliners could be expected to fit such a demanding description.

Sport and culture were two areas of the utmost importance to the communist regime. In the first, East Germany could – as the medal tables showed – claim to be a sporting superpower. As for culture, ever since Walter Felsenstein's reign at the Komische Oper it had played a pioneering and leading role in the staging of opera. It was a country rich in musical talent and its three main orchestras, the Dresden State Orchestra, the Leipzig Gewandhaus and the Berlin Symphony Orchestra, were celebrated internationally. It could boast opera and lieder singers of the stature of Theo Adam and Peter Schreier, the trumpeter Ludwig Güttler and the horn player Hermann Baumann. In the visual arts the official demand for socialist realism had a dampening effect, but East Germany's museums and galleries, and notably East Berlin's, were well stocked with treasures.

Cultural distinction, pursued by the politicians as a means of heightening East Germany's international profile, was not wasted on a people who, in the absence of western distractions and diversions, were tremendously culturally aware. It was really a case of 'opera for all' with low seat prices, high standards and an opera house in every major city and two in East Berlin. I remember talking to a street sweeper outside

Leipzig's Thomaskirche about Bach, 'unser grosser Komponist' (our great composer), and to a war widow out shopping in Dresden about the architectural taste of Augustus the Strong. I never ceased to be amazed by mothers taking their smallest children to museums that would daunt many adults in the West. One morning in East Berlin's Pergamon, whose classical collection boldly challenges that of the British Museum, I was stopped in my tracks by a four-year-old asking his mother a very pertinent question about one particular Hellenic statue. His two slightly older sisters and a still younger brother listened intently to her reply without lapsing from their scrutiny of the white marble god. At first I thought I had stumbled across a remarkable family, but the longer I spent in East German museums, the more precociously interested and impeccably behaved children became evident. On a tour of the elegant Schloss Friedrichsfelde, a fine pink and white two-storey baroque house built originally for a wealthy Dutch merchant in Berlin, two girls, aged eight and nine, were fascinated by more than the outsize felt overslippers visitors had to wear to protect the floors. Their questions were full of curiosity and intelligence. East German children were well educated and, without exposure to video and computer games, retained old-fashioned virtues and enthusiasms. It was one of the very few good things to be said for the old regime.

Sport and a good dose of culture were to bring me back to East Berlin a few weeks after the Torgau and Colditz anniversaries. This time the International Olympic Committee was meeting there, a useful opportunity for Herr Honecker to burnish his country's image abroad. On no pre-revolutionary visit to East Germany was I made to feel so welcome, not only by the Germans.

No sooner had I arrived in my room at the familiar Metropol Hotel than a slightly out of breath, eye-catchingly dressed

French girl with almost waist-length dark hair knocked on the door with a 'Press kit', in fact a gift of a small 'designer' briefcase – white with flashes of red and blue, like the outfit she was wearing – containing all kinds of similarly designed requisites, from pens and stationery to a cigarette lighter inscribed 'Paris 1992'. Paris, competing with half a dozen other cities, was lobbying hard for the right, and accompanying profits and prestige, to stage the 1992 summer Olympics. It was to be an unsuccessful bid, but not before delegates and journalists were showered with presents and regaled with an extravagant buffet where more fine champagne was consumed than East Berlin could have seen in the previous decade. It was unsubtle, but very French and quite delicious.

Erich Honecker, sitting in the front row of the magnificently restored Schauspielhaus with his education minister wife, Margot, from whom he was separated, led the applause at the concert in honour of the eighty-two delegates. Like so many East Bloc leaders, he always managed to appear to be clapping himself. The elegantly arched and latticed Jehmlich organ, surmounted by a golden lyre between two music-loving dolphins, opened the evening with Bach's Toccata in D minor. The *pièce de résistance* was Beethoven's Ninth Symphony, as it was to be at Christmas 1989 when the American maestro Leonard Bernstein came to the Schauspielhaus to conduct a concert of celebration for East Germany's peaceful revolution and the overthrow of the Honecker regime. In the finale's setting of Schiller's 'Ode to Joy' Bernstein insisted that the word *Freiheit* (Freedom) should be substituted for *Freude* (joy). How comfortably ignorant of the course history was to take, and how falsely secure, Honecker was at that gala concert early in June 1985.

After years of neglect and bursts of bad building in the 1960s and 1970s, the East Berlin authorities had at last in the 1980s woken up to the fact that the city possessed the best of the former Prussian capital's architecture and that war-damaged buildings might be better restored than demolished. East Berlin became an even bigger building site as scaffolding started cloaking venerable ruins and Polish workers, who had proved their skills in the meticulous restoration of Warsaw's Old Town, joined East German experts. Of a number of major restoration projects undertaken in the heart of the city, that of the Platz der Akademie, as the Gendarmenmarkt had been renamed in 1950, and the Schauspielhaus, its centrepiece, was by far the most successful.

The eighteenth-century French and German cathedrals on either side of the square, with their matching domes – one of Frederick the Great's architectural ideas – had remained ruins into the early 1980s. Both had suffered terribly, along with the Schauspielhaus, in Allied air raids in 1944–5 which reduced them to burned-out shells. On early visits to East Berlin I remember the sad sight of the crumbling Corinthian porticos of the two churches, plants and trees sprouting from the cracked pediments, netting cast over the capitals to prevent flaking stone from falling. With its almost perfect symmetry and breadth, this had been, if not Europe's, then certainly Berlin's finest square. Slowly and with great care, behind ugly corrugated-iron screens and with towering orange-painted cranes disturbing the once harmonious skyline, it was being brought back to life: first the Schauspielhaus and the French cathedral and then the German church, due to be completed in the 1990s.

It was not the first time the Schauspielhaus had risen from the ashes. The previous National Theatre building completed in 1802 by Karl Gotthard Langhans, best known as the architect of the Brandenburg Gate, burned down in a fire on 29 July 1817. The following April Karl Friedrich Schinkel won the commission to rebuild it, incorporating the surviving exterior walls and the columns of the portico. Completed early in

1821 and reopened in May with a performance of Goethe's *Iphigenie*, the result was one of Schinkel's masterpieces, strongly classical but highly functional, with a stage, concert hall and ancillary rooms. There was even an entrance passage for carriages under the broad sweep of steps so that theatre- and concert-goers could alight directly into the building when it was raining. The wonderful decorative detail of the interior suffered from neglect and then changes in taste later in the nineteenth century, so that by the time Allied bombs wrought their destruction in February 1945 little of the original Schinkel decoration was left. But his plans, not only architectural but for much of the interior decoration, had survived and a reconstruction was begun which restored the exterior to its original state and created a convincingly Schinkelesque neo-classical interior where its adaptation to modern requirements was necessary. Dazzling crystal chandeliers cast their bright light on exquisite marbling, pastel-hued wall-paintings and the most delicate gilded plaster work. There can be little doubt that the result would have won the approval of the great architect who had said, 'Being historical does not mean clinging solely to what is old or repeating it, for that would be the death of history; to act in the spirit of history one must continue with the past in giving rise to something new.'

The rebuilt and refurbished Schauspielhaus opened amid great acclaim and with a gala concert of music by Weber, Mendelssohn, Nicolai and Richard Strauss on 1 October 1984. Inevitably Honecker was there to witness the applause and appreciation for Berlin's and surely Europe's most attractive concert hall. It was a late lesson for the communist regime: that more points were to be scored at home and internationally by a good restoration of an historic building than by its brutal replacement with some modernist fantasy. If only twenty years earlier Schinkel's bomb-damaged Bauakademie (Building Academy), a seminal work in the history of architecture, could have been spared and as carefully renovated. Instead it was torn down to make room for one of East Berlin's most abominable architectural creations, the Ministry for Foreign Affairs. Like a huge coffin covered in polystyrene packing, it makes nonsense of the careful counterpoint achieved in the heart of Berlin by its foremost eighteenth- and nineteenth-century architects.

The French cathedral, the 'French Church in the Friedrichstadt' which served Berlin's once significant Huguenot community, was restored with the same care and attention to detail as the Schauspielhaus. The panelling and gilded wood carvings that encased the original organ of 1755 were by a stroke of good fortune packed away safely in storage when the church was bombed in 1944. A new instrument, particularly suited to the playing of French classical music, was created by the Eule organ builders of Bautzen to fit the old baroque casing. Carillon bells were installed in the tower that could play Bach chorales and Mozart and would ring across the square on the stroke of the hour. On the way up to the tower, somewhat unecclesiastically, a wine restaurant was opened offering sustenance to cathedral visitors during the day and concert-goers from the Schauspielhaus in the evenings. The balustrade immediately beneath the cupola presented an all-round view of the once fine heart of old Berlin. The cathedral itself was not entirely given over to Mammon, being still used by the French Reformed and Friedrichswerder church parishes and Berlin's Ecumenical Association.

Its history was certainly unusual. A small French Reformed community serving the court in Berlin was already in existence in 1672, but it swelled to about 5,000 after the revocation on 18 October 1685 of the Edict of Nantes, which had underwritten religious tolerance. The result was an exodus from France of about 200,000 Huguenots. Brandenburg-Prussia, recovering from the devastation of the Thirty Years War, was one of the countries to welcome them. England was another.

Already on 29 October with the Edict of Potsdam, Elector Frederick William offered Brandenburg-Prussia as a new home to those seeking refuge. By 1700 some 20,000 Huguenots had settled there, forming about 50 colonies with their own pastors, schools, mayors and judges. Berlin itself attracted about 6,000 or a quarter of its population at the time. The Huguenots brought a wealth of talent and skills to a city which was still economically backward. They rose to influential positions at court and in the army and were to play important roles in commerce, science and the arts.

In 1701 work was begun on the French and German cathedrals by Louis Cayart and Martin Grünberg respectively. Cayart, who had trained under Vauban as a builder of fortifications, including the fort of Verdun, died the following year, and Abraham Quesnay, otherwise known only as an architect of orphanages, took over. The French cathedral was dedicated in 1705 and the German church three years later. But their most famous attributes, their matching domes (one of Frederick the Great's inspired whims influenced by Rome's Piazza del Popolo), were added between 1780 and 1785 to designs by Carl von Gontard carried through by his pupil Georg Christian Unger after the unfortunate collapse of the German church's cupola in July 1781. The two towering domes were built purely for show and do not even open into the churches. In August 1785 a key to the tower was symbolically presented to the French Reformed community, which was to use its rooms for a sacristy, offices and soup-kitchen. Today, apart from the restaurant, it houses a library, offices and a Huguenot museum.

The bomb-battered once bustling Gendarmenmarkt was returning to life and regaining some of its former elegance. It was repaved, trees were planted and the houses round about either restored suitably or re-created in a style that was in character with the surroundings. East Berliners and western

71

visitors began to flock back to what for forty years had been a ghost square haunted by its ruins. The newly opened Arkaden Café on the corner was perpetually full.

In March 1986, a month after the Soviet-Jewish dissident Anatoly Shcharansky was exchanged in a spectacular East–West spy swap at the snow-covered Glienicke Bridge, a deal of a very different kind was negotiated at top level. Friedrich Schiller, the great German poet and dramatist – or at least his Carrara marble likeness by the popular late nineteenth-century sculptor Reinhold Begas – was to return to the place he had occupied since 1871 in front of the Schauspielhaus. In exchange for Schiller, who had been held in the West ever since the war years, East Berlin agreed to return twenty-nine late eighteenth-century relief portraits by the sculptor Johann Peter Echtler to the tea salon of the small Pfaueninsel Castle on the Wannsee. They included depictions of Moderation, Innocence, Peace, Abundance, Virtue and Gratitude. West Berlin would also receive the Calandrelli Nymph, a statue which had formerly graced a fountain by the Villa von der Heydt on the Landwehr canal.

Much of the hectic construction programme under way, the sudden interest in repairing historic buildings after years of neglect, had a political objective. In 1987 Berlin was to celebrate its 750-year-long history, an occasion for which the authorities in the West were making elaborate and extravagant preparations, disbursing generous subsidies. But the historic core of Berlin, its architecturally most significant buildings, and indeed 90 per cent of its past, lay in the East. It was only early in the twentieth century that the centre of the city spilled west of the Brandenburg Gate and its previously rural environs were gobbled up by rapid industrial expansion and residential needs. East Berlin, richer in history, could not allow itself to be upstaged by the wealthier West. It too would be celebrating the anniversary which presented another opportunity to sharpen its international profile, raise its standing and strengthen its claim as 'Hauptstadt der DDR'.

Despite all the rebuilding activities in the Platz der Akademie, the main focus of attention was on the area around the Nikolaikirche (Berlin's oldest church), the Nikolaiviertel. This was the historic core of the city, where in the twelfth and thirteenth centuries the trade settlements of Berlin and Cölln merged into one. But what a team of architects headed by Günter Stahn endeavoured to achieve here was more radical and ultimately less successful than the parallel project at the Platz der Akademie. His plans were altogether more adventurous; he would re-create earlier styles rather than restore. For the narrow streets, he designed pseudo-medieval or period buildings, which were then constructed with modern materials. The result was unauthentically spick and span, an East German Camelot or Disneyland, which yet enjoyed a certain popularity both with visitors and the over fifteen hundred East Berliners who lived there. It may have looked like a period setting, but it was modern and functional. Some of the flats, for example, were designed with handicapped people and wheelchairs in mind. Another argument in its favour was that it could instead have suffered, like the nearby Alexanderplatz in the late 1960s, the much worse fate of being transformed into an uncompromising modernist landscape.

Apart from the Nikolaikirche, three buildings, however, succeed, and for particular reasons. Two of them, the Ephraim Palace and the Nussbaum Inn, were moved here from elsewhere and the third, the Knoblauch House, is one of the few original buildings in the Nikolaiviertel.

The Ephraim Palace was originally built between 1761 and 1767 by Friedrich Wilhelm Diterichs, one of the masters of Berlin baroque, for Veitel Ephraim, the Jewish banker, court jeweller and leaseholder of Frederick the Great's royal mint. He provided grain and salt for Frederick's armies and through the mint financed the king's wars. By steadily reducing the precious metal content of the coins he earned Frederick some twenty-nine million thalers and an additional fortune for himself, and ruined the purchasing power of the currency. The king, who approved of the practice as 'state policy', remained discreetly in the background, while his banker gained general opprobrium. The palace's eight Tuscan columns, which were to be tastefully crowned by gilded balconies and putti, were provided by Frederick the Great from booty plundered in the war with Saxony, coming from the palace of Count Brühl, the Saxon minister. But the whole splendid rococo creation, long considered 'Berlin's most beautiful corner', was completely dismantled in 1935 during building work on the Mühlendamm Bridge and put away as numbered pieces into storage. Like so many other works of art, when Berlin came to be divided ten years later, they were stranded in the wrong half of the city. But in 1983, following the precedent of the repatriation to the East of the neo-classical statues that had adorned Schinkel's Schlossbrücke in exchange for the pattern books of the Königliche Porzellan Manufaktur and before the deal involving Begas's Schiller statue, the Ephraim façade was also returned to East Berlin. In 1983–4 it began to be carefully reconstructed some sixty feet from its original site, opening as a museum, gallery and café in time for the city's 750th anniversary. It was a notable achievement and the finest element of the ambitious Nikolaiviertel project.

The inn Zum Nussbaum, originally built around 1570 on the nearby Fischerinsel, was also transferred to the Nikolaiviertel and an appropriate walnut tree planted outside. Its reputation rests largely on the popular late nineteenth-century caricaturist Heinrich Zille, who found in its smoke-filled rooms many of the Berlin types he was to portray so engagingly. It is still cramped and busy, with an acrid smell of sweat mingled with stale tobacco and an abundance of Berlin atmosphere.

Another leading member of the Jewish community during

the reign of Frederick the Great, the silk merchant Johann Christian Knoblauch – by all accounts a more attractive personality than Ephraim – commissioned the fine baroque family house in the Poststrasse in 1759. Later given a neo-classical façade, it was to stay in the hands of the family until 1928. The playwright Lessing, the Jewish philosopher Moses Mendelssohn and the von Humboldt brothers, the prominent Berlin academics, were regular visitors at the Knoblauch House, which survives and stands out as one of the quarter's few original buildings.

The Nikolaikirche itself has a longer history than any Berlin church, dating from around 1230, but it suffered terribly from nineteenth-century restorers and from war damage. For centuries the Gothic church's single asymmetric pointed tower was a distinctive feature of the Berlin skyline. But as part of a radical and unnecessary overhaul in the 1870s – and only after much controversy – the neo-Gothic renovators directed by Hermann Blankenstein substituted twin towers, completely redesigned the interior and installed a massive organ. The towers were burned down in an air raid in June 1944 and the nave caught fire during furious street fighting in April 1945 between die-hard Nazi units, including boy soldiers decorated personally by the Führer, and the Red Army. Weakened by the elements, the vaulting finally collapsed in 1949 and the Nikolaikirche remained a ruin until repair work began in 1980. The result was mixed, the modern materials making the church seem clean, cool and detached from a long history rooted in Berlin's solar plexus. Its use as a museum rather than place of worship exaggerated its aloof, artificial atmosphere. The great irony was that an admission fee was now being charged to one of the city's newest museums, where since the earliest days of its 750-year history the people of Berlin had come to pray. The decline in spiritual values seemed to be symbolized by the workman who, when asked the way to the Nikolaikirche, could only respond with a shrug of his shoulders.

The workman was busy outside another church that had been secularized, but this time more successfully. The Friedrichswerdersche Kirche – on the other side of the river Spree behind the Crown Prince's palace – is Schinkel's Gothic masterpiece in Berlin. Having graced the Prussian capital with its finest neo-classical buildings, Schinkel fulfilled Crown Prince Frederick William's commission for a twin-towered Gothic church in the Werdersche market, although he had initially provided designs for classical alternatives. In 1826 Schinkel had travelled to England to inspect the British Museum and seek ideas for his Altes Museum. He also studied industrial architecture and workers' dwellings in Manchester and returned with his notebooks brimming over with sketches, ideas and observations. When it came to the Friedrichswerdersche commission, he let himself be influenced by the Gothic country churches he had seen in England and the result, apart from the north German red brick Schinkel so favoured, is strongly and strangely English in the heart of Berlin. Dedicated in 1831, the church would fit well into an Oxford or Cambridge collegiate setting. It was soon complemented by his Bauakademie, finished in 1835 on an adjacent site and demolished by the East Berlin authorities in an inexcusable act of vandalism in 1962. The Bauakademie was considered among Schinkel's most original achievements, fusing medieval structures with Greek detail. It was rightly to play a seminal role in German architecture. Schinkel himself moved into a flat on its top floor, where, after a stroke, he died in October 1841.

As if to make up for their earlier infamy over the Bauakademie, the East Berlin building authorities decided to restore meticulously the Friedrichswerdersche Kirche, which was badly damaged in April 1945 and subsequently allowed to decay. Another of Berlin's finest buildings was to be saved on account of the approaching 750th anniversary programme. It was not to be revived as a church but as a Schinkel Museum, documenting in its upper gallery the life and work of Berlin's most gifted architect. The pews were not returned to the nave, which became a gallery of neo-classical sculpture, placing together works by Schinkel's contemporaries and friends and including some of his own terracotta reliefs from the ill-fated Bauakademie. The interior was exuberantly light, well lit from the tall, arched windows – those at the end brightly coloured and patterned as elegantly as a Hermès silk scarf. Perhaps partly because of its much shorter life as a place of worship compared with the Nikolaikirche, but principally as a result of the integration of detail – whether door handles, decorative carvings, stained glass or panelled wooden pulpit, the work of one inspired mind – it succeeds as well in a secular as in a religious function. And in this case the East Germans chose a highly suitable secular use.

So in the early 1980s, spurred by the sense of history required for the 750th anniversary celebrations, they were beginning to take the right architectural decisions after years of misguided socialist modernism.

Wandering down those still bullet-scarred, shell-pocked streets of East Berlin, most of which had mercifully survived the modernist developers, all kinds of surprises were possible. None was more startling and exhilarating than that to be found halfway down the Grosse Hamburgerstrasse. Suddenly a gap between two particular cannon-peppered house corners revealed a jewel of early eighteenth-century elegance wholly unexpected in this run-down quarter once notable for its Jewish community. I stopped and stared and was staggered. Here was a church as out of the Berlin character as the Friedrichswerdersche, though this time we were not in rural England but in Wren's City of London. Tucked away off the road in the manner of St Bride's, Fleet Street, it was like a perfectly formed pearl inside a heavily encrusted, blistered oyster shell. The Sophienkirche's tiered tower, added in 1732–4 by Johann Friedrich Grael, miraculously survived the bombing and street fighting all around as Hitler's capital crumbled, and today it stands proudly as Berlin's only original baroque tower. Seventy metres high, it adds distinction to a skyline which has been drastically altered by war and modern development. Its perspective from the bottom of the Krausnickstrasse would be a credit to Venice or Paris, cities more gently treated by fortune. The long grey-stoned body of the church – visible only side-on from the Sophienstrasse – dates from 1712 and is quintessentially English. In its graveyard lies Leopold von Ranke, 'the first modern historian' (whom Thomas Carlyle considered 'Dry-as-Dust') and great-uncle of Robert Graves.

Untouched apart from a late nineteenth-century neo-baroque interior redecoration, the Sophienkirche continues as a parish church and provides the axis of one of Berlin's few remaining eighteenth-century streets. Walking down the Sophienstrasse is as uplifting an experience as the first close-up sighting of the church. It begins with a pleasant corner café, the Sophieneck, with a charming little adjoining garden, and on the other side of the street there follows a fine sequence of trade and craft premises: a ladies' tailor; goldsmith; Boris Schoenherr, maker of woodwind instruments. It ends with a paper factory, hand-weaving studios, a barber and a caster of tin figures. Taking the Sophienkirche for St James's, Piccadilly, this is Berlin's nearest to Jermyn Street. Finally, as one is about to leave this enchanted world and return to the twentieth century and the soulless Alexanderplatz, a small puppet theatre beckons on the right with performances of Mozart operas. What hidden pleasures this outwardly austere, communist-ruled city still had.

But East Berlin was not typical of East Germany; it was the communist-promoted flagship, the socialist metropolis. On account of the approaching 750th anniversary programme, the authorities poured 1.3 billion marks investment into the city while the impoverished provinces continued to decay. Much of historic Dresden, once one of Europe's most magnificent cities, the erstwhile 'Florence of the Elbe', remained in the ruins in which it was left by Allied bombers on 13/14 February 1945.

Berlin also had special qualities of its own, which the communist authorities did not need to promote and could not discourage. The dry sense of humour and resilience of its people stood out. Whether toiling in the grim conditions of late nineteenth-century factories or enduring the chaos that followed the First World War or the bombing and destruction of the last war and the loss of individual liberty under Nazism and later communism, that sense of humour survived. 'Berlin wit is worth more than beautiful surroundings,' the philosopher Georg Hegel observed as early as 1830.

The International Olympic Committee delegates, ferried from one presentation and reception to another, cannot have seen much of the real Berlin during their June 1985 visit, but enough perhaps of the luxury hotels and gala concerts to be convinced that things were not so bad in the socialist German state. Sport, which so often can bind people together, can also hoodwink them. Those who came to Hitler's 1936 Berlin Olympics left convinced that German fascism was not the scourge some made out. They enjoyed the hospitality and saw a modern, prosperous city, well organized and efficient. On a smaller, less significant scale, Erich Honecker was conducting a similar public relations exercise almost fifty years later. To crown the event the delegates were invited to a display of sporting prowess and music at the vast Palace of the Republic, which so brashly occupied the site of the former royal palace. Luxury buses came to collect the guests from their hotels a few hundred yards away for an evening of entertainment provided by young gymnasts, former Olympic medallists and even a group of athletic pensioners. From my seat at the top of the enormous auditorium, surrounded by pairs of unsmiling, blue-shirted and yellow-scarved boy members of the FDJ, the communist youth movement, I watched this extraordinary spectacle of well-rehearsed sporting virtuosity. It really was a brave new world, where discipline over mind and body was perfected at the expense of any individualism. East Germany's sportsmen and women were, after the communist rulers, the country's élite. I looked down to the distant front row and there was Erich Honecker with a pursed smile, clapping as usual.

He was watching the generation born in the years after he had personally supervised the raising of the Berlin Wall, excelling in sport and displaying total loyalty to the socialist cause. Having himself been charged with the setting up of the communist youth movement at East Germany's inception, he always felt close to young people despite his own advancing years. He was sure he enjoyed their support, just as he felt certain that the people of East Berlin appreciated what communist rule had accomplished for them and their city.

In reality they looked West, compared and felt cheated. Honecker's intense feeling of pride in East Germany's and East Berlin's socialist achievement was, despite outward appearances, shared by few ordinary East Germans. Though indoctrinated and rigidly regimented, their obedience was only ensured by the pervasive control of the omnipresent Stasi. They could hardly be expected to be 'workers and peasants' by choice, but they were not allowed to choose. East Germany had been declared by its communist rulers to be 'The Workers' and Peasants' State'.

Part 2

EAST EUROPEAN
NEIGHBOURS

5 Southern Bohemia by Bicycle

An appropriate starting-point for an adventure in Bohemia is the rough and tumble of the crowded visa section of the Czechoslovak embassy in Vienna. The taxi stopped by a fine honey-coloured town house and the consular entrance was immediately apparent from the long queue of impatient visa applicants that snaked into the street. Buried deep among their number, unruffled by the chaos and armed with a pair of scissors, four pieces of carbon paper and some glue, was John Nicholson. We had arranged to meet to submit together our visa applications for a cycling expedition beginning the following day in southern Bohemia.

I set to work right away, cutting a couple of passport photographs to size, pasting them on to the top two of the five application sheets and then sandwiching the carbon paper in between before completing the forms. It was a tricky procedure with which Nicholson was well familiar and therefore suitably equipped. To have admitted to being a journalist on such a trip to pre-revolutionary Czechoslovakia would have brought unnecessary complications, so we declared ourselves to be musicians. This might have been absolutely true in the case of Nicholson, who would sing in the chorus of the Vienna State Opera and with the Arnold Schoenberg choir, and partly accurate with regard to Richard Bassett, the third member and guiding spirit of the trio, who apart from writing for *The Times* played the horn at parties and friends' weddings. But my claim was rather spurious. If asked, we decided, I was the conductor, the music director. Nicholson, displaying a civility to which the surly consular official was quite unused, handed in his and Bassett's passports and visa forms and I added mine. We should return in an hour or so to collect them. We gave authenticity to our claim, not altogether intentionally, by ad-journing to the Max Reinhardt Academy next door for a late breakfast. If the Czechoslovak secret service vetted the em-bassy's visitors as closely as they might, which was extremely unlikely, they would have been impressed by our mingling with the music students, a number of whom Nicholson knew well. They came from all over the world – from as far away as America and Japan – to study in Central Europe's musical capital. The academy was named after the great director who before emigrating to America in 1938 had revolutionized theatre in Berlin, Vienna and Salzburg. I remember my mother telling me how as a young girl she was auditioned and given a small part by Reinhardt in *The Miracle*, the *tour de force* of the exquisitely beautiful Diana Cooper.

We returned to the still chaotic visa office; the queue re-mained long and patience short as the invariably brief consular hours were coming to an end and many would clearly be stranded or, despite 'urgent family business' entreaties, even tears, turned back. But our passports were stamped with the necessary red and blue ink and Bohemian lion that embellished a Czechoslovak visa and, after paying our fee, we were glad to leave the confusion.

Early the following morning we were to meet at Vienna's Franz Josef station on the Prague train. Bassett and I walked down the platform and chose a compartment near the front of the train, but there was no sign of Nicholson. A whistle blew, the train started, stopped, shuddered and moved on again. We eyed somewhat dubiously the unshaven young man stretched out asleep by the compartment window; he seemed oblivious of our conversation. A pity about Nicholson, we thought, whereupon, clutching a battered rucksack, he slid back the door and joined us. He had jumped on the train as it was leaving and walked the length of it to find us. We transferred to the restaurant car, which had begun its journey in East Berlin and was in the hands of an affable and rather under-worked Berliner. His only clients, we ordered scrambled eggs and tea with bread and strawberry jam, followed, as the morning progressed and the frontier neared, by East German beer. We would disembark at Gmünd, the last station on the Austrian side, and pick up bicycles we had reserved there. The bicycle hire service offered by Austrian railways was ideal for such expeditions. We paid our deposits, adjusted the seats and handlebars and set off downhill on the short ride to the border.

The surprise shown by the Austrian customs officials as we cycled past was slight compared with the absolute astonish-ment of the stout, grey-uniformed Czechoslovak border guard when we arrived at the red, white and blue barrier that marked the frontier. The cyclist was still an almost unknown phenomenon in Eastern Europe, where it was assumed that every westerner owned a fast car.

He asked to see our passports, took them and told us to wait. As he pushed open the green-painted door of the České Velenice border post, we surveyed the scene: the flagpole; the tank traps, some overgrown with straggly weeds, by the side of the cracked, worn road, ready to be moved into place in an emergency. It was a picture which cannot have changed since Hitler's troops violated the border and drove into Czechoslo-vakia almost fifty years earlier. The border official returned, his bulky body swaying with the brisk steps of his walk, and lifted the barrier. A little out of breath, he signalled that we should leave our bicycles outside the wooden office, asked us where we were going and for how long, and ushered us into the modest building. The main part of his role now over, he stood to the side while a female colleague sitting behind a glass partition as in a bank analysed our papers further and calculated exactly how much hard currency we would have to exchange for our time in Czechoslovakia. Completing her sums, she made her demands with a smile enhanced by the crimson lipstick she was wearing. That and her loudly dyed blonde hair seemed to offer feminine compensation for the masculinity of her uniform. The atmosphere was becoming pleasantly relaxed for a border post. A more senior officer, older, with thinning hair and steel-rimmed glasses, came out of his office clutching a bundle of papers, glanced at us, said good day and went into another room. We asked our original border official for the best cycle route to Český Krumlov. Although no great distance away, it was as if we were pressing him to recommend the quickest way to Rome. After many hums and haws he eventually pointed to exactly the main road we wanted to avoid. We thanked him and, as an afterthought, he asked us if we had cameras or anything else to declare. We assured him we did not, said goodbye and set off down the road. As we moved off, I saw him lift the front of his cap, mop his brow with a handkerchief and return to the hut.

Our first few hundred yards in Bohemia were in the wrong direction. We cycled into the altogether insignificant town of České Velenice instead of striking out immediately on a country road that would take us through fields and woods to our goal, Český Krumlov. Down the cobbled street we went, under the railway bridge, past yellow and grey buildings with small piles of household lignite dumped outside. Our bearings were clearly wrong and remained so until, emerging at the other end of the town, our eyes were caught by a remarkably buxom, fair-haired girl indulging in the favourite East European pastime of leaning out of a window and watching the world go by. We stopped to ask the way, but before she could give a coherent answer she was pulled back and replaced by her suspicious husband or father, an oil-smeared mechanic who showed us the right direction.

We cycled back through the desolate town and then found the country road that for a time continued parallel to the railway track. It may not have been the most direct route to Český Krumlov, but it was certainly attractive, and had the great advantage of being almost traffic free. It was not yet midday and we had plenty of time. After a mile or so we broke off away from the railway, taking a turning to the left and meandering along agreeably through fields and forests that displayed a rich range of golden-brown autumn colours. Then, when we approached the crest of a hill, the idyll was slightly jarred by the presence of a tall watchtower, though its purpose was not at first clear. After a quarter of an hour the riddle was solved. As we progressed through the woods we saw rows of concrete ramps, bunkers and an assortment of military hardware: we had unwittingly stumbled across a Soviet missile base, carefully concealed near the border. Fearing that our cycling expedition might come to a premature end and certain that our entry into the woods had been monitored from the watchtower, we hastened on and were relieved to emerge from the restricted area unchallenged. It was a reminder of the dense Soviet military presence in Eastern Europe, similar to the concentration of Russian troops I had come across in travels around Leipzig.

After this first taste of adventure we traversed more gently undulating, long-harvested fields, meeting neither man nor machine, until we descended to the pleasant town of Nové Hrady. In the far corner of the broad early nineteenth century town square was an alehouse packed with men enjoying large mugs of light golden beer, something for which we thirsted. We left our bicycles in the corridor and were lucky to find a table by the window. We were instantly brought as much beer as we could drink. Food was another matter, for this was no restaurant, but Nicholson, a natural quartermaster, had made up some sandwiches in Vienna and we had chocolate to follow. Czechoslovak beer, already second to none, can hardly be more appreciated or better earned than after a spell of hard cycling.

It had a restorative effect even if initially it may have slowed our post-prandial progress. But more to blame was the much hillier country we encountered next. Ideally, lunch should be followed by a long, leisurely downhill ride. The Austrian railways bicycles had three rudimentary gears, which were of little help with the sometimes relentless Bohemian hills. The broad cross-country views we had been enjoying began to be curtailed by a fine, disagreeable drizzle and the cool autumn temperatures dropped a telling few degrees. The only compensation was that the uphill ascents were rewarded with extended, exhilarating downhill swoops, past farmsteads with shrieking geese and barking dogs, through villages which, however modest, were yet graced by small baroque churches or chapels. This was a Bohemia where time had long stood still. Only an occasional battered tractor or family car hinted at progress.

Our descent had by now brought us to the town of Kaplice. We were soaked from sweat and rain, beginning to tire and little more than halfway to Český Krumlov. It was getting dark and a break was overdue. The steamed-up window of a small hotel only half concealed a roomful of beer drinkers and card players. Like the saloon bar in some Wild West settlement, it was the natural stopping place. But instead of tying up our horses outside we locked our bicycles together. It was to be an unfortunate mistake that would bring a tiresome entanglement with the secret police. Until now, apart from the border formalities and the restricted Soviet military zone, we might have forgotten that we were in a state still rigidly ruled by communists. Weary, wet and unsuspecting of the trouble that lay ahead, we entered the muggy, smoke-filled room and sat down to three glasses, as is the local custom, of tea.

Fortified, we paid the small bill, assembled our belongings

and left. Austrian railways had issued combination locks with the bicycles and the one we had secured them with would not unfasten. We took it in turns trying to coax it open, playing with one permutation of numbers after another, although we were fairly sure which we had set. It remained stubborn. Linked by this iron-chained umbilical cord, the bicycles were inseparable, immovable. Gradually our performance was attracting an uncomfortable amount of attention. In the West we would have been taken for rather clumsy bicycle thieves. Fortunately, in this obscure corner of Bohemia we were the only likely owners of such machines. Passers-by were stopping and were joined by those entering or leaving the hotel. Drastic action was needed. Bassett returned to the hotel bar and asked for a mechanic with a wire-cutter. So great was the invariable poverty of spare parts and machinery under Eastern Europe's state-managed socialist systems that one could safely assume that every male of adult age was by necessity something of a mechanic. So out came Václav. But before going down the road to pick up wire-cutters, he decided to try and force the combination lock with his bare hands – unsuccessfully. Meanwhile, a sinister young man in a grey anorak had joined the small crowd and asked to see our passports and visas. He spoke in flawed English and introduced himself as John.

Preoccupied with the bicycle business, we at first paid little attention to him. Who on earth was he? And why should he see our passports? His manner was highly irritating and untiringly persistent. Obviously he was a member of the secret police, but why should we show we knew? The very distance the other members of the crowd kept from him was indicative. Still composed, he responded to our 'But who are you?' with a wave of an identity card which manifestly did not declare him to be a 'secret policeman'. An impasse had been reached: we were unwilling to show any documents to an official out of uniform and his few sentences of English had reached their limit. Václav had returned with a splendid-looking outsize pair of wire-cutters. He looked at John with disdain and settled down to cutting through the chain.

John was unhappy. He was clearly frustrated that the three dubious characters he had discovered near restricted border areas were not impressed by his authority and so far no one was backing him. What promotion might lie ahead if he was personally responsible for the arrest of three western agents! But his training taught him not only to be suspicious but to retain his composure. He remained unpleasantly polite.

Time was slipping by; soon Václav would have severed the chain. John had an idea. He ordered one of the boys watching to find the schoolmistress, who spoke English. Just as Václav cut through the last link and we felt like raising a cheer, she arrived, a dignified but slightly perturbed woman in her late thirties.

'The man here, who is a policeman, says you must give him your documents,' she said, repeating something we had been only too well aware of for the last twenty minutes.

'Please tell him that we are very happy to show our papers to a policeman or person of authority in uniform.'

John, for the first time showing signs of more than irritation, hissed, 'Wait here, I come back immediately.' He jumped into a Skoda parked on the other side of the road and drove off at speed.

This was the right moment to reward Václav for his excellent effort. We all returned to the bar where the trusty black-moustached mechanic chose his reward: a largish glass of Fernet Branca, an acquired and clearly local taste, as it was shared by most of his friends. The moment we left the bar again an army jeep driven by a smartly uniformed soldier armed with a Kalashnikov rifle drew to a halt outside. Next to him was John with a triumphant smile. The crowd had stayed to watch the sequel. The soldier, who looked extremely puzzled, rapped his heels, saluted and, in Czech, asked us for our documents. The schoolmistress translated. We at once gave our passports to the soldier, who hardly glanced at them before passing them on to John. He peered at the papers intently under the street lamp. But the longer he looked, the clearer it became that we were only doing exactly what we had declared on the forms. We were following our stated itinerary, even if we were running late.

Rather sour, he eventually returned the passports and visas and asked us where we were going. To which we replied, as he might have guessed, Český Krumlov. The soldier, clearly impatient to return to more military duties, saluted and drove off in the jeep. John was left standing on the pavement, having scored no points at all. But it was not quite the last we were to see of him.

We thanked Václav again and cycled away from a town where we should never have lingered. We had a great deal of cycling before Český Krumlov, much of it uphill. It was still raining, pitch dark and cold. This was the less appealing side of cycling. None the less, at the end of the day there would be a justified sense of achievement. After the trouble with the combination lock, the Austrian cycles presented a new problem: my headlight stopped working, which meant that on the unlit country roads at least two of us had to cycle together. A fairly desolate and exhausting hour went by. We passed through two or three villages, but otherwise were riding by fields which we could not make out in the inky darkness. Occasionally a car rushed past and for a fleeting moment I was jealous of its speed and comfort.

We were approaching a small town, the last, we hoped, before Český Krumlov itself. It was already after 7 p.m. A group of bored young people were congregating outside the cinema and Nicholson checked the directions with them. As we waited for him by the traffic lights, a familiar beige-coloured Skoda slowly coasted past, driven by a man in a grey anorak. There could be no doubt; it was John. We thought that the same Skoda might have been one of the cars which had overtaken us earlier. Obviously he had nothing more interesting to do on a cold and wet autumn evening than tail three weary cyclists.

The final stretch was to prove unexpectedly exhilarating. According to our calculations, we would complete it within an hour – a prospect which made increasing fatigue bearable. And as so often in cycling, our determination and application were soon to be rewarded, in this case by one of those long downhill runs that make Bohemia such good bicycle country. We dismounted for a particularly demanding hill – which we did not dare think might be the day's last – and then free-wheeled down, endlessly it seemed. How long could it last? In the dark one could see nothing but the road just in front, which made it reminiscent of one of those wild, helter-skelter rides at the funfair. The twisting road reflected shiny black in the rain and as the pace quickened, hands became sore from squeezing the brakes. Down, down we went, faster and faster. The bicycle was rattling and shaking madly on the rough road. And then finally and gloriously we saw the castle of Krumlov ahead, a mighty image despite the driving rain and gloom. Without stopping we bumped through a sixteenth-century arch and across a narrow footbridge that straddled the Moldau (Vltava) and so, bringing our bicycles to a reluctant halt, entered Krumlov. It was the end of a wild, extended descent that no funfair could have provided at whatever price.

We had reached our goal. All that we needed now was a room and some food. We went straight to the Hotel Krumlov in the corner of the main square, an attractive green-grey early nineteenth-century building, its façade decorated by four thin white Corinthian pilasters surmounting an arcade of three pointed arches that sheltered the entrance. But our first attempt at securing accommodation was fruitless; the hotel was fully booked and the girl receptionist, beautified by an extravagant perm of dyed blonde curls, referred us to a smaller establishment up the street towards the church. Full of red plush and with a cloying, stale smell, this seemed distinctly unpromising. But it quickly lost any relevance as an older, rather disagreeable woman wearing a black woollen shawl made clear that no rooms were available anyway. So we decided to return to the Krumlov and adjourn to its busy dining-room in the hope that by the time we had finished a meal something would materialize. Our tactics were both sound and successful. For following an excellent dinner of pork and dumplings and a good quantity of life-enhancing Bohemian beer, we emerged to find an altogether prettier receptionist greet us with a broad smile and the offer of a fine three-bedded room that overlooked the square. Apparently a coach party of Czechs had failed to arrive. After a day that had begun in Vienna and had seen us complete more than fifty miles on bicycle, quite apart from our entanglement with tiresome John, the secret policeman, it was extremely good news and cause for celebration.

It also proved a rule I had once been taught in Africa, that tenacity and patience invariably pay off. I had arrived in Freetown, Sierra Leone, with Colin Legum of *The Observer*, the doyen of Africa correspondents, and a hundred or so other journalists who had come to cover an African summit meeting. Weary from the long flight, Legum and I were left at a Chinese-built sports stadium and told there was no more accommodation. I protested and pointed out that this had been guaranteed before. 'Don't bother to argue, it's too hot. Come and sit down,' Legum said, finding a table with two chairs. He pulled out a bottle of malt whisky from his suitcase and shouted to a passing African, 'Boy, can you bring two glasses?' The bewildered young African obeyed and Legum poured out two generous measures of the dark-hued liquid, removed his panama hat and sat back. We expended no more energy during the next hour or so other than that required to lift the glasses and mop our brows dampened by the humidity of the African night. Proving Legum's law, one of the Sierra Leonean officials then returned to say that he had found a twin room in the athletes' quarters, which we could have if we did not mind sharing. Patience was rewarded, and I would have had a good night's sleep but for the airless conditions and the fact that Legum seemed to puff away at his Havana cigar even in his sleep. 'Legum of the Damned', his less respectful colleagues called him.

Back in Český Krumlov, we were in such good spirits that despite our physical fatigue we were reluctant to retire to our prized room. It was Friday night and there was a measure of life in the old town. Two doors along, the adjoining building, also early nineteenth century but painted yellowish brown and with narrow white Doric pilasters and rounded arches, was clearly the epicentre of Krumlov's night-life. A queue of young people wound up the narrow stone stairs, stopping in front of an iron gate where a tough-looking individual sat behind a table. It was the town's discothèque and entry was not an easy business, involving an indeterminate vetting procedure. Some persistence and payment of a couple of hundred crowns secured our entrance. It was a very East European disco: a room punctuated by tables whose occupants were furiously dancing on a cramped dance floor in front of a blaring band playing western rock music with eastern verve. On the near side, up a couple of steps, was a bar, brightly lit in pink with a bow-tied barman occasionally mixing outrageously coloured cocktails but more often dispensing 'juice and vodka', watery orange or grapefruit juice enlivened with vodka, the young person's drink anywhere in the Soviet empire. Bassett and I more cautiously had some French brandy we had spotted on the top shelf, proof that this was an above-average Czech establishment. Nicholson meanwhile had gravitated with remarkable alacrity to a table tightly hemmed into a corner of the dance floor where he had spotted an apparently single girl of gypsy appearance. Before we could moisten our lips with the precious Courvoisier, he had enticed her on to the dance floor – a credit both to his charm and tactical sense as it was only a matter of minutes before her jealous-looking boyfriend returned from wherever Czechs go to powder their noses. Luckily the large amount of juice and vodka he had evidently consumed seemed to neutralize his passion, if not hers.

Having tasted Krumlov's night-life and so much else during the day, we retired to our hotel dormitory and slept as soundly as one would expect after so much physical exercise.

Saturday dawned with a golden autumn sun that suited the ancient town well. The previous afternoon's relentless rain had been banished eastwards, across Moravia to Slovakia. Český Krumlov is one of those extraordinary East European towns that has been bypassed by the march of time. For much of its history it was but a fief of the powerful Schwarzenberg family, who had their seat in the massive, forbidding castle that is unassailably built into the rock. It is marked by a fine thirteenth-century tower with Renaissance additions, which like some fat, luxurious fountain-pen dominates the town's skyline from afar. The Schwarzenbergs, driven back to Austria in 1945, had long maintained the economy of Krumlov, or Krumau as it was known in German, as well as a private army. Their departure deprived the town of its soul and much of its life, though according to the superstitious the family ghost, a white lady, stayed behind and continues to haunt Krumlov.

The narrow cobbled streets run steeply between decaying sixteenth- and seventeenth-century houses, some of which have remained deserted since the princely family left. To boost the drastic decline in the local population, the communist authorities decided some years ago to import homeless gypsy families, who have begun to give the medieval town an altogether different character.

In the town square, more intimately proportioned than the castle, the Schwarzenberg arms are emblazoned in four medallions on a sixteenth-century building that is almost Italianate in mood. Among them is the lion of Bohemia and a shield that depicts somewhat gruesomely but memorably a raven picking out the eyes of a Turk, an allusion to a battle honour gained against the Ottoman armies.

The castle itself is suitably daunting, reflecting a princely authority that lasted much longer than post-war communism. But as in Torgau on the Elbe, it is the Russians who first impress with their brown bears lazily and hungrily roaming the drained moat. Stone bridges, adorned with cannon-balls and statues of martial saints in armour, lead through austere sixteenth-century arches deep into the castle precincts. As a fortification Krumlov Castle is impressive: its external walls merge into the rock and present a sheer drop down to the Moldau; its access from the town is protected and limited by the moat, bridges and courtyards that serve a perfect defensive purpose. As a residence of such a powerful and wealthy family, it could have offered surprisingly few comforts and relief other than its rococo chapel and eighteenth-century theatre. The rooms are muddled and cold, with elegance sacrificed for security. But in times of peace its extensive, well tended and designed gardens must have given pleasure, combining formal beds with wooded avenues, a small lake and an outdoor theatre. Their recent upkeep was hardly a communist priority; the once so carefully manicured lawns were only occasionally mown and allowed to brown for lack of regular irrigation. Rarely pruned, the roses have become quite wild. As for the capricious fountains, they had long ceased to celebrate the magic setting or mirror the family's affluence and taste. Abandoned and neglected, they would not even play for the people any more.

So satisfactory was our room that we decided to make the Hotel Krumlov our headquarters for another night. But we would not lose our mobility; we would split the day into two cycling expeditions: one before lunch to the monastery and church at Zlatá Koruna, followed by a late afternoon sortie to Rosenberg (Rožmberk). This was decided over a breakfast of scrambled eggs, always when possible enlivened with onions in Bassett's case, rolls, strawberry jam and tea, a combination that can be relied on throughout Eastern Europe. Nicholson automatically filled a few extra rolls with strawberry jam to take with us. But before setting out we would reconnoitre the town further.

Although dominated so much by its castle, Krumlov has some compelling features, none more so than the uneven rows of medieval houses that line the Moldau at the foot of the rocky crag. At this stage high in the Bohemian Forest the river, still narrow, clear and quick, hardly hints at the broad magisterial sweep it attains by the time it reaches Prague.

The ride to Zlatá Koruna was easy paced, along small country roads that traversed gentle fields bordered by apple trees and odd patches of pine forest, the pungent smell of which delighted the senses. After little more than an hour we plunged down a steep hill that took us into the village near where the old monastery, now a museum, was tucked away. We were in time for a guided tour, joining a class of Czech schoolchildren who took special delight in donning the bulky felt overslippers and sliding about the polished floors. They were a little less absorbed in the history of their surroundings than the ten-year-olds I had come across in East Germany. Was this the fault of a less thorough education system or were they just less serious? The guide turned a large and ancient key in the heavy oak door of the monastery church and it swung

open heavily with a perfectly pitched creak. A narrow shaft of
sunlight cut through the cavernous Gothic interior, revealing
marble memorials to long-forgotten princes and abbots. There
was an aroma of must and dust and a certain chill, but no
feeling of decay. Isolated in the Bohemian Forest, this once
busy church had escaped war and pestilence and stood unrav-
aged by time. It seemed to be only under wraps, ready for a
full return to use when required. Perhaps its pews were occupied every night by the ghosts of monks continuing to celebrate
mass in the presence of the two Ottokars, kings of Bohemia,
interred in ornate baroque tombs either side of the altar. After
the last of us had filed out, the massive studded door swung
shut on its worn iron hinges and the church returned to its
now usual darkness. The small chapter house, finely vaulted in
red brick, was by contrast a model of lightness, the cloister a
place of perfect repose. In the cloister yard some of the
spandrels were strangely painted with islands and ships against
a deep blue sea. How the monks must have mused.

It was foolish of the Czechoslovak communist authorities to
try to suppress monastic orders. Faith is invariably strength-
ened by persecution. While in western countries freedom
of thought did not help monasteries recruit novices, the
Roman Catholic orders continued to attract young people in
communist-ruled Czechoslovakia despite, or perhaps because
of, their having to operate underground. Over the border in
Bavaria several monasteries have had to close in recent years
since only a handful of ageing monks were left to carry out
duties and maintain traditions.

Our thoughts turned from monastic life to dumplings and
beer, which no doubt preoccupied the monks of Bohemia too.
We followed the trail of the schoolchildren to a small inn
which was busy serving both, along with chunks of pork,
Czechoslovakia's staple meat.

Bolstered by lunch, we studied our maps and charted a

different route back to Krumlov. Before leaving the village we stopped to admire an immaculate 1928 dark blue Skoda limousine parked outside a dilapidated cottage. The contrast was striking, but it illustrated how rural Czechoslovakia seemed to be frozen in another age, as well as the national passion for fine vintage cars.

The ride back to Krumlov, skirting more fields and forest on a slightly busier road, was uneventful except for an uneasy moment on the final downhill run when I heard a clatter, braked and found that, shaken by the relentless cobblestones, my bicycle had finally and irretrievably shed its rear light. Our roadworthiness was diminishing daily.

We felt we had a lot of mileage left in us yet and pressed on directly for Rosenberg, cycling through Krumlov and emerging with the Moldau on the other side. Gently we descended with the river, the road curving as the Moldau began to meander. An elderly couple crossing a bridge asked us where we were from. 'From England,' the man repeated, tapping his stick against the ground. 'Ah England! Churchill! We remember him. We fought side by side then,' he added with nostalgic warmth and a measure of pride, before waving us on and wishing us well. Houses gradually gave way to trees and the forest thickened. The smell of pine was intoxicating. A few miles on we heard the penetrating whirring of chain saws and soon after came across piles of logs stacked high on either side of the road. A primitive-looking wood-pulp or paper factory followed. It hissed, thumped and puffed up clouds of dirty smoke. Piled outside among the corrugated-iron outbuildings was a dazzling mountain of cobalt-coloured powder, and a little further on a bigger one of yellow sulphur. What alchemy was afoot so deep in the forest? The road ran on, always alongside the Moldau, our view of it regularly obscured by a curtain of trees. It was undemanding cycling without the steep hills we had grown accustomed to. As the late afternoon sun reddened and cast its glowing light on the hills that rose on the other side of the river, a strange, deep moan echoed across the valley. A few minutes later it reverberated again, even more painfully. We halted to listen. Once more it groaned. It was a stag rutting.

The light was beginning to fade when, turning another bend, we sighted on the opposite bank of the Moldau the castle of Rosenberg, a coal-black block perched on a rocky crag surrounded by forest. These Bohemian castles were massive and gloomy, suggestive of hostages fettered in dark, dank dungeons, and strange secrets. The 'Prisoner of Zenda' could have been held in any, or Florestan if Beethoven's *Fidelio* were to be given a Bohemian setting. Before the advent of cannon and gunpowder, they must have been almost impregnable. This was a stronghold of the Rosenberg family, who held sway in the region before the Schwarzenbergs and who, like the houses of York and Lancaster, adopted a rose as their emblem.

By the time we reached the town it was quite dark and deserted. Its few inhabitants had retired for their evening repast and perhaps some television, or a concert on the radio. Only the lights of a solitary inn burned brightly. Inside amid the blue-grey haze of cigarette smoke were half a dozen men drinking draughts of beer after work. Those who lived alone were waiting to have a meal brought to them. A black and white television set attached to the wall was showing a concert performance of excerpts from Italian operas. The pallid-faced young landlord brought the beer, his buxom wife took the orders. We were offered pork schnitzels and dumplings, for which we were grateful even if so far on this trip we had failed to get away from pork. Eastern Europe is no place for those who cannot eat pigmeat.

The return trip to Krumlov involved retracing our tracks on the same road for about eighteen miles: a good after-dinner distance on a cold and black night. Nicholson now had the only working headlight, so we had to cycle abreast, pulling to whenever car lamps pierced the gloom. Occasionally a bat flapped above, adding an atmospheric touch. All we needed as we cycled through the dense forest were a few rattling skeletons and perhaps an owl hooting. Instead there was the steady murmur of the Moldau, now no longer visible, the moon too pale even to reflect in its rippling waters. If our original descent into Krumlov had all the excitement of the funfair big dipper, then this night ride was as spine-chilling as the ghost train. There was no lingering and we made much better time than on the outward ride, finally clearing the forest and plunging deeper down the valley to Krumlov. As it neared, the castle tower loomed distinctively ahead and to the right the sharper lines of the Church of St Vitus with its rocket-shaped Gothic spire. We swept in through the bottom of the town and crossed the pedestrian bridge over the Moldau more quickly than we had estimated. We were back at base.

Though physically quite exhausted after another day during which we had cycled a good fifty miles, we had enough pep left to give the discothèque another try. This time we were confronted with the Saturday night queues, which were hopeless. As a tame alternative we toured the town, though we were tempted when we found workmen had left a ladder against the back of the discothèque building. Risking an encounter with the not necessarily secret police, we positioned it against a second-floor window which was half open. While I kept cave, Bassett and Nicholson ascended to find themselves in an empty kitchen, the door of which was firmly locked. Behind it they could hear the blaring music; they had almost made it. Admitting defeat, we withdrew for an early night, which in view of the next day's unexpectedly full programme was fortunate.

We rose early and before breakfast walked up the hill to the

Church of St Vitus for mass. The long, narrow nave was well filled and we were lucky to find places. Old people predominated and some in their dark green Austrian *Tracht* had the air of old Schwarzenberg retainers. Standing outside in the gentle morning sun after the congregation had filed out, we came across the same couple we had talked to on the way to Rosenberg, the man who admired Churchill. Their Anglophilia seemed to be enhanced further by our early appearance in church.

Fortified by the usual dependable breakfast of scrambled eggs, we packed up the few items of our kit and bade Český Krumlov a fond farewell. It had been a particularly good stop. We decided that our next destination should be České Budějovice, best known by its German name of Budweis and for its fine beer. We would cycle there directly as the signs were that the fair autumnal weather would not hold. Half the distance we managed undisturbed on an agreeable minor country road before having to move on to something bigger, where traffic, and especially a regular flow of lorries, limited enjoyment.

Located by the Moldau on a plain at the foothills of the Sumava or Bohemian Forest, Budweis is a prosperous and prominent town with its own bishop. As we arrived it began to rain and there was no sense in wheeling the cycles about the town centre, so we left them at the railway station's left luggage office. Budweis was bustling with an activity we had not yet found in Bohemia. For a Sunday and one which was becoming quite wet, the streets were surprisingly well populated. Although industrial, producing steel as well as its celebrated beer, it is a town of some elegance, rich in eighteenth-and early nineteenth-century buildings. Most remarkable is the spacious main square, which has extraordinary breadth and is on a scale that dwarfs the finest squares of Prague. It is flanked all around by arcaded buildings, the most striking of which is the Renaissance-style town hall erected in 1730. Facing it is the Hotel Zvon, which translates as 'bell' in English. It looked promising for both food and accommodation. We were shown and took a good-sized, inexpensive room on the first floor with four beds. As it turned out we were hardly to use it. Ready for lunch, we went downstairs to the busy dining-room, which was full of boyish-looking Czechoslovak conscripts enjoying their leave with extra-strength (twelve degrees) Budvar ale. If they were lucky they came with their girls, but the less fortunate had to make do with their own company and the beer. We shared a table with four rosy-faced conscripts, half-drained ale mugs in front of them and behind on the wall, ranged on hooks, their peaked, red-banded caps neatly hanging in a row. At a small table nearby a young soldier was seriously, though not confidently, courting a fine-featured, high cheek-boned, blonde beauty. The promise of the restaurant was quickly shown by the offer of trout, duck and even boiled beef, apart from pork. We celebrated our escape from pigmeat by ordering two trout and potatoes and one boiled beef with dumplings, with, of course, several rounds of the famous beer. The green-overalled waiter was especially attentive as he had hopes – later realized on a small scale – of inducing us to change some Austrian schillings for Czechoslovak crowns. The black market, so visible in Prague, extended even to the provinces.

It was no weather for further cycling and we would have more than enough the next day when we were due to return to Austria. Instead the afternoon was spent exploring Budweis, its churches and broad, gas-lit, cobbled streets. Though blackened by industrial pollution, it was largely unspoiled and had a harmonious skyline, its buildings rarely rising above three storeys. We found the cathedral in time for the end of evening mass. It was full and there were more young people than in Český Krumlov. Near the back there were even several soldiers in uniform, which, in view of the state's rigid anti-clericalism, cannot have done their chances of promotion any good. It was another sign of how so many Czechoslovaks chose to ignore the communism that was thrust upon them and live their lives in the certainty that their belief in other values would prevail. It was a passive resistance which two years later was to make possible the most gentle and joyous of the revolutions that was to sweep Eastern Europe, the 'velvet revolution', as Czechoslovaks proudly came to call it.

On our return to the Zvon via deserted side streets, the flickering light of the gas lamps reflected on the wet, shiny pavement suggested a Budweis stuck in the nineteenth century. I half expected a hansom cab to clatter past, its bowler-hatted driver protected by an oilskin.

But back in the hotel and passing the kitchen on the way to our room, we were brought sharply up to date by the sight of a fair-haired girl sitting there knitting. Clearly conscious of the latest trends in western fashion, she had raised the hemline of her white kitchen dress, transforming it into an eye-catching mini. We exchanged smiles through the open door.

This time the waiter, fishing for another opportunity to change money illicitly, found us a corner table to ourselves. The beer came without asking and we chose two portions of duck and red cabbage and one boiled beef, all accompanied by *knedliky*, the ubiquitous and wholesome dumplings. We repaired afterwards to the bar on the first floor, where we could have a glass of *slivovice* within sight of the kitchen door. A rapport was established and an agreement reached that once kitchen work was over we could take Milena and her girlfriend Helena, who seemed more actively employed behind the sink, to the best nightclub in Budweis, the Savoy. By about 11.30 p.m. they were free and we set out together across the square for the Savoy, despite its name a far from smart establishment which served overpriced vodka to raucous rock music. We each had to buy a card which the waiter marked every time a drink was ordered, a dangerous form of credit. The dance floor was as cramped as at Krumlov. But no sooner were we beginning to become familiar with the procedure than suddenly, half an hour after midnight, the music stopped, the lights went on, the waiters came to clear the tables and tot up the drinks marked on the cards. As these were absurdly expensive, we had to pool together the last crowns on us to extricate ourselves with honour.

It was a premature, unsatisfactory end to the evening so the girls suggested we should all go to a friend's flat for a nightcap. This, I thought, might be stretching their hospitality – but why not, we decided. Budweis's streets by night were empty and even more evocative than earlier, like some redundant stage or film set. The walk to the flat was long but invigorating. We arrived at the soot-blackened nineteenth-century building and rather sheepishly rang the top bell. After a few minutes a bleary-eyed young man opened the door, clearly the boyfriend of the girl who soon joined him. Once the initial surprise passed, they greeted Milena and Helena and three strangers as if it were nothing out of the ordinary to drop in for a drink at such an hour. Up the creaking stairs we went, led by the girlfriend with a finger on her lips. Apparently she had a difficult neighbour, an older man who was a Communist Party official. The most glamorous of the three girls, she worked as a waitress at the Zvon bar. I had sighted her there earlier in the evening. The boyfriend, Milan, was studying at the university, having completed his military service. Like young people throughout communist-ruled Eastern Europe, they thirsted for contact with the West and, once a few cushions had been distributed on the floor of the modest but cosy flat, they were eager to open discussions. But first something suitable had to be found to drink, so Milan and Nicholson, always the quartermaster, left in search of a bottle. Within an hour they were back with a Slovak wine they had procured at a bar on the other side of Budweis. It said something for Czechoslovakia that this was possible at 2 a.m.

The talk mirrored many conversations I remembered with young East Germans: the anti-Russian feeling, resentment of the Soviet military presence, conscription, frustration over limitations on travel and the poor choice of consumer goods. But the young Czechs were more exuberant, showed greater irreverence to authority and were less serious and *angst*-ridden than their East German counterparts. They had an anarchic streak, and certainly displayed neither gloom nor doom. Helena, who with her short dark hair and muscular body had the look of a trained swimmer, was the most serious of our circle – when Milena described her as 'a bit of a party girl' she was clearly not referring to her love of going out – but she was more relaxed than East German girls of her age.

They found it hard to believe that we had cycled from Austria. Why on earth didn't we have a car? And why come to Budweis? For the beer? When we said we had been given visas as musicians, they exclaimed with spontaneous enthusiasm, 'Jazz!' Their knowledge of western rock music was encyclopaedic, but there was something especially adventurous and risqué about jazz, which in Prague had become identified with popular opposition to the communist authorities. In the circumstances the idea of three English jazz musicians touring Bohemia by bicycle had an air of excitement and danger. We never really had a chance to deny the roles projected on us. In fact we were expected to live up to them. And so the night passed, in conversation and, until they had to be abandoned for fear of rousing the grumpy neighbour, in English party games as at some childish birthday. It was a bizarre night in Budweis.

Finally, as the sun was preparing to rise, we thanked Milan and his girlfriend for such memorable hospitality and gingerly slipped out, led downstairs by the girl – as before with her finger to her lips. The neighbour was an early riser and must not sight us. We escaped into the dawn feeling groggily elated. We had managed a minor adventure.

As we walked light-footed back to the Zvon, the streets began to fill. It was only 5.30 a.m., but people were hastening to their workplaces in a mechanical stupor. It was Monday morning. Twenty minutes later, a few hundred yards from the Zvon, Nicholson, who less than four hours earlier had bought a bottle of wine, stopped at a stationery shop to purchase some Christmas cards while I found some Cuban cigars. Behind the drab communist-imposed discipline and austerity, all kinds of things were possible in Czechoslovakia. As the Zvon's kitchens – without Milena and Helena, who were now belatedly claiming their day off at home – were opening for breakfast, the three of us retired to our fine four-bed room for three hours' sleep. More we could not afford as our visas were running out and we had a good sixty miles of cycling to the Austrian frontier.

By the time we emerged, feeling rather frailer than before, the Zvon breakfast-room was uncomfortably crowded, packed with soldiers and their friends. There was only one harassed waitress and apparently little food left. A power cut then plunged the chaotic scene into darkness, the final inducement to leave and have our breakfast elsewhere. The railway station proved a good choice, offering the scrambled eggs, rolls, strawberry jam and tea we craved for. It was just after 10 a.m. when we retrieved the bicycles and set out on the homeward run. The first stretch, taking the main road out through the industrial suburbs, was penance for our overindulgence the previous night. Breathing in the noxious fumes of the passing lorries was punishment for having been overfamiliar with this Bohemian town on so short an acquaintance. But within an hour we could transfer to a minor road and wind our way pleasantly through orchards and fields. My only regret was that, lagging behind a little, I missed a timely opportunity taken by Bassett and Nicholson. Just as we were approaching a long uphill climb a tractor and trailer full of hay swerved into the road in front of us. They were near and quick enough to grab the back of the trailer and let it pull them to the top. I had to sweat it out under my own steam.

Třeboň lies halfway between Budweis and the border, surrounded by a garland of small lakes and birch forest. Wherever fish features on Czechoslovak menus, carp or trout 'Třeboň' is to be found. The explanation became apparent as we cycled over a causeway that bisected one of the lakes. On either side carp, the national fish, and trout were busily breeding in special pens. It was about 1.30 p.m. when we skirted the town wall and entered Třeboň's sandstone medieval gate, passed the brewery and found the main street. There was a touch of East Anglia about its Gothic architecture, comfortably juxtaposed with arcaded Bohemian Renaissance buildings. Nothing more modern than the late nineteenth century post office disturbed the picture. An inn opposite lured us to a late lunch, not of carp or trout but duck, dumplings and Třeboň beer. Sitting smiling with a male friend at a corner table was the pretty receptionist from Český Krumlov. She spotted us immediately. To our embarrassment, we did not quite have enough crowns to pay the bill until Nicholson went out to change an Austrian note at the post office. There was no hint of a black market in this town so famous for its fish.

Třeboň was the last serious stop in our progress to the border, a very grand finale in cycling terms. The hills became gentler, the forest thicker. As we went by at a steady pace we disturbed and sent running herds of hundreds of deer. We could see them raise their heads as they picked up our scent, tremble and then in a rippling wave run away, striding over obstacles with elegant agility.

We paused at a crossroads to ask an old peasant woman who was raking a vegetable patch outside her cottage to take a snapshot with Nicholson's camera of the three of us and our faithful but battered bicycles. She gave us the broadest smile that broke like the sun across her weathered, leathery face, framed tightly by a grey and blue checked headscarf. This was too much for her, so she called her husband to press the Instamatic while she beamed at us. A few miles on we passed a stately former monastic building and, as the clock on its onion-domed tower showed five minutes to four, Nicholson and Bassett posed for a final photograph under its fine wrought-iron gate surmounted by Bohemian lions.

On we pressed, the late afternoon sun casting a cool glow over the tall pine forests. For the first time we began to feel the chill as a cloudless sky allowed temperatures to drop sharply. Tank traps scattered at intervals by the roadside indicated that we were approaching the border. Down a penultimate hill we descended to the undistinguished frontier town of Nová Bystřice, which straddled the road half a mile from the well-guarded border. Fortune had always favoured us, and so it did as we entered a small smoked-out inn to dispose of our last few coins. Three teas and two bars of chocolate were possible, and as we warmed our cold, stiff fingers against the hot glasses of tea, the band struck up. The town's wind and brass band, in dark-blue, gold-braided uniforms, had adjourned to the next-door room to have a final warm-up and practice for some local occasion. What marvellous old instruments they had, including the serpents – distinguished ancestors of the tuba – Donizetti loved to write for. For three semi-bogus musicians it was a fine farewell to an enchanted corner of Eastern Europe.

6 The Bohemian Spas: In Goethe's Footsteps

Another, more recently fashionable Bohemia lies in the north-west of modern Czechoslovakia, abutting Bavaria and southern East Germany. The Bohemian spas first flowered in the late eighteenth century, reaching the peak of their bloom and the height of fashion a hundred years or so later. Emperors, tsars, crown princes and maharajas congregated there to sip the restorative waters and dazzle with their entourage. Like so much else, however, the spas were allowed to fade and wilt under more than forty years of communism. Their proximity to the frontier saw them initially turned into garrison towns; then privileged party and trade union officials from throughout the East Bloc came for subsidized holidays and cures. But now, as in their heyday, the spas stand free to benefit from their situation at the heart of Central Europe, from which the barriers so unhappily thrown up by communism have been removed. Czechoslovakia's 'velvet revolution' has returned to the westerner's itinerary the most popular of turn of the century destinations: Carlsbad (Karlovy Vary), Marienbad (Mariánské Lázně) and Franzensbad (Františkovy Lázně). No longer as elegant as when they were graced by the future Edward VII and half the crowned heads of Europe, they yet retain a unique charm, ripe for rediscovery.

The 36-year-old Goethe was sent here in 1785 to take the waters by his patron Duke Carl August of Sachsen-Weimar, who was concerned about the health of his court favourite. The duke likened the most brilliant star of Weimar's firmament to a plant that needed a long time to recover from harsh weather. It was the beginning of an almost forty-year-long relationship with his 'dear Bohemia', where the great German poet and man of science declared he 'always liked to be'. In fact his love of Bohemia was to see him spend 1,114 of his days there, 431 more than in Italy, which was to play such a seminal role in his life and work. He stayed in Carlsbad a dozen times, in Marienbad on three occasions and in Teplitz (Teplice) once. The longest of his Bohemian trips was the tenth in the momentous year of 1812. It lasted 136 days, from 1 May to 13 September. The shortest was the third in 1790 when he made a three-day Bohemian stop on his way to Silesia. The visits were an opportunity to bathe in and sip the invigorating waters, to socialize with visiting nobility and royalty and to come across leading contemporaries. The muses of poetry and music brought off an extraordinary coup in 1812 when Goethe met Beethoven in Teplitz in July and then again two months later in Carlsbad, encounters which were so pregnant with expectations that they were bound to disappoint. Nevertheless, Beethoven could write in a letter to the poetess Bettina Brentano of his high regard for Goethe, whom he described as 'the nation's most precious jewel'.

The spa regime, which saw Goethe rise to be the first to bathe at five in the morning and substitute mineral-rich water for at least some of the wine he loved to imbibe so much, appealed to his hypochondria. An attack of kidney-stone colic led the Weimar court doctor to advise Carlsbad in the first place. Stomach and digestive complaints, gout, catarrh and leg sores were to dog Goethe for much of his life. But it was not an ailing cripple who courted and won the not merely platonic admiration of the succession of talented, beautiful, aristocratic and always much younger women who were his fellow spa guests. He immersed himself in Bohemian history and was fascinated by its rich geology, which he explored on frequent trips in the region. Like so many visiting cards, a host of memorials, statues and plaques to Johann Wolfgang von Goethe are today scattered liberally around north-west Bohemia.

Emulating Goethe, we would begin our tour of the spas at Eger, or Cheb as it is called in Czech. But while his trips originated further north in Weimar, ours began well south, in Vienna. It was back to the Franz Josef station with Nicholson and Bassett, seven months after the expedition to southern Bohemia. This time Nicholson was only there to see us off; a choir practice detained him until the following night when we hoped to meet at one of Carlsbad's most notorious addresses, the Grand Hotel Pupp, absurdly renamed the Grand Hotel Moskva by the communists. The Prague train showed the greatest patience, shuddering, inching forward and back but never starting until the ageing Viennese porter, a damp cigarette in the corner of his mouth and a bicycle under each arm, had deposited his load in the guard's carriage. He stepped off, took the cigarette from between his lips and waved at the stationmaster, who lowered his flag and off trundled the train, two minutes late. It would take the familiar route to Prague, where we would detrain and catch the afternoon connection to Eger.

The train drew to a halt just before the frontier station at České Velenice. A team of green-uniformed border guards and customs officials boarded and conducted a meticulous search of each compartment, lifting up every seat. It was a long wait, enlivened only by the arrival of the cashier, a portable cash box slung round her neck with a leather strap, who worked out and demanded the amount of hard currency we had to change for the number of days we were spending in Czechoslovakia. Our visas were then stamped with the date, place and a fine depiction of an old steam engine. When we had crossed by cycle the previous October, they could hardly be expected to have an extra stamp with a bicycle, so instead our passports were imprinted with a smart open tourer of 1930s vintage. Similarly, arrival and departure stamps at Prague airport bore the image of a biplane reminiscent of a competitor for the Schneider Trophy. These delightful mementoes of a bygone age of travel were one of the few rewards for the time and trouble involved in securing a Czechoslovak visa during the years of communist rule.

How tantalizing it was to arrive in Prague, the fairy-tale city, with little more than an hour between trains! It gave us time for a brisk walk past the Powder Tower, weaving through the Old Town to Charles Bridge. We reached the point – marked by his statue – where on the orders of King Wenceslas IV the martyr St Jan Nepomuk, the country's patron saint, was thrown bound and gagged from the bridge into the Moldau, only to be swept up heavenwards by angels. There are two differing versions of how the canon of St Vitus's Cathedral incurred the king's wrath. According to the first, Jan Nepomuk became embroiled in a dispute between the archbishop of Prague, with whom he sided, and the king. The second, later disseminated by the Jesuits who were eager to create a popular Catholic saint to counter the Protestant hero Jan Hus, was that as the queen's confessor Jan Nepomuk refused to reveal to Wenceslas her confessions. Canonized in 1729, Nepomuk has since been the patron saint not only of Bohemia but of bridges, and his name invoked against slander and watery perils. From our miraculous vantage point on the spot where the unfortunate Nepomuk was hurled over the bridge into the water on 20 March 1393 we surveyed this most marvellous of European capitals before reluctantly turning on our heels for the station.

The Eger train was waiting and due to depart in five minutes. In Vienna we had been told that the bicycles would be sent straight through to Eger, where we could pick them up at the customs office. Nevertheless, we thought it prudent to check that they were safely stored in the guard's carriage. We slid open the door to find three railway officials: a lady ticket collector with heavy blonde curls under her scarlet cap and lips adorned with cherry-red lipstick, a male colleague of porcine appearance and an older, distinguished-looking inspector. But there were no bicycles. The platform clock showed three minutes to departure. We peppered the officials with questions. Why weren't the bicycles there? Where could they be? The two younger ones shrugged their shoulders and showed no interest in the fate of our future transport, only looking at their watches. But the grey-haired inspector slowly stepped off the train and called to a burly porter who seemed to be deriving immense, childlike enjoyment from driving a small tractor that pulled a succession of empty trailers. Spilling out of the small seat, wearing his cap smartly, his boyish pose was rendered ridiculous by a heavy drooping moustache which gave him the appearance rather of one of Simón Bolívar's lieutenants. He reluctantly halted the tractor and came over to the inspector. I checked my watch: one and a half minutes left. There followed one of the most curious scenes I have ever witnessed at a railway station, a theatrical *tour de force* worthy of the final act of Mozart's *Don Giovanni*, which was first performed with such success in Prague. The platform suddenly opened and closed and Bassett and the moustached porter disappeared into the bowels of the earth, leaving me standing on the platform with the inspector. Only a thunder-clap was lacking. The train started hissing, its steel wheels grinding impatiently against the rails. I looked at my watch, at the platform clock, time was up. We were into extra time. I was resigned to a night in Prague, not Franzensbad. A minute later the great steel plates of the platform creaked open to reveal Bassett seemingly much his usual self and the porter bearing the two bicycles. The train started moving and the two younger rail officials, stretching out their arms, helped pull us into the guard's carriage. The porter had thrown the bicycles in and I managed to slip a twenty-schilling note into his palm. By the time we had got to our feet and dusted ourselves down, the train had cleared Prague station.

Bassett had seen extraordinary things in his brief time in the underworld. A maze of criss-crossing passages and rooms; the bicycles were stored in one, while in another, around a table and under a solitary unshielded light-bulb, a group of porters were playing cards and smoking, visibly astonished at seeing an intruder from the outside world. Prague is full of subterranean surprises, as I was to discover again some time later when I saw a military band, complete with instruments, disappear after the pavement opened up off Wenceslas Square.

The drama over, we found an empty compartment, sat back and enjoyed the splendid scenery that passed: the spectacular crossing over the railway bridge that spans the Moldau with its panorama of old Prague, the smaller art-nouveau stations on the outskirts of the city, the mighty Karlšteyn Castle perched on its rocky crag and the diverse succession of valleys, fields and forest that follow. We pulled the window right down to cool ourselves, letting the curtains flap wildly in the draught. The lady ticket collector came and punched our tickets without a word about the recent excitement in the guard's carriage, offering only a flicker of recognition in her pale blue eyes. And so the journey passed peacefully, through industrial Pilsen (Plzeň), Czechoslovakia's beer capital – the Burton of Bohemia – with its busy platforms, and on past Marienbad, a jewel of a station where princes once alighted, to the train's final Bohemian destination, Eger.

There we disembarked as border guards and customs officials boarded to check passengers continuing their journey over the border to Bavaria. The Eger equivalent of the tractor-driving porter in Prague was a quite different proposition. She was another of the cool, efficient blondes who seemed to be the mainstay of Czechoslovak railways. Immaculate in a tight-fitting blue uniform and smart red cap, she accompanied us to the guard's carriage and herself lifted the two bicycles out without allowing any help. Along with a few parcels, they were loaded on to the first of the tractor's trailers and driven off with great seriousness to the customs office. Unlike her counterpart in Prague, driving the mini-tractor was clearly a duty not a pleasure. We followed her to the office, where we completed customs formalities with an affable young man who was quite perplexed as to why we should want to bring in bicycles and take them out again. If we weren't going to sell them, why had we brought them? When we pointed out that they were not even ours, but belonged to Austrian railways, he was even more confused. Never having dealt with such travellers, he did not persist in his questioning and was only too pleased to give directions to Franzensbad, wave us on our way and shut his office.

The old centre of Eger is rich in history and has changed little since Goethe's day. It can justly claim to be Czechoslovakia's finest border town with its picturesque market square, pastel-painted houses, fountains and delicately wrought iron signs marking shops and inns. In 1634 Wallenstein, the statesman-general who played such a dominant role in the Thirty Years War, was treacherously murdered here by his own officers on the orders of Emperor Ferdinand. Only five years earlier (1628–9), created duke of Mecklenburg after a series of notable victories in north Germany, he had resided in great splendour in the Renaissance castle at Güstrow. Wallenstein's end (in a room that today lugubriously forms part of the town museum) was transformed into one of the great tragic plays of German theatre by Schiller in 1798–9, the very time that Goethe, his Weimar contemporary and friend, would stop at Eger on his way to Carlsbad.

We finally mounted the bicycles we had brought all the way from Vienna for the gentle downhill run from Eger to Franzens-bad, the pearl of the Bohemian spas. After half an hour or so on an empty road under a soft evening sun, we entered the town by a majestic avenue of horse-chestnut trees heavy with pink and white blossom. It is the smallest and most unspoiled of the celebrated trinity of Bohemian spas – Franzensbad, Carlsbad and Marienbad – that nestle so comfortably in valleys surrounded by dense pine forest. The buildings have an eighteenth-century elegance, uniformly painted in *Kaisergelb* (imperial yellow) and adorned with white stucco work and detailing. With its extensive parks, colourful flower-beds, spa buildings and two bandstands – one of them, a paradigm of good taste, has a delicate white lace-like carved wood canopy and busts of Mozart and Beethoven – the town has preserved a certain smart tranquillity. But under communism the once fashionable hotels that were previously filled with wealthy guests taking the waters were converted into rest homes (*dùms* in Czech) for state organizations and workers on cures. The choice of accommodation for casual visitors was therefore limited. But a few doors away from where Beethoven stayed in 1812 is the Hotel Slovan, a modest, medium-sized establish-ment which has preserved extraordinary caryatids on the stair-case inside despite a rather brash recent refurbishment. As in Krumlov, the hotel was initially declared full, but half an hour of dogged negotiation and persistence by Bassett while I guarded the bicycles outside eventually secured a room over-looking the attractive avenue running down to the famous Francis Spring. Legum's law had once again prevailed.

But relief at obtaining beds was soon qualified by a singular lack of success in finding anywhere or anything for dinner. Our appetites were sharp after only a Czechoslovak railways omelette for lunch and our first exercise of the expedi-tion. Both the elderly man employed as the hotel's porter/

receptionist and a curious red-shirted, blue-jeaned, more than middle-aged character who was loitering by the reception were pessimistic about our chances of discovering food. A short tour of the town quickly proved them correct. As in Goethe's and Beethoven's day, guests at Franzensbad should not delay dining: after 9 p.m. it is practically impossible to obtain either food or drink. The town, and so its visitors, retires and rises early.

Somewhat dispirited we stepped back into the Slovan to be offered beer from the hotel stock by the dubious-looking man in the Lacoste shirt. He spoke good English, which added to our suspicions, and introduced himself as Robert. 'I get you two beers,' he said, turning round to give the elderly retainer the order in Czech. We did not want to be ungracious and we were thirsty, but Robert was hardly our cup of tea. Was he a secret policeman or a pimp? We sat down with him and three bottles of Pilsner Urquell. He said he was a businessman who did a great deal of travelling to and from the border – which hardly allayed our doubts. He had a son in London who ran a restaurant and would be coming over for a visit later in the summer. Another question mark. Dressed in the Czechoslovak national colours of red (designer shirt), white (tennis shoes) and blue (trousers), adorned with a heavy gold bracelet, rings and necklace, and smelling strongly of cologne and corruption, Robert was hardly a typical fifty-year-old Czech. But he did clearly represent the collaborator class, those who through some compromise had done well under communism and could lead a remotely western life, those who had money and could travel, those with privileges denied to the majority. His was not the spontaneous hospitality of the ordinary Czechoslovak, but the fawning of someone with an interest. What it might have been we did not linger to find out. Nor did he learn more about us than that we were two Englishmen cycling in Bohemia. Less than two years later in free, post-revolutionary

Czechoslovakia, where revenge was so generously eschewed, had Robert become an honest entrepreneur or had he quietly retired on his ill-gained profits?

There was an early morning cacophony as Franzensbad awoke. I looked out of the window to see the street milling with middle-aged East Europeans on errands or on their way to take the waters. Further up the avenue there was a hubbub that seemed to come nearer in stages. Now it was at Beethoven's house, soon it would be outside the hotel. Against the mild morning sun I saw a large orange water-tanker advance slowly. Like a mechanical elephant, it lowered its trunk at each of the concrete boxes filled with geraniums that lined the street. Then with a great whoosh it disgorged gallons of water on each and was manoeuvred noisily to its next position.

Whether for plants or people, water was very evidently the major concern here. From the sixteenth century the prized local water was known as 'Egerwasser' (Eger water). In the eighteenth century the baroque architect Balthasar Neumann undertook an unfulfilled project to pipe the spa water to the commercially more important town of Eger where he was born. The spring water was being prescribed for digestive and other disorders even then, and the baths had a reputation for helping women with child-bearing and gynaecological problems. Jugs of the highly valued liquid were widely exported well into the last century. Goethe, who came to Franzensbad thirty-three times, for years had it sent to Weimar, in 1808 dispatching forty jugs to his wife, Christiane.

The main drinking well, called the Francis Spring after the Habsburg emperor, is enclosed in a small but perfectly classical Doric rotunda, bearing the date 1793 when the Eger doctor Bernhard Adler founded the spa town. Inside is a fine array of shining brass pipes and taps, and a white-overalled old woman dispensing the life-enhancing waters that are tapped from deep below the surface and are remarkably rich in minerals. The water is so strong – like a stiff gin and tonic – that it is difficult to drink more than a beakerful at a time. Those on a 'cure' promenade about the gardens or along the cool classical colonnades, sipping at regular intervals from curiously shaped porcelain beakers with snouts, a strange-looking ritual to the uninitiated.

Across the park with its colourful flower-beds is the bath house where in Goethe's day, according to one contemporary account, the women guests opened their barrage of daily fashion dressed in eye-catching negligées. 'The women themselves do not play the main role, this is taken over by their wardrobe. At the spring in the morning the most elegant negligée attracts the most looks, while the most tasteful dress clinches victory in the afternoon, what it covers – whether a skeletal frame or formless colossus – is apparently irrelevant,' wrote Maria von Ebner-Eschenbach (quoted in Hermann Braun and Michael Neubauer, *Goethe in Böhmen*). Nearby is a larger pump room, with a theatrical exterior but cavernous and church-like inside. Here after another change of dress the fashion-conscious spa guests could parade anew while this time sipping the water. Some 170 years later the women could no longer be described as either fashionable or elegant.

We left Franzensbad by another of its parks, passing the exquisite bandstand where musicians were with gusto playing Viennese waltzes and polkas by Carl Michael Ziehrer and Czech marches by Václav Vačkář. Once again fortune had contrived a musical send-off.

The cycle ride from Franzensbad to Carlsbad must be one of the best in Europe. A day is needed to complete the almost fifty miles comfortably. Keeping to the narrow country roads, free of all but agricultural traffic, the journey begins across gently undulating country ideal for cycling. Past farmsteads and small settlements at Lesinka, Hněvin and Hartoušov and across the Sazek and Plesna streams, it is countryside that has hardly changed over centuries. The only concession to the twentieth century was the ageing yellow biplane on a crop-spraying mission, which in a Buchanesque display swooped low and menacingly to investigate the curious spectacle of two cyclists. More traditionally, farmyard geese and watchdogs cackled and barked in alarm as we cycled by.

Up to Kaceřov, which has an attractively modest rococo church and late nineteenth-century schoolhouse, its brickwork unusually embellished by various exotic animals, including crocodiles and kangaroos, the ride was easy. It became hillier as we approached Maria Kulm (Chlum nad Ohří by its Czech name), but the twin spires of its magnificent baroque church always remained in view to encourage us on.

From 1806 Goethe used to break his journey to Carlsbad here after being overcharged for lunch at Zwodau (Zwota). The pilgrimage church is one of the finest in the region, part of it built by Giovanni Santini (born in 1667) and the remainder by Marcantonio Canevale to plans by Christoph Dientzenhofer (1655–1722), most famous for the exuberantly baroque Church of St Nicholas in Prague. But unlike his Prague masterpiece, the Maria Kulm church, dedicated to the Virgin Mary, who is reputed to have appeared miraculously in woods here, is sadly neglected. Now on the path of neither pilgrims nor tourists, it has been a poor candidate for government funds despite its architectural merit, and the local parish priest and his house-keeper have had to struggle to acquire basic building materials to preserve it from complete decay. Maria Kulm used to be especially noted for its Whit Monday processions, which at-tracted pilgrims from far and wide. In his notebook for 2 May 1812 Goethe's valet John noted: 'On our journey to Carlsbad we rested by the church and very devotedly watched the procession of pilgrims with their crosses and flags.'

Standing before this powerfully baroque church, having

never lost sight of it against the glorious curtain of 'the Blue mountains' that opens on the proscenium of 'the Emperor's Forest', is a thrilling experience we readily shared with the great German poet. Opposite the church was an old grocery shop, which outside had a finely inscribed black plaque recording in German Goethe's visits in 1806, 1807, 1808 and 1812. Inside we found bottles of good Czechoslovak Pilsen beer and nuts which we took for refreshment on one of the tree-shaded iron benches in the deserted square that faces this half-forgotten Marian shrine. The shopkeeper had greeted us much as her forebears must have welcomed Goethe himself. Otherwise we were quite alone until an old woman climbed the hill and entered the shop, leaving her wooden cart outside while she bought potatoes. Maria Kulm, once so crowded on feast days, was eerily empty.

We knocked on the church door. After two or three minutes there was a clatter and the hollow crack of an outsize key turning in an ancient lock. A middle-aged woman poked her head through the gap left by the quarter-open door. She had a gentle smile and a sparkle in her eyes that reflected her pride in showing this great charge of hers to a pair of latter-day pilgrims. There was a certain magic for her in the mention of our English provenance. As a small girl at the end of the war she had some complicated connection with a Scottish soldier and his family, had perhaps even been there, but her account in German was not clear. However, her picture of Britain as a land of tolerance and freedom was quite vivid. 'You know how important John Wycliffe was for us Czechs? You know the influence he had on our Jan Hus? And together we stood against the Nazis,' she added, jumping more than five centuries and generously forgetting how Chamberlain had sold Czecho-slovakia out to appease Hitler. Like the pensioner we had met at Krumlov, she preferred to remember Churchill and how Free Czech pilots had helped win the Battle of Britain. 'Our revenge for the loss of our country, though we continued to pay a heavy price.'

The priest was away on pastoral duties, leaving his church in the sure hands of his trusted housekeeper. She told us the story of the church: how the Virgin Mary had appeared to foresters in the woods here and a church was already to be found on the spot in 1383. There are two versions of how the new church was funded. According to one, local robber bands brought to justice in Eger were compelled to hand over their stolen treasures for the church; the other, even more romantic explanation involved a courageous young girl inducing the bandits to give up their evil ways and donate their booty to the church rebuilding programme. This account became widely popular in the nineteenth century through the melodrama *The Bandits of Maria Kulm* by a friend of Goethe, the Carlsbad bookseller C. Cuno.

Leaving a couple of Austrian banknotes towards the next rebuilding programme, we thanked the good housekeeper and left the church wiser about the Bohemian achievements of Christoph Dientzenhofer, Canevale and Santini, not to mention the robber bands of Maria Kulm.

The following stage was wonderfully undemanding, with our cycles free-wheeling past Bukovany and Citice while we marvelled at the rich green landscape and the distant blue hills. But there were suggestions that the rural idyll would not be indefinite: two tall chimneys, their tops marked out for aircraft in a red and white check pattern, towered in the middle distance and, as the road curved round in a great arc, ungainly mechanical diggers could be seen chewing away a hillside like grotesque insects. The sudden, jarring evidence of industry and open-cast mining was a reminder of how in the late nineteenth-century Bohemia was already celebrated not just for its verdant forests and hills but also as the industrial heartland of the Austrian empire. Under post-war communism the industrialization was brutally extended with no regard for what was one of the most beautiful natural regions in Europe.

We finally plunged down into the industrial town of Sokolov, with its rows of smoking chimney-stacks and air heavy with pollution. Though hardly attracted by its exposed industrial architecture, blackened and rusting, and cursing its filthy air, we realized that it was our last chance for lunch. Near a children's playground and opposite a large red brick church by the river Ohře we found a simple restaurant with a free table on its terrace. For the first time we would be able to have a meal with our bicycles standing next to us. We had become attached to these simple machines lent to us by Austrian railways, which had almost gone astray in Prague. We were quickly greeted by two charming, smiling young waitresses, one blonde, the other dark haired, both with azure eyes, who seemed to vie with one another to take our order of roast chicken and dumplings and bring us cooling beer. They were an unexpected vindication of our stop in this hell-hole. As I wiped a handkerchief across my brow I saw it turn quite black. Our descent into Sokolov had transformed us into chimney-sweeps in all but dress.

Hoping to spin out the competition between the delightful waitresses of Sokolov, we then ordered ice-cream. But to our surprise and disappointment it was brought by a waiter who simultaneously issued the bill, which was a pity for the tip. The ice-cream, however, was excellent – as it tended to be throughout the Soviet empire – if not quite as delicious as the product I remember once tasting on a hot summer afternoon in Kiev. The answer was in the *smetana* (cream), which was thick, fresh and free of any additives and, thanks to state subsidies, cheap and readily available.

Sokolov, a more than passable meal and the winning waitresses had detained us long enough. Our goal, Carlsbad, beckoned. The time had come to cycle out of this industrially blighted valley and regain the hills of the true Bohemia.

It did not take long to return to the world of romance and discover one of those Bohemian castles that Rupert of Hentzau could have put to mischievous use. Loket, dominated by its bleak medieval castle perched high on a hill overlooking the river Ohře, could equally well have provided a setting for one of Dornford Yates's inter-war adventures. Indeed a place called Loket features in one of his novels, but he transfers it to Austria. Loket derived its former name, Elbogen (Elbow), from the abrupt bend of the river Ohře round the rocky eminence on which the town is attractively situated. The river rises in the highlands of Saxony but most of its course is in Bohemia amid spectacular mountain scenery, until it finally flows into the Elbe (Labe) near Litoměřice. Predictably, Goethe came to Loket; his statue stands magisterially in the cool shade of overgrown trees on the outskirts of the small town, opposite a tiny, sadly neglected rococo chapel of almost doll's house proportions. In the town square marble plaques outside the principal, apple-green-painted inn record in Czech and German Goethe's visits in 1807, 1808, 1810, 1811, 1813, 1819 and 1823. It was at the White Horse Inn (Zum Weissen Ross), destroyed in a fire that swept the town in 1825, that Goethe attended a birthday party in 1808 for the dark-haired Silvie von Ziegesar – one of his spa flames, who was thirty-six years younger – and then on 28 August 1823 celebrated his own seventy-fourth birthday in the company of Frau von Levetzow and her three daughters. The eldest, Ulrike, was the last great passion of the poet, though at nineteen she was fifty-five years his junior. Goethe was given Rhine wine and a cake by Frau von Levetzow, as well as a cup of the finest Bohemian crystal engraved and inscribed with the names of the three girls: Ulrike, Amalia and Berta. Ulrike inspired the poet's 'Marienbad Elegy', which has been described as 'the profoundest of his love-poems, deeply individual and yet deeply generalized – an old man's symbolic farewell to the last of his loves and to the world which only love can make significant' (David Luke in Goethe, *Selected Verse*).

Past a tall baroque Corinthian column, theatrically surmounted and surrounded by statues of saints and angels, the apex of Loket's long, narrow main square, it is a steep climb to the forbidding castle, said to have been founded in 870. The core of the impregnable building, which successive occupants repeatedly extended, dates from 1234 and for some time sheltered the young Charles IV and his mother. Neither Hussites nor later Swedes in the Thirty Years War succeeded in taking such a formidable fortification. Now abandoned, though earmarked for restoration, we found entry barred by builders' fences and barbed wire. This was clearly another Bohemian town that had depended on its baron for a livelihood. Without a ruling family, the castle left empty and decaying, Loket had little purpose. Its streets were deserted and had a ghostly air even on a fine early summer afternoon. It was as if the town had emptied after some dreadful deed.

On leaving the town we discovered one of Loket's secrets, a rough woodland path that runs along the Ohře towards Carlsbad. We turned our bicycles on to it, glad to escape from the road, and for seven miles we meandered along with the river amid magical silvan scenery. Rivers are a cyclist's delight, as I had been first convinced on bicycle rides by the side of the Zambesi, which offered extravagant wildlife and the risk of a sudden encounter with a crocodile or hippopotamus, and later riding by the Rhine, with its romantic castles, ruins and endless barge traffic, or by the winding Moldau on the trip to Rosenberg. The Ohře was no exception, the route becoming dramatic as the path expired by a sheer rock face, the Hans-Heiling-Felsen, only to be transferred to the opposite bank by a rope and wood bridge swinging precariously over the river. These jagged, forest-enclosed cliffs made a deep impression on Goethe, reflected in his writing during the 1810 and 1811 Carlsbad visits.

The rough, wild path along which Goethe, marvelling at nature's repertory, had trod, his mind constantly brimming with ideas, was replaced on the other bank by a smooth, level road, newly laid and tarred by Czechoslovak army engineers. We found the sappers surveying their handiwork, which had left stretches of tar still soft under foot. The excellence of this obscure road, leading to a frail, swaying bridge that would not have been out of place straddling some Andean ravine, was a riddle. Gradually rising out of the steep valley cut by the Ohře, it led us sedately to the modest town of Doubi.

We emerged at the end of the town by drab blocks of workers' flats and, disinclined to linger, cycled out of it along the busy main road for a couple of miles until we reached a turning to the left that cut through tall pine forests for the final stage to Carlsbad. It was hard, uphill pedalling for an hour or so. Like the vaulting of a great Gothic cathedral, the tops of the towering trees met high above us as we proceeded along this natural nave. The sunlight filtered through in weak patches as if condensed by stained glass, catching in its broken rays particles of dust dancing in the air. The silence was almost oppressive. Then suddenly, as if by some Hansel and Gretel magic deep in the forest, a rustic wooden building appeared in a small clearing, complete with chairs and tables outside: a place for refreshment. And then the climax of the day, the glorious downhill descent, the evening air heavy with the smell of pine, into the valley and to the great spa of Carlsbad.

The town gained its name and reputation from Emperor Charles IV, who in the first half of the fourteenth century came across its curative waters while hunting. Long favoured by diverse royalty, it can boast the longest and most distinguished history of any of the Bohemian spas. It is, as a result, the grandest.

The bulk of Goethe's spa visits – thirteen, including the last in 1823 when he was based in Marienbad – were to Carlsbad, of which he wrote in a letter to his wife, Christiane, on 16 July 1807: 'I know of no more agreeable or pleasant stopping place and will stay here a while . . . One can mingle here with high society or be quite alone, as one wishes. And I can find and do here everything which interests me and gives me pleasure' (author's translation).

He added: 'Weimar, Carlsbad and Rome are the only places where I would like to live.' Next to each other in the heart of the spa are three pension houses where the poet stayed: the White Hare (Weisser Hase), where he had rooms on his first visit in 1785, and, on either side, the Three Red Roses (Drei Rote Rosen, today the 'Mozart' house), where he was quartered the following year, and the Golden Ostrich (Goldener Strauss), where, coming from Marienbad, he stayed in 1823 to be near Frau von Levetzow and her three daughters (notably Ulrike) who were also housed there. A short stroll away behind some horse-chestnut trees, the faded yellow Posthof, a coffee, concert and dance place much frequented in Goethe's time, remains popular today.

From the forest we entered the top of the town and Carlsbad's splendid past immediately became apparent: the glistening gold of the onion domes of the orthodox church, built in the last century for the use of visiting members of the Russian imperial family and their entourage, and further down the more sober late Victorian red brick Anglican church. Unlike at Marienbad, where the Anglican church is in a desperate state of decay, the Carlsbad Protestant community can still manage a sparsely attended Sunday service in what is now an Evangelical church. The Victorian and Edwardian stained glass, oak pews and the threadbare hassocks once lovingly stitched by English matrons all survive. So does a memorial to the right of the altar which, adding a transatlantic note, recalls one of the church's benefactors who came a long way to restore his health: Henry Le Clercq of New York City, 1852–1909.

At the foot of the hill we neared the centre of the town, moving back earlier into the nineteenth century. An eye-catchingly stylish white stuccoed villa stood out, built as a home for convalescing imperial officers, with appropriately martial reliefs of rifles, bayonets and lances decorating its exterior, and a magnificent iron-columned colonnade running along one side. The villa's military function was rightly, even if with a regrettable loss of panache, maintained under communism.

It was time to dismount as we wandered the length of the pedestrian area along the river, through the heart of the once fashionable town with its faded elegance and sometimes bombastic nineteenth-century buildings; past the long, flamboyant colonnades where those taking the waters stroll before queue-ing to refill their beakers, and the dilapidated souvenir shops that for a few crowns sell roses petrified by the sulphurous water or small porcelain jugs encrusted with the thick yellow-brown deposit it leaves. A more appetizing local speciality, to be found a few doors along, are the Carlsbader Oblaten, large but almost transparently thin wafers, deliciously filled with nut or vanilla cream. The best come in green tins bearing stylized drawings on the lid of the Virgin Mary, a church cupola and a serpent.

Two hundred yards further down the promenade is the Elephant, a café and cake-shop the excellence of which is more typical of Vienna than Bohemia. Prague, for all its qualities, knows no establishment like this. So good is the patisserie and coffee that its red plush seats are never unoccupied.

Then, as the river bends in a final right angle through the old centre of Carlsbad, comes the grandest of grand hotels, the Pupp. This great, wedding-cake-like nineteenth-century edifice, weighed down by its almost vulgar abundance of Corinthian columns and pilasters, a mass of architectural icing, epitomizes the most obviously fashionable of Bohemia's spas. Its name changed to the Moskva by the communists, who incongruously crowned so bourgeois an institution with a huge red neon star, the 'velvet revolution' saw both rapidly removed and the affectionate reinstatement of the long familiar Grand Hotel Pupp. It has a distinguished pedigree, having been founded as early as 1701 by Augustus the Strong of Saxony; he had a 'Saxon assembly room' built, to which a 'Bohemian hall' was added twenty-five years later. Then in 1760 Count Chopek brought to Carlsbad a master cake-maker, Johann Georg Pupp, who strategically fell in love with, and married, the daughter of the wealthy local patissier. With their considerable combined resources, they brought the original two buildings together and founded both the Pupp and a dynasty to run it. Subsequent Pupps strove to turn their charge into the greatest hotel of the Austrian empire. The prolific Viennese architectural duo of Helmer and Fellner, responsible for opera houses throughout Central Europe, including the Carlsbad theatre, were called in to build an extravagant *fin de siècle* banqueting hall where 700 guests could be seated before a concert platform complete with an organ of 4,778 pipes and 66 registers. There was a dazzling ballroom with a great glass skylight and 358 opulently furnished rooms, their capacious tiled bathrooms equipped with the latest developments in late nineteenth-century plumbing. The long corridors were filled with classical statuary and overembellished with elaborate cornices and columns. Florid wrought-iron balustrades, gilded plaster work and a profusion of Bohemian crystal chandeliers and stained glass completed the grand hotel's uninhibited decorative plan.

It was at the Pupp, amid the potted palms and to the strains of Strauss and Lehár, that the notorious traitor Colonel Redl handed over to his Russian contact the entire Austrian battle order on the eve of the First World War.

And it was here that we finally arrived towards eight in the evening, having left our bicycles outside with the bemused but extremely courteous, dark blue and gold liveried porter. Our room was predictably of generous proportions with a high, fine white stucco ceiling. Parting the thick curtains revealed a view of the main courtyard, where a plaque recorded that Beethoven had stayed here in 1812. The outsize bathroom with its giant bathtub ensured an invigorating soak, enlivened by the provision of Carlsbad pine oil, that banished any saddle weariness.

The old black telephone rang discreetly. I lifted the heavy receiver: 'Sir, there is a "Pan" Nicholson waiting for you downstairs.' We had completed our rendezvous with a precision that would have done credit to an SOE operation. There was just time to dress for dinner.

7 Prague, the Golden City

There is an opera by Smetana which tells the fantastic story of Libussa. According to legend this eighth-century queen, though the youngest of three daughters, was chosen by her father Krok, prince of Bohemia, to succeed him. Among her many virtues was the gift of prophecy. She rightly predicted that she would wed a farmer called Premysl, but, more significantly, she handed down to her subjects another prophecy: 'I see a town, the glory of which will reach the stars. There is a spot in the forest which the river Moldau encircles, and which to the north the stream Brusnice secures by its deep valley; and to the south a hill, which from its rocks takes the name Petřin, towers above it. When you have reached this spot you will find a man in the midst of the forest, who is working at a door-sill for a house; even mighty lords bend before a low door. From this you shall call the town which you will build there "Praha".' The derivation is said to be from the Slavonic *prah*, a doorway. And so, according to legend, Prague arose.

Libussa and her father had lived on the rocky crag called Vyšehrad which overhangs the Moldau on its right bank. The train bringing me from Carlsbad trundled past Vyšehrad's abandoned wooden station as I marvelled at the unfolding panorama of Zlatá Praha (Golden Prague), its myriad towers and pinnacles sharply defined in the late afternoon sun.

My picture of Prague was still a rough sketch, in need of completion. My mother was born in this fabulous city before the First World War in privileged circumstances. Her parents kept town houses in Prague and the imperial capital, Vienna, where as a young girl, dressed impeccably in white lace, she was taken by carriage to the Stefansdom (St Stephen's Cathedral) for her confirmation. Her mother was of an old Austrian family who had long served as courtiers; on her Czech father's side there was a tradition of service in the imperial army which Colonel Julius Pisarowitz, obsessed with horses, maintained in the cavalry. The Great War saw him dispatched to the Alpine battlefields of north Italy, where in the mountain passes the Austrians were locked in bloody combat with Italian troops, blasting them with fearsome Skoda howitzers made in the factories of Pilsen. The Armistice and the collapse of the worn-out Austrian empire saw the creation of modern Czechoslovakia, a model republic which my grandfather enthusiastically embraced. He was quick to volunteer for the newly formed Czechoslovak army and was promoted to the rank of brigadier-general. Only the premature death from heart disease of his wife marred for him a period of such national promise. He heaped his affection on my mother, indulging every whim of hers and loving best to place her on one of his huge bay mounts. He missed her greatly when in the early 1930s she went to the Sorbonne to complete her studies, never to return to her beloved Prague except for a visit on the eve of the Nazi take-over to seek her father's permission to marry the Englishman she had met in Paris. Approval was instant on account of my father's equal equine obsession.

In May 1945 this English son-in-law, borne by an American tank, entered Prague and made straight for the house looking on to the castle. The door was locked, the caretaker had a grim report: the old soldier had been taken away and shot two weeks earlier. The Prague uprising, which should have been synchronized with the city's liberation by Soviet troops, was premature and my grandfather, along with scores of others, had paid the price. My father found the freshly dug grave and planted a small, red-berried mountain-ash tree there, fulfilling an often expressed wish. As a child I remember two stories in particular about the grandfather I never knew: that he carried a small silver box into which he deposited his cigar ash, to be saved as toothpowder, and that he took great pride in being one of the few officers in his regiment who did not need to wear a corset.

Growing up during the heady years of the first Czechoslovak republic, my mother had many tales with which to regale me of this uniquely beautiful city and how it had earned a reputation then second only to Paris. Hatred of the Nazis, who had desecrated so civilized a city with the swastika and its perverted ideology, was matched only by detestation of the communists, who had tried the impossible, making such a golden city drab.

Prague's good fortune was that its historic buildings, if not its people, were largely spared by the Second World War. Two American air raids were recorded towards the end of the war, causing some damage to an industrial suburb and one of the city's modern bridges. The most serious loss was the town hall in the Old Town Square, which the SS burned down as they withdrew. The adjoining clock tower dating from 1474 with its wonderful astronomical clock, one of the city's great sights, was lucky to survive. It was a luck Dresden, the Saxon capital and cultural rival on the Elbe, was denied.

The Carlsbad train deposited me at one of Prague's outlying stations where I transferred to the swish new Soviet-built metro, which twice took me back and forth under the city without a ticket before I alighted at the right stop, having belatedly taken advice from an army major who, judging by his well-stuffed briefcase, had something to do with the Defence Ministry. Like Moscow and East Berlin, Prague's streets and stations were always peopled by uniformed officers hurrying to their offices, a feature of communism. Was it a result of military overstaffing or a constant indication of preparedness for a war footing?

A room had been negotiated at the Alcron, not the oldest,

dating from the 1930s, but still Prague's most elegant hotel, conveniently situated just off Wenceslas Square. Though communism had instilled in the staff a superficial surliness, as so often was the case, their confidence and trust could with patience be earned, encouraged in true Central European fashion by an occasional bribe. I was surprised at the positive response from the lady telephonist when I dictated a telegram I had promised to send on arrival to a countess in Austria. The Habsburg empire may have been long dead but it was not forgotten. It was clearly remembered as a period of more benevolent rule, of greater liberty. It reminded me of my KGB-vetted secretary in Moscow, who, when I was not looking, cut out every picture and article in the British Press on the royal family for her own scrapbook. Starved of glamour by years of communism, it was perhaps to be expected that covert, even if vicarious, nostalgia for forgotten royalty existed in these countries.

Anna, an exquisite product of cool north German and fiery Montenegrin stock, had arrived after a day-long but never dull rail trip across Germany and Bohemia in the unlikely guise of a harpist. Admission to being a journalist would have been grounds enough in those days for a visa refusal, or at least an over-long delay. She had assumed an instrument which nobody was likely to ask her to play. After my unnecessary meanderings on the metro, we had met in another perfectly executed prearranged rendezvous in the modern orange and black underworld beneath Prague's main western railway station. Any contemporary producer of Gluck's pioneering opera *Orfeo ed Euridice* could learn from this station, exuberant art nouveau upstairs and a cavernous latter-day hell below, full of Furies. It was from this netherworld that I snatched Anna, never daring to look back.

Pre-revolutionary Prague was a very different story from communist-ruled East Germany. It was less efficient, more chaotic and colourful, but it too could be sinister and, hardly surprisingly, it was sometimes disturbingly Kafkaesque.

The hotels were watched, the rooms bugged and Wenceslas Square was infested with black-market money-changers, a good percentage of whom were *agents provocateurs*. There were also, needless to say, the prostitutes whose real pimps were the secret police. But there were too many more worthwhile distractions for any of this really to matter. No wonder that Václav Havel* and so many other stout, persecuted souls smiled at adversity. Inspired morally and intellectually by their city and its past, they had higher priorities, knew greater things and had learned above all to be patient. History had given them heroes, whether the defiant early fifteenth-century reformer Jan Hus, the Protestant nobles executed after their defeat at the battle of the White Mountain in 1620, Tómaš Masaryk, the founding father of modern Czechoslovakia, or Jan Palach, who set himself alight in protest at his country's rape by Russian tanks in August 1968. Crushingly oppressed after the stifling of the Prague Spring, they could survive by developing a natural superiority complex over their thuggish tormentors. They knew that their time would come sooner or later. It came rather earlier than most expected.

In 1923 an English officer, writer and artist strongly drawn to this ancient country, newly revived, wrote of the aftermath of the battle of the White Mountain in words that were to have an echo under another oppressor, during the years of communist rule: 'Then the Jesuit-ridden Habsburg entered Prague and laid his heavy hand on all Bohemia, almost to the undoing of its people. But it is a wonderful thing, that power of a strong race to survive treachery and oppression until the

---

* 'Hope is a dimension of the spirit. It is not outside us, but within us. When you lose it you must seek it again within yourself and in people around you – not in objects or even in events' (Havel, *Letters to Olga*, London, 1989).

time comes when it can reassert itself' (Lt-Col. B. Granville Baker, *From a Terrace in Prague*).

It was almost twenty years since I had last seen Olga. Then, a year after the suppression of the Prague Spring, having to leave her husband behind as a hostage and with an absurd allowance of only two pounds sterling, she was allowed to come and stay with us in London. In the ideological upheaval that followed the Russian intervention she had lost her teaching post. She had grown up with my mother in the house that looked on to the castle and in spite of Nazis and communists was too patriotic ever seriously to have contemplated leaving her homeland.

Punctually at 10 a.m., smartly dressed in a white and pale lilac checked suit, her fair brown hair neatly permed, she nervously entered the Alcron lobby. Recognition despite those twenty years was instant and emotional. Neither of us had apparently changed that much. We kissed clumsily and Anna, no stranger from correspondence between my mother and Olga, was introduced. In the hotel foyer – the colour of Colman's English mustard and art deco furnished – we sat around a table, ordered coffees and reminisced about London in 1969: eye-opening first impressions for her of a huge, pulsating city full of pageantry and intoxicating freedom. Her memory was faultless; she even recalled an essay I had written in my last year at school on Jan Hus.

The excited meeting in the Alcron was only an opening encounter to plan a programme for our Prague visit. The next day, Saturday, Olga would meet us for a tour of the old city. We would be in expert hands, for since being forced to give up teaching she had become an official guide. That evening we would go to her home for dinner. Meanwhile, we would be left to our own devices, though we had an imminent fixture with Bassett and Nicholson, who, stopping on their way from Marienbad back to Austria, were due to join us for lunch under the life-sized silver nude – a Czech Josephine Baker – that so alluringly graced the Alcron's dining-room.

But first we decided to test the Alcron's dry martinis which, I had been told, rivalled those of Harry's Bar in Venice. They did. The grey tail-coated head waiter then ushered us to our places by the statue, the focal point of the room whose predominantly old pink was pleasingly relieved by the starched white table linen and Bohemian crystal. As in Vienna, a basket of *Kipferl*, small, delicate rolls of bread embellished with caraway, poppy seed or salt crystals, were offered after the menu. Then a tray of extra-curricular hors-d'œuvres, the most notable and recommendable of which were the cornets of Prague ham stuffed with freshly grated and creamed horse-radish. Among the fish were, predictably, both trout and carp 'Třeboň Art'. There was fried chicken, a recipe I remember well from my mother (though hers was certainly better), and the duck and pork so prevalent on Czech menus. As the bottle of rich red Moravian wine and the precious mineral water arrived, the Marienbad cyclists entered, thirsty and hungry and delighted to have completed another rendezvous with such precision.

If there is one opera which should be seen in Prague, it must be Mozart's *Don Giovanni*, first performed there with notable success on 29 October 1787. Mozart himself conducted the première at the Nostitz Theatre, later known as the Tyl. After the tribulations of Vienna,* where, for all his battling, he was never accepted as a court composer, his popularity in Prague did much to lift his spirits. Prague productions of *Die Entführung aus dem Serail* and *Le nozze di Figaro* had already

---

* In a letter dated 12 July 1789 Mozart wrote: 'Fate is, unfortunately, most unkind to me, but only here in Vienna, so that I can earn nothing, however much I try.'

captured the public's enthusiasm, leading to the commission for *Don Giovanni*. The warm reception given to *Figaro* in Prague was in marked contrast to the meagre interest shown in Vienna, where it was performed only nine times over an eight-month period at the Burgtheater. In the first monograph on Mozart, published in Prague – itself worthy of note – in 1798, Franz Xaver Niemetschek wrote: 'The opera impresario Bondini commissioned from Mozart a new opera to be performed at the Prague theatre next winter; Mozart gladly accepted, having seen for himself how his music is appreciated and well performed in Bohemia. He used to repeat this to his Prague friends. He liked Prague, an appreciating audience and genuine friends.'

Mozart, moreover, was able to cock a snook at the Vienna establishment and directly at the imperial court, which cold-shouldered him for ten years, by giving his new Prague opera a revolutionary note which was as pertinent in 1787 as it was to be two hundred years later. In thirty-three bars of the *Don Giovanni* score, marked off in red pencil in the original performing manuscript, Mozart makes a call for political freedom which, according to contemporary accounts, was spontaneously taken up by the politically aware Prague audience joining in. 'È aperto a tutti quanti, Viva la libertà,' sings Don Giovanni as he opens his house to all in the masked ball scene towards the end of Act 1. To which everyone ('Tutti' in the score) responds, 'Viva la libertà!' – a seditious reference which significantly (to escape the imperial censor) is not to be found in the libretto published in Vienna shortly before the Prague première. As so often during revolutionary periods, the stage was used for statements which could not yet be made on the streets.

The original Tyl opera house having long been closed for restoration, *Don Giovanni* was to be performed that Friday at the Smetana Theatre, which in pre-communist days was known as the New German Theatre and used for German-language productions: a worthy creation – with a delectable white and gold, red velvet interior – by the ubiquitous Helmer and Fellner late in the last century. My mother's family had a permanent box in the theatre and in December 1920 at the tender age of not quite eight she recollected only too well being taken by her mother and father to *Don Giovanni* with her best friend Lizzi, a daughter of a fellow officer who lived in a fine house overlooking the Moldau a few yards from theirs. While my mother was thrilled by the ghostly statue of the Commendatore accepting the invitation of the dissolute Don and his entry in the closing scene, to the accompaniment of bass drums and a thunderclap, to sup with him, it was all too much for Lizzi, who, to the consternation of the grown-ups, flooded the box. No doubt as a result of this deeply imprinted memory, as well as the plot's unmatchable whiff of sulphur and sin, it was to remain my mother's favourite opera for the rest of her life. Alexander von Zemlinsky, a friend of Mahler and himself a not inconsiderable composer, had conducted that Prague *Don Giovanni*. Born in Vienna in 1871, Zemlinsky was described by Arnold Schoenberg as 'the first of living conductors'. My mother's brother, eleven years older than her, had abandoned chemistry to study music with him.

Standing on the steps of the theatre and keeping our eyes peeled, we managed with only five minutes to spare to secure a pair of tickets for the sold-out performance from a talkative New Yorker whose escort was otherwise detained. 'Have a nice evening,' she said after reluctantly accepting West German marks in payment – to anyone else the most sought after currency in Prague.

While we were ticket hunting, a black Rolls-Royce drew up before the theatre in inimitable fashion, a small Union Jack pennant flying on its right wing. Out of it stepped a ruddy-faced, silver-haired man, the most musical of former British premiers, Edward Heath, in the company of Her Britannic Majesty's ambassador.

Our tickets, by one of those astonishing coincidences that pepper life, were for box seats and, if I remembered my mother's description accurately, 'Lóže 7' must have been her family's box.

It was the same solid Václav Kašlík/Josef Svoboda production, conducted by Zdeněk Košler, that had been staged at the Tyl for the best part of twenty years before the theatre closed for restoration and it transferred to the Smetana. Musically the performance was chiefly notable for the appearance as Leporello of Walter Berry, veteran of the Vienna State Opera. As a 25-year-old, Berry had sung Masetto in Furtwängler's celebrated 1954 Salzburg production of *Don Giovanni*, the great conductor's swansong.

Breakfast at the Alcron is taken in the ante-room of the main dining area, under brightly coloured stained-glass panels of national flags, with erstwhile communist states strongly but not exclusively represented. So, for example, Canada can rub heraldic shoulders with Cuba, while New Zealand sits incongruously by Mongolia. As we emerged from this amusing if outdated geography lesson, Olga appeared, impatient to initiate us into some of Prague's many secrets.

We descended bustling Wenceslas Square (Václavské náměsti), Prague's Piccadilly, for the ancient core of the city, past the green and white Tyl Theatre, inelegantly clad in scaffolding, through the fruit and flower market by which it is colourfully set, wending our way past glorious baroque and rococo buildings which too hastily, and foolishly, can be taken for granted, until from the Malé nám., with its iron-caged sixteenth-century fountain, we arrived at the Staroměstské nám., the Old Town Square. It was in this magnificent square, dominated today by the surviving tower of the town hall and its extraordinary fifteenth-century astronomical clock, the twin towers of the newly restored Teyn Church, its palaces and medieval guild buildings and, at the bottom, the gracefully proportioned baroque Church of St Nicholas by Kilian Dientzenhofer (not to be confused with the even more imposing St Nicholas's built by his father, Christoph, on the other side of the Moldau) that the flower of Bohemian nobility, twenty-one in number, was taken to the scaffold after defeat at the battle of the White Mountain. The Protestant martyrs took their last sacrament at the old church, which the Jesuits pulled down to make way for the new St Nicholas's. Today a later chapter in history is reflected in its splendid chandelier modelled on a tsar's crown. At the same time as St Nicholas's was raised the Hussite symbol of a large chalice that was emblazoned on the front of the Church of Our Lady of Teyn (the principal church of the Old Town since 1310) was replaced by a brilliant golden, lozenge-shaped image of the Virgin. But Bohemia's Protestant hero was to return in more modern times. The 500th anniversary of his execution at the stake in Constance was to see the unveiling of a sprawling bronze monument to Jan Hus in 1915, not uninfluenced by Rodin's *Burghers of Calais*, which, however, stands far more happily in the shadow of Westminster.

We lingered, as every passing Prague citizen and visitor does, in front of the great astronomical clock to see it perform on the hour. The whirring, the chime and the gyrating carved figures carried through their hourly ritual, none more convincingly than that of Vanity holding his head back to admire it in a mirror, or the skeleton representing Death, which had particularly delighted my mother as a child.

Taking the Karlová, we were quickly at the Charles Bridge, which, dating from 1357, perhaps more than any of Prague's riches has come to symbolize the 'Golden City'. Olga stood by the deeply compassionate statue of St Anne to point out the route she used to swim with my mother up and down the

Moldau, from the swimming school down river up to the great arches of the bridge. I recall my mother telling me that it was a tough but exhilarating swim, notwithstanding the dirty water or the dead rats that floated in it. Her house was clearly visible from here.

We advanced down the great bridge with its slight curve, stopping from time to time to admire its fine statues and the view – Hradčany Castle and St Vitus's Cathedral crowning the hill, or, looking back, the National Theatre, its shining, gilded roof like the lid of a giant jewel box – and pausing again at the spot where St Jan Nepomuk met his martyrdom. At the furthest end on the left is a splendid group of statues that includes a pot-bellied janizary, known to Olga and my mother as the 'Prague Turk'. As small girls they had delighted in clambering up and counting the number of buttons on his well-filled tunic.

On the far side of the bridge we had reached the Malá Strana (Small Side), an area unspoiled by time, picturesquely sandwiched between the river and Hradčany Castle. This is Prague at its most romantic, with its narrow, gas-lit, cobbled streets that still remain thoroughly eighteenth century in character. Carriages are called for, bearing periwigged and powdered men and women to their palaces or back from the theatre. Plaques record the houses in which Mozart and Beethoven stayed. When Milos Forman made his film *Amadeus*, he needed to look no further for his film set.

After allowing ourselves to be stunned by the baroque majesty of Christoph Dientzenhofer's St Nicholas's and its pulsating, almost dizzying use of space, we passed the more modest Gothic Church of St Thomas, where Olga had married her first husband, Josef, to find ourselves before the huge Palais Waldstein, built for the formidable Wallenstein in the 1630s. Twenty-three houses were pulled down to enable Giovanni Marini and his team of architects and landscape gardeners to create a suitably regal residence for the warrior statesman. In its gardens, amid magnolias as old as the palace and by a bower of black yew trees where Wallenstein would confer with the ambassadors of kings who sought his alliance, my mother had played with Lizzi and Olga. Her house was opposite, U Železné Lávky 8 (By the Iron Chain Bridge 8). Willow trees have since grown in the small park in front to form a thin veil between the rather over-ornate pink and white façade, with its central statue of St Francis, decorative urns and garlands, and the palace opposite. Above rises an unimpeded view of the austere, humourless lines of the castle and the soaring Gothic pinnacles of St Vitus's. To the left the Charles Bridge can be seen confidently straddling the Moldau. With communism this tallest and most elaborate wedge of houses, so favourably placed, was hardly surprisingly given over to apartments for party officials. Its post-revolutionary fate remains uncertain.

Opposite, near the Waldstein Palace, stairs rise to the Hradčany, hugging the hill and offering magnificent views of the city and its graceful towers and spires, bisected by the shimmering Moldau. Prague is forever beautiful, whether glistening like gold under a clear blue summer sky, or becomingly wearing its winter apparel of white. From these stairs the Malá Strana, its numerous elegant palaces and gardens turned over to foreign embassies and diplomatic use, can best be surveyed.

The hill itself is comprehensively occupied by the castle until suddenly, out of one of the courtyards, like a huge rocket on its launching pad, soars the towering, flamboyantly Gothic Cathedral of St Vitus. It is to Prague what Notre Dame is to Paris, the great church for state occasions, where after the miracle of the 'velvet revolution', the venerable, ninety-year-old archbishop, Cardinal Tomasek, who for years had been a solid buttress of faith against the communists, led a service of thanksgiving, complete with *Te Deum*, for Havel as president

Above: A view of East Berlin and the river Spree from the Reichstag, its skyline graced on the left by the elegant tower of the Sophienkirche and cluttered on the right by the modern blocks of the Alexanderplatz.

Below: A ritual abandoned with unification: changing of the Guard at the Schinkel Neue Wache on Unter den Linden.

Left: Seat of the revolution: Leipzig, the Church of St Nicholas (Nikolaikirche), from which after Monday prayers the weekly demonstrations started that toppled the communist regime.

Below: Leipzig station.

Above: 'Here you bite on granite!' Allied prisoners playing volleyball at Colditz Castle.

Below: A smoke-blackened land: the chimneys of Espenhain.

Left: Waiting for the bus in Cottbus.

Below: Splendidly decorated, modestly supplied: a butcher's shop in Halle.

Opposite, top: Český Krumlov, its massive castle rising magisterially above the river Moldau (Vltava).

Opposite, below: Franzensbad, avenue leading to the Doric rotunda of the Francis Spring.

Left: The richly decorated ballroom of the Hotel Pupp, Carlsbad.

Below: Carlsbad: taking the waters by the palm-lined colonnade.

Above left: The celebrated astronomical clock in Prague. Dating from about 1410, this magnificent time–piece is set in the old town hall and includes moving figures and a crowing cock.

Above right: Prague: view of St Nicholas's, the former Jesuit church designed by Christoph Dientzenhofer and his son Kilian.

Right: The Loreto Church in Prague, another inspired work of the Dientzenhofers.

Above: Prague: Charles Bridge in winter.
Below: Prague: Malá Strana.

Above: Warsaw: the meticulously reconstructed market place of the Old Town.

Right: The Neptune Fountain Gdańsk.

Opposite, top: Revolution in East Berlin: 'Long Live the Prague Spring!'

Opposite, below: Berlin: the Arsenal (Zeughaus) building.

Right: Potsdam: the Neues Palais, Sans Souci park.

Below: Cecilienhof, Potsdam.

Above left: Schwerin, the castle park: one of four allegorical figures at the base of the equestrian statue of Grand Duke Friedrich Franz II.

Above right: Brandenburg Cathedral.

Opposite, top: Dresden on the Elbe: the ruined castle, Hofkirche and Semper opera house.

Opposite, below: Dresden's Zwinger: the Wall Pavilion surmounted by Permoser's 'Hercules Saxonicus', an allegory of Augustus the Strong.

Above: The Wartburg: scene of Luther's translation of the New Testament and of Wagner's opera *Tannhäuser*. In the distance the town of Eisenach, birthplace of Johann Sebastian Bach.

Above: Erfurt, dilapidated capital of Thuringia.

Below: Erfurt: Marktstrasse.

Left: Weimar: the double statue of Goethe and Schill outside the National Theat

Below: Part of Goethe's ho on the Frauenplan in Weim and, on the left, convenient situated next door, the Whi Swan Inn, a Napoleonic cannon-ball still lodged in its wall.

of a free Czechoslovakia. Bohemian history echoes through the vast spaces of this church, the origins of which can be traced back one thousand years. Its Gothic transformation came, like so much else in Prague, in the mid fourteenth century during the reign of Charles IV, first with the French architect Matthias of Arras, who took Narbonne Cathedral as his model, and then under that most sensitive of craftsmen Peter Parler, whose hand is so clearly discernible. But it was to become an endless building project, like that of the great Gothic cathedral in Cologne, and was only completed in 1929, appropriately during the flowering of the first Czechoslovak republic.

Its bejewelled Wenzel or Wenceslas chapel, dedicated to the saint and the work of Peter Parler, is embellished with some thirteen hundred cut and polished semi-precious gems from Bohemia, as well as Gothic wall-paintings. The ring on the door is said to have been grasped by the pious king as he was cut down by his pagan brother Boleslav in 935. Treasure fit for a king's ransom is to be found five chapels further on in that dedicated to St Jan Nepomuk, with its inordinately lavish and flamboyant solid silver raised tomb, designed by Fischer von Erlach and completed in 1736.

Emerging from the cathedral, we were quickly reclaimed by the surrounding castle from which kings and, in more recent times, presidents governed. Until the November 1989 revolution and the people's dispatch of Havel 'to the castle', its use was hardly a point of attraction. The goose-stepping guards at the main gates, threateningly surmounted since 1768 by aggressively posed Titans, gave an air of unwelcoming authority. One of the favourite propaganda pictures disseminated by the Nazis was of their storm troopers stamping through these front gates watched approvingly, it seemed, by the Titans with which they had so much in common. It was the same after the stifling of the Prague Spring when the hard-line communist leaders of the Warsaw Pact could assemble here in security, knowing that they had achieved their heartless task and successfully suppressed a nation. In front of the gilded mirrors and beneath the elaborate Bohemian crystal chandeliers, they unashamedly toasted their ignoble achievement with Russian vodka. Today it is a happier story; the Titans are still there, but now they guard over a popular playwright–president who spent enough time in prison to appreciate the meaning of freedom for his people. A theatre designer friend of his has devised gentler uniforms for the presidential guard, who now perform a less martial drill routine under the Titans' gaze.

The castle's Vladislav Hall, completed in 1500 by Benedikt Ried, is the grandest of secular Gothic halls with majestic vaulting. It was used as a banqueting hall for coronations and for tournaments, a remarkable feature being the Rider's Staircase, which allowed knights to enter the great hall on horseback. It still provides the setting for acts of state, including the now democratic election of the president.

It leads to the very much more modest council room that was the scene of the dramatic events of 23 May 1618 when two Catholic councillors were thrown from its windows in an act that precipitated the Thirty Years War.

Beyond the castle lies the loveliest of churches, the Loreto, its spirited façade the inspired creation of the Dientzenhofers. Its lightness, long lines and elegant tower are as easy on the eye as the heavily baroque Černín Palace opposite is displeasing. Francesco Caratti's design has a monumentality that is out of place in Prague and, quite suitably, the palace was taken over as a barracks in the nineteenth century and as the Foreign Ministry after 1932. It was from an upper window of the Černín Palace that during the communist take-over in 1948 Jan Masaryk, foreign minister and son of Czechoslovakia's first president, fell to his death in a modern and no less chilling case of defenestration.

Approaching the square in front of this forbidding palace,

we found it filled for the day with an impressive array of vintage Skodas and Tatras, a reminder that before the war Czechoslovakia produced some of the finest and most sporting roadsters in Europe, and that afterwards the collecting and maintenance of old cars was something of a national hobby and a welcome distraction from communist drabness.

Apart from its Dientzenhofer façade (1721–4), the Loreto is full of riches. Chief among them is the Casa Santa around which it is built, a copy of the Holy Family's house in Nazareth which, according to legend, angels bore to Loreto in Italy at the end of the thirteenth century. The Prague Loreto is modelled on Bramante's High Renaissance Italian version and was completed in 1631. A cannon-ball from the 1866 Austro-Prussian war remains very neatly and tactfully lodged in the heavenly cloud behind the angel Gabriel in the annunciation scene on an upper relief of the Casa Santa. The Loreto also has a dazzling collection of treasure, among which is an incredible twelve-kilogram monstrance of gilded silver designed by Fischer von Erlach and embellished with no fewer than 6,222 diamonds.

Near the entrance to the treasury is a side chapel with a most extraordinary saint, the 'Heilige Kümmernis' (Holy Sorrow). No saint fascinated my mother more as a small girl and she would linger at the Loreto for hours, staring at this radiantly dressed effigy of the saintly and beautiful princess who prayed every night that God would make her so ugly that she would be rejected by the prince she was expected against her will to marry. On her wedding day, she awoke to find that her long raven-black hair was matched by a fully grown beard. Her prayers had been answered, the marriage was called off and she retired content to a nunnery.

There is too a story worth relating about the Loreto's twenty-seven bells, which were cast in Amsterdam in 1694 and installed by the Prague clockmaker Peter Neumann. In the nearby poor quarter, behind the baroque Capuchin monastery, there once lived an old impoverished widow with twenty-seven children and a purse hidden away with twenty-seven silver coins. Plague was raging through the city and one child of hers after another perished. At the death of each child she gave a silver coin for the Loreto's bells to be rung. As she returned home from burying her last child she was also struck down by fever and thought, my dear children, I was there to make sure the bells pealed for you, what can you do for me? At that very moment, as she passed away, the Loreto's bells rang, playing a heavenly melody.

Descending the castle hill and returning to the Malá Strana, I was eager to see another church that I remembered hearing about during my childhood: St Maria de Victoria (St Mary of Victory). The oldest baroque church in Prague (1611–13), it had been originally planned for the city's German Lutheran community, but the defeat of Protestantism at the battle of the White Mountain saw it handed over to the Carmelites. The figure of the Victorious Mother of God, with crown, sceptre and shining halo, set in an arched niche above the portal, is the earliest free-standing baroque statue on a Prague church façade and was to be widely copied throughout Bohemia. However, it was the Pražské milostné Jezulátko or Prager Jesulein, the Infant Jesus of Prague (revered throughout the Latin world as the Bambino di Praga), that made the church such an important place of pilgrimage. This two-foot-high wax figure of the infant Christ came to Prague from Spain as part of a dowry in the sixteenth century and was presented to the church by Polyxena von Lobkowitz in 1628 with the words, 'I am giving you what is dearest to me, honour this sculpture and it will bring you good.' Soon afterwards Ferdinand II unexpectedly decided to give the Carmelite convent considerable financial support, and its vines on the Petřín brought in a bumper harvest. During the plague none of the Carmelites succumbed; constant prayer to the Infant Jesus during the Swedish army's siege of Prague ended in its withdrawal and when the figure was taken into the streets to be revered by the people, the blind could suddenly see, the deaf hear and cripples threw away their crutches. Ever since, the brilliantly attired, gold-crowned doll has been an object of deep veneration, not only in Prague. My mother had come across the Jesulein, resplendent in an extravagant, high baroque silver case made in 1741 by Johann Pakeni, when she attended German masses at the church and afterwards always kept a figure of the Prague Jesus in her bedroom. In 1702, it is recorded, a thief was deterred from stealing the Jesulein's precious regalia by a voice saying, 'I am Jesus, whom you are persecuting.' The empress Maria Theresa herself embroidered a dress for the figure with gold thread, and today its clothing is regularly changed, drawing on a wardrobe of thirty-nine costumes.

That evening we were to meet up with Olga again for dinner at her home. Václav, her second husband, a retired translator who was a compulsive BBC listener and, though well into his seventies, a bull of a man, came to the Alcron to pick us up. We took the metro, then a tram to an address some way out from the centre. The small top-floor flat was a far cry from the house looking on to the Hradčany where Olga had lived in pre-communist days. But it too had a view, if not so compelling, and, she insisted, being modern, was far more practical. But the past was not entirely forgotten: as we sat in the cramped room at the dining table and enjoyed cornets of Prague ham adorned with tomatoes expertly cut into roses, I admired the fine eighteenth-century painting on the wall of the martyrdom of St Barbara. It was small enough to have been rescued from the old house and was as good as any of the pictures I had seen in the Prague National Gallery.

Less than eighteen months later, on 17 November 1989, the communist fabric finally cracked. The Berlin Wall had amazingly opened a week before and Czechoslovaks took to the streets to show that anything the East Germans could do, they could do better. They rallied in Wenceslas Square and, rattling their house and car keys in unison, created a cacophony that was to be the death knell of the communist regime. In a desperate bid to crush the openly expressed dissent, the police tried to beat the demonstrators into submission on 17 November. A year earlier they had done the same. This time they hounded protesters into the side streets and brutally assaulted them. Despite erroneous initial reports that a student had been killed, and the fact that hundreds were seriously injured, the first miracle of the revolution was that there were no fatalities. The police action was a grave miscalculation – one which may even have been deliberately engineered by the KGB to bring about political reform. Instead of silencing protest, their brutality mobilized the whole population, which flooded the streets and paralysed the capital, all the time rattling their keys, a Dance of Death for the hated regime. Within days the revolution had been won. Though inspired by the changes in East Berlin, the Prague revolution was pushed through and happily concluded while the East Germans were still deliberating how far to take theirs.

Václav Havel, the diminutive, plucky playwright, stood side by side on the balcony in Wenceslas Square with Alexander Dubček, the dignified hero of the 1968 Prague Spring. The crowd roared its approval. 'Havel na Hrad!' (Havel to the castle!) they shouted. They had found their leader; to hell with the communist stooges. And the communists were powerless; they had lost all support: from the workers, from the military, even from the rank and file police who resented their manipulation by the STB secret police. Without the backing of Russian tanks, the communist cause was finished. Only six months previously a favourite joke in still hard-line controlled Prague was that if Gorbachev was to carry on with his reforms Czech tanks would have to be sent to Red Square to restore orthodox communism!

More than twenty-one years after Warsaw Pact troops invaded Czechoslovakia, killed at least eighty-two people and ousted Dubček, the tables had been turned completely. The people had triumphed. Havel's words, 'Truth and brotherly love vanquish lies and hatred', were recalled and printed on posters bearing his impish image. Dubček, unbowed by years of humiliation, returned as speaker of a democratically elected parliament. Unlike in East Germany, there were no calls for revenge. The Czechoslovak character was quite different, preferring to live and let live. And so the discredited communist leaders were allowed to retire quietly, shrink away and be forgotten, all except for the particularly reviled Prague communist boss Pavel Stepan, a greasy, corrupt, middle-aged communist who had to answer for the excesses of 17 November. He was later tried and given a modest prison term. Under the arches on the Národni 28 Rijna, between Wenceslas Square and the National Theatre, where the walls and pavement were still splattered with student blood, candles and flowers were placed and a bronze plaque attached to the wall in remembrance of a memorable date in Czechoslovak history: 17 November 1989.

Returning to Prague three months later was a bizarre experience. It was as if people had learned to smile again, like the funny head emblem of the revolutionary movement OF – Obsčanské (Civic) Fórum – depicted on badges, posters and T-shirts: a couple of dots marking the eyes and a cursory line for a mouth in the O. Havel was everywhere, in shop windows, fly-posted in the street or worn on lapels. Shortly before the revolution, the general secretary of the Czechoslovak Communist Party and former prime minister had declared Havel 'a nobody'. Now the playwright's portrait was propped up against the equestrian statue of St Wenceslas, appropriately next to a picture of another non-person under communist rule: Tómaš Masaryk, Czechoslovakia's founding father. If Havel had not been such a modest and humorous individual, and if his smile were not so infectious, such a personality cult might even have appeared sinister. But the ubiquitous presence was only an expression of joy and symbol of reassurance after more than forty years of communist misrule.

Statues of Stalin were being sold off for the common good. In the north Moravian town of Zabreh the municipal authorities, raising funds for the modernization of the local hospital, negotiated with American and West German buyers for the sale of their over life-size statue for around thirty thousand dollars. 'The new owner will not only receive a unique curiosity, but will also be supporting the fight of the Czechoslovak people for freedom and democracy,' the authorities promised. In Prague Czechoslovakia's first communist leader, the late Klement Gottwald, had his name removed from a metro station and a bridge.

Most change was gradual, gentle and in character with this strange, dream-like revolution. Supplies of bottled beer for home consumption remained variable, with butchers' shops, as before, often proving an unlikely source. Mineral water could still only be obtained in restaurants. The first few neon lights furtively appeared in Wenceslas Square, though the transition to capitalism was conducted without the indecent haste seen in neighbouring East Germany. Olga and others were mainly concerned about the soaring crime rate, which rocketed by several hundred per cent in the first few post-revolutionary months. This was attributed to one of President Havel's magnanimous but perhaps injudicious early acts: a pardon not only for political prisoners but also for many common criminals who were cooped up in the country's prisons. As the revolution had robbed the police of their previous surfeit of authority, the magical streets of Prague were no longer so safe. The high profile of gypsy pimps and their prostitutes in leading Prague hotels became darkly intertwined with the beginnings of drug trafficking. Writing in the already relaxed 1920s, an Englishman noted how the pleasure area had then been extended and how 'the supposed taste of foreign visitors is catered for in a style that is international, and in places even a trifle *décolleté*'. As elsewhere seventy years on, morals had slipped further. Political and personal freedom, to the disillusionment of many a starry-eyed idealist, clearly, also had its price.

But in the city of Kafka and the good soldier Švejk a very special black humour continued to prevail. Over the large mugs of frothy Pilsner Urquell in the Golden Tiger (U zlatého Tygra), they talked of the dreams Havel has had lately. He is back in prison, sitting on his bunk and recounting to his cellmates how he was once president. 'Give us another!' they guffaw, shake their heads and tell him how after all these years in the jug, he has finally cracked.

8 From Warsaw to the Prussian Riviera and the Wolf's East Prussian Lair

Platform 10 at West Berlin's Bahnhof Zoo railway station was tightly packed with Poles waiting to return home with outsize parcels of western shopping. The older generation – the women in black dresses and men in brown suits – carried large bags and baskets of oranges, bananas, kiwis and pineapples, chocolate, coffee and pallets of lavatory paper. Younger men and women, uniformly wearing blue jeans, were burdened with giant-size containers of soap powder and disposable nappies, as well as a wide assortment of electronic equipment: computers, televisions, radios, recorders and a popular make of Japanese electric organ. They were all waiting for the 1315 train, which, as on most days, was running at least half an hour late. It was coming from Paris and would finish its marathon journey in Moscow.

In the summer of 1989 Poles were among the privileged East Europeans who could travel freely. Warsaw, encouraged by the more liberal course steered under Mikhail Gorbachev in the Kremlin, was pioneering reform in Eastern Europe. The trade union movement Solidarity, whose popular success at the beginning of the decade had led to fears of Russian intervention and seen it banned with the imposition of martial law in December 1981, had broadened into a political party and been brought into government, where it was soon to play the leading role. Enterprising Poles were able to travel West with what hard currency they had managed to graft, or with produce they could sell, and translate it into western goods which were highly sought after at home. Huge profits, the equivalent in some cases of several months' wages, could be made from one trip to the nearest western destination, West Berlin.

I had been urged earlier at the ticket office to invest the equivalent of one pound in a seat reservation and had wisely followed the advice, though on the platform I had increasing doubts over how effective this would prove. When finally the express trundled in, forty minutes behind schedule, it was met by a tremendous scrum. But the Poles were well practised: the men fought their way on to the train, lowered a window, and the women passed the goods through. Seats had meanwhile been bagged in a compartment or places in the corridor. It was just as well that nobody seemed to want to get off, for it would have proved extraordinarily difficult. Battered, I managed to squeeze on to the wrong end of my carriage. The train moved off. Somehow I had to battle my way to the other end and find my compartment. Holding my suitcase high above my head, like an African porter fording the Limpopo, I advanced slowly, compartment by compartment, until I reached the one where I had, according to my reservation slip, been designated a window seat. It was, predictably, filled to bursting point, not only with travellers but down the middle with large suitcases, for which there was no room in the overhead luggage racks. Timidly I mentioned that the corner seat should have been mine. Far from arousing hostility, it was immediately liberated with a smile, as it might have been in Britain but never in Germany, where reservations are the gospel of the railway and woe betide any transgressor. I was clearly sharing the compartment with six Poles, which was confirmed a moment later when the older woman opposite offered me some bread and salami and the girl in the other corner came up with peppermints.

Grinding its way around a bend of the gloomy river Spree and, past the Reichstag, traversing the Wall – still formidable only five months before its demise – the overladen train had in a few minutes reached its next stop, East Berlin's Friedrichstrasse station. It was to be a long wait and as the sun streamed through the dirty, cracked glass panes of the station roof, the temperature in the compartment mounted. The window was right down, but, with the train stationary, it made little difference. A fat black fly enjoyed buzzing from one passenger to the next. My previously reliable watch surrendered to the heat and remained on western time. The unsmiling East German border guards had boarded the train and, barking to the passengers in clipped German – 'Alle 'raus! Alle 'raus!' – ordered them to get off. Watching the Poles file out submissively was a sinister sight that evoked jarring memories of a not so distant chapter in modern German history. I could not quite understand the purpose of the exercise. Why on earth did we all have to leave the train having only just got on it? But then the German logic became apparent: those of us who had the good fortune to have seats were allowed to stay on board and the border guards could move freely in the corridor as our transit visas and tickets were checked. It was our turn; the official snapped our passports open and shut. Momentarily surprised by the sight of a British passport among so many Polish ones, he quickly regained his impenetrable manner and demanded five marks for a transit visa. Winks and suppressed smiles cannoned from one Pole to another. Their thoughts could be read in capital letters. Once the seated passengers were sorted out, those who had been herded on to the platform were readmitted on completion of their formalities. The whole uncomfortable performance took fifty minutes and was the typical East German contribution to an already tiring trip.

The train jumped back into life again but only as far as Berlin Hauptbahnhof, where a handful of East German travellers boarded and we had a further wait. When eventually we trundled out of the city's industrial suburbs, the express, while not exactly living up to its description, gained some momentum. Red brick factories with tall chimneys spouting black and murky white smoke looked as if they had survived the combined efforts of British and American bombers and all the time maintained some sort of outdated production. Thick forest followed, also, it seemed, from another age. Deer were disturbed, as they might have been here long before the age of the locomotive. It was another Germany through which we were travelling, passing old, run-down houses, smallholdings, simple cars, rough roads; where in the West there would have been garish advertisements for ladies' underwear or cigarettes, there was only the odd red pennant or a hoarding bearing the name of a socialist factory. The East was another country.

We were approaching the border at Frankfurt on the Oder, the last stop in East Germany. The Polish passengers roused themselves from their slumber, and snatches of suddenly animated conversation volleyed back and forth across the compartment. A precious bar of chocolate was split, as if in celebration of the return home. The train moved on over the Oder, dirty and fast flowing, into Poland. Before long it was the turn of the Polish border guards and customs officials to make their rounds. The guards gave the floppy blue, silver eagle embellished Polish passports only the most cursory of looks. A British passport elicited a half salute, a stamp recording the Kunowice crossing point and a word of welcome.

'Very different to those East German guards earlier,' I said to my Polish neighbour.

'But we were allies in the war, against the Germans,' she replied with a broad smile that revealed several gold teeth.

The customs officials, fearing either too much work or undue unpopularity, merely asked the passengers whether they had anything to declare, ignoring the wealth of electrical equipment and contraband of every description stashed away in and outside the compartment. The passengers unashamedly denied having anything declarable.

'They're more worried about what we take out, especially antiques,' my neighbour explained.

After East Germany's factories and forests, the Polish plain unfolded, a quite different landscape: agricultural as far as the eye could see, with huge fields of potatoes and beet, followed by rolling expanses of barley and wheat. Very occasionally a battered red tractor could be spotted at work, but much more common were sturdy horses, pulling carts or ploughs, slowly, laboriously, though with the great advantage that they, unlike the tractors, never needed spare parts that were unobtainable.

At Poznań, a hub of industry and commerce as well as one of Poland's most ancient towns, the train cleared. Only a few travellers stayed on board for the still long haul to Warsaw. After being so cramped that crossing one's legs was impossible, I was left alone to savour the space of the suddenly evacuated compartment. The train heaved out of the former fortress town, which, strategically situated on the river Warta, had until 1296 been the residence of the rulers of Poland and possessed among its attractions a fine cathedral, castle and Renaissance town hall. I pulled the window right down and, invigorated by the cooling wind, watched the shadows lengthen over the sun-drenched fields. It was evening and still bright by the time the train stopped at Kutno, where a crocodile of white-frocked small girls was excitedly assembling on the opposite platform after their first communion.

After eight and with still a couple of hours to Warsaw, I decided to explore the restaurant car. It was a primitive affair compared with what Czechoslovak, or even East German, railways had to offer. Instead of white-clothed tables and menus, there was a snack bar and round stand-up counters to which one could take one's refreshment. The attendant doubled as a cook and prepared me a plate of scrambled eggs and bacon well up to the high standards of East European egg dishes. This with a basket of bread and an acceptable Polish beer, though but a pale reflection of its unrivalled Czech equivalent, came to less than two Deutsche Marks, a paltry sum by western standards. But deserted and dirty, the buffet car was no place to linger and, besides, I had left my suitcase in the empty compartment. On the way back I rather worryingly saw two policemen holding a rather rough-looking character in the corridor. All was well, however, and I contentedly settled down with a book for the final stretch to Warsaw.

Warsaw's central station is a dark, modern construction, another tracked Hades to be escaped from at the earliest opportunity. Before long I spotted among the crowd two distinctive figures, Bassett and Baxter, whom I knew from Trinity days, at the top of the escalator. We exited swiftly to the waiting taxi and headed for the *Times* flat at Rozbrat, in a distinguished if shell-scarred turn of the century building agreeably situated near the Lazienki Gardens, where Bassett resided. There a bottle of good champagne was on ice and there were mouth-watering, thinly cut slices of salami, bought the day before in Yugoslavia's troubled southern province of Kossovo.

The wanton wartime destruction of Warsaw by the Nazis and the fierce street fighting that accompanied its liberation suggest a far more desolate capital. But Warsaw followed the phoenix's example and rose from the ashes, its old centre lovingly and laboriously restored and many of its boulevards retaining their eighteenth- and early nineteenth-century character and elegance.

The Lazienki Gardens are a particular delight, with long, leafy avenues of ancient trees whose bullet and shell scars bear witness to Warsaw's wartime ordeal. Originally a bathing place and hunting lodge graced this spot, which so enchanted King Stanislas Augustus that from 1767 to 1788 he built for himself a château, or Petit Palais, several villas for the royal retinue and his 'building of delight' – a small open-air theatre, with marble terraces running down to the edge of a limpid lake; the stage itself is embowered in shrubbery on a tiny island. It is still a magical corner, full of romance, known to many a young couple who come here to while away summer evenings. The château is adorned with allegorical statues that are gently mirrored in the lake, together with the Corinthian columns and pilasters of its front. Inside, the salons are splendidly decorated with frescoes and reliefs, recalling a more extravagant age.

The western end of the park leads to another château, the Belvedere, set in its own attractive, English-style gardens and serving as the unpretentiously stylish residence of Poland's president. Here and in the coolly classical buildings along the broad, lime-shaded Ujazdów Boulevard, the Champs-Élysées of Warsaw, there is a strong feel of Paris, underlying the bond established between the countries in the last century. In 1806 Napoleon had made Warsaw his headquarters.

It was therefore not altogether inappropriate that we should be walking down the Marszalkowska in search of a young Polish countess recently returned from Paris. She was not at home, only the growling mastiff that kept a jealous guard over her. We consoled ourselves with Russian caviar, suitably accompanied by Polish vodka, followed by trout and rounded off with wild strawberries at a recently refurbished restaurant nearby; it was well placed to cater for the diplomats whose embassies were scattered around. Polish menus are always unpredictable undertakings, with advertised items unavailable and unlisted possibilities – some quite promising, such as the caviar hoarded after a recent visit by the Soviet leader – suddenly emerging with the prospect of a dollar payment.

The Nowy Swiat (New World), an attractively broad boulevard with a distinctly Biedermeier character, led us towards the Old Town. Its early nineteenth-century buildings, of a uniform three storeys, form a graceful, slightly curving line, which at the Church of the Holy Cross (where Chopin's heart is preserved) merges into the Krakowskie Przedmiescie, a lively thoroughfare that disgorges into the Castle Square.

It was just by a flower stall here that a clear, strong but girlish voice rang out and set heads turning: 'Richard! Richard!' It was the Polish countess waiting for a bus; like all great cities Warsaw was surprisingly small. We agreed to drop by later in the evening for a drink. 'En Varsovie on s'amuse,' said Napoleon, and one could not dispute such a conclusion in this most Parisian of East European capitals.

The nucleus of the city is the Royal Castle (Zamek Krolewski) in the Castle Square, first built by the princes of the duchy of Masovia. Before the war a balustrade existed halfway up the onion-domed central tower, which used to be a popular public viewing point. Hard by the red-stoned castle, which when not used by kings of Poland had been the residence of Russian governors-general, stands the bronze statue of King Sigismund III, atop a lofty marble column, holding a large cross symbolizing the triumph of Roman Catholicism in Poland.

The Old Town, the Stare Miasto, is just around the corner, with its narrow, crooked, cobbled thoroughfares and quaint cramped buildings. But the eye is deceived, for the old quarter was mercilessly razed by the Nazis, only to be meticulously and perfectly reconstructed stone by stone after the war. The result is a triumph of restoration, which could and should have been copied in many other European cities ravaged by the war. Polish restorers have ever since enjoyed an unequalled reputation and exported their skills to neighbouring countries such as East Germany, which belatedly and slowly turned to the task of repairing their historic buildings. Now, as before, the central square is filled on market days with small booths selling garden produce and fiacres are parked waiting to pick up passengers for a gentle but expensive trot around the Stare Miasto.

However, not even the offer of a handful of dollars could induce the luxuriantly bearded driver at the head of the queue to take us back to Rozbrat. Instead we walked back to the castle, found a Polski Fiat taxi and returned, passing a fairly violent riot outside the Communist Party headquarters where student protesters were locked in battle with the Zomo riot police. Feeling was running high in the wake of the recent Tiananmen Square massacre of students in Peking. While in June 1989 the Polish Communist Party was in the process of gradually relinquishing power to democratic forces, it had not yet completely abdicated.

That evening we found a Who's Who of the new Poland at a farewell garden party given at the residence of the Australian ambassador: Solidarity spokesmen, economists, historians, pianists and composers and a remarkable bearded poetess of a certain age draped in heavy amber beads. There was a mood of optimism on the part of the Poles, a certain frivolity shown by the Australians, but nobody had yet fathomed how the Polish political transformation was to prove the catalyst of the remarkable series of revolutions that were to rock Eastern Europe later in the year. The Poles were pleased for Poland, though somewhat nervous that the democratization process could still backfire. They wanted to bring Poland back into the western fold to which, they were convinced, it rightly belonged. Similar sentiments were to be expressed a few months later in other East European countries when they began to be freed from their communist shackles.

A pleasantly informal dinner followed at the departing first secretary's house. A very *petite* Polish designer, who drew attention to herself by the shortness of her elaborately pleated black party dress and the severity of her ballerina hair-do, joined the number. An hour or so later there was dancing on the table and we still had to visit the countess and the notorious nightclub at the People's Palace. 'En Varsovie on s'amuse,' I remembered.

We left clutching a case of Pimm's, which was not destined to return to Canberra, and wandered down at least two of the tree-enveloped residential streets before we stumbled across a taxi.

It was late enough for the countess to have wondered whether we would take up her invitation. We rang the bell and the dog barked ferociously. She held the huge brown and black hound back and brought an ice-cold bottle of Stolichnaya from the kitchen, a Polish tribute to the best of Russian vodkas. Glasses were filled, raised and instantly downed by the countess and Bassett. Baxter, who on an evening in Poland more than ten years earlier had been a victim of Polish hospitality and had had enough vodka to last a lifetime, was more cautious and took two gulps. I followed his example.

Glaring at us with piercing black eyes, the countess snapped disparagingly, 'But if you are men you must be able to drink your vodka in one.' For her eighteen years and girl-like figure she was quite formidable. I did not want to argue that in less haste I felt I could savour the clear spirit more. Instead I concentrated on redeeming my standing by getting on with the dog, which worked.

Sitting among the elegant eighteenth-century furniture, under the ancient family portraits and with a fine old Persian carpet on the white-painted wall, it was hard to imagine that Poland had been through more than forty years of communism. Having become homesick in Paris, the countess had returned to take over a great-aunt's flat overlooking the boulevard, only a couple of hundred yards from the president's residence. There was a patriotic fervour among many Poles which set them apart from their East European neighbours.

The next stop was the Palace of Culture, the vast ungainly Stalinist skyscraper which the Soviet dictator presented as an unsolicited gift to the Polish people. Built between 1952 and 1955, this gargantuan pile dominates the Warsaw skyline with its 800-foot-high spire – more than twice the height of St Paul's Cathedral. During the day more than 6,000 people work in the building and tens of thousands pass weekly through its doors. It has been calculated that in its first 35 years of existence 150 million people attended some 250,000 events in the People's Palace. Its 42 floors provide space for 4 theatres, 3 cinemas, 2 restaurants and an assortment of museums and galleries, as well as sports and leisure facilities. In the basement – beneath the offices of the Polish Academy of Sciences, several university departments and a number of learned societies and institutions – was the nightclub for which we were heading.

It was perhaps too late even for this, but it was a striking enough example of Warsaw's nocturnal culture to be worth a view. A rock band blared centre stage with an abundance of feeling but not a note of artistry. I had heard better bands in Moscow, Kiev and Prague, quite apart from Český Krumlov, where the same medley of dated western hits was given with a uniform but rather compelling Slavonic exuberance. The dance floor around was filled with energetic couples. We chose an empty table to one side and a wan-faced waiter quickly brought a bottle of vodka and, wisely, one of mineral water. Amid the curling cigarette smoke and red plush, it was a wonderful picture of low life, viewed, as it were, from the dress circle. The bar was teeming with gap-toothed prostitutes of Hogarthian appearance besieging willing western business-men too drunk to know better. In our splendid isolation we enjoyed some of the best vodka I can remember, limpid and pure, and had no difficulty resisting the approach some time later of two hags, one in a mini-dress of poisonous green and the other in electric blue, of unbelievable hideousness. Such witches would have certainly done fearsome credit to a modern production of Macbeth.

The band had exhausted itself and its audience, and both began to pack up with that feeling of frustration endemic to such establishments. Salvaging the remains of the vodka bottle for future consumption, we surfaced into the starry night, picked up a taxi at the foot of the palace's great sweep of steps and cruised home through the empty streets.

As arranged, Bogdan arrived soon after nine the next morning. His Polski Fiat was packed in the back with jerry cans of spare petrol. We were heading first north towards the Russian border and the former German province of East Prussia. Our goal was Hitler's bunker headquarters at Kętrzyn, the Wolf's Lair (Wolfsschanze), where he so narrowly escaped assassination on 20 July 1944. Afterwards we would strike north-west for the great port of Gdańsk, still known as Danzig to Germans, and the nearby resort of Sopot, once the pearl of the Prussian riviera.

Driving through Poland, like taking the railway, underlined the agricultural bias of the economy. No sooner were we across the river Vistula than road traffic was impeded by carts and horses heavily laden with produce. By the side of the road berries of various kinds were for sale, the best undoubtedly the tiny, deliciously sweet wild strawberries. As a further hazard, mongrel dogs ran alongside the road, which every so often would be completely blocked by livestock transferring from one field to another. Bogdan, though a somewhat erratic driver, was used to all this and put his foot down when the road was clear. As so many East Europeans, he took motoring very seriously. On a trip to Germany he had bought a special, illegal device which, discreetly attached under his dashboard, warned of approaching police radar traps. The Fiat, though well past its prime, was carefully nursed and attended. Nevertheless, Bogdan admitted that he was saving up hard currency to buy a Volkswagen Golf on his next trip West.

The landscape of endless rolling fields, punctuated by villages made up of buildings of a distinctly Russian nineteenth-century character, began after a couple of hours to give way to very different country: the Prussian lake district, an area peppered with generally small lakes and extensive woods, where the villages took on a German, Wilhelmine air. The extensive estates of the former Prussian Junkers were now farmed by Poles using the same old methods; the horse still prevailed over the tractor. Lines of communication were provided by long straight roads lined by poplars or birches. It is country more suited to the horse and carriage than the motor car, and when the former owners return to view or reclaim their old property, they will find little has changed since the day their families left.

Kętrzyn itself is a small town of north German appearance, its red brick railway station, civic architecture and villas all the products of the period of rapid economic expansion which Germany experienced at the turn of the century. The remains of Hitler's hide-out are some way from the town, concealed in thick forest, truly a wolf's lair. It was from here that he directed his war on two fronts, until early in 1945, with the Red Army closing in, the headquarters became untenable and were abandoned for Berlin. So impregnable was this rabbit warren of huge reinforced concrete bunkers and underground tunnels hidden among the birch trees that hundreds of tons of Russian explosives failed to destroy it after the Nazis had fled.

Today the bunkers that had been the nerve centre of the Nazi war machine lie wrecked in the dense woods: great slabs of concrete and steel jut out awkwardly at jagged angles, camouflage netting is still entangled in the trees. But the remarkable engineering of Krupp and the work of AEG and Siemens is still visible.

'Fantastic!' exclaimed the West German pensioner on seeing the vast – appropriately biggest – Goering bunker used by the Luftwaffe supremo, Prussian prime minister and Hitler's designated successor. 'What an achievement, the best of German industry,' added Werner Hollweg, a seventy-year-old retired sales director from Hanover.

'We were young then, we were enthusiastic. They sent us young soldiers to Poland, to Belgium, to France and, ach, then to Russia. We saw places we would have never gone to, Germany ruled Europe. These were golden times for us, until the terrible mistakes. Hitler's decision to invade Russia, the Jews . . .'

The pensioner's unusually frank words came after he had made sure he was not speaking to a Pole but a German-speaking Englishman. Marvelling at the scale and complexity of the headquarters, he had dropped behind from his tour group which in the meantime had moved on to the next bunker.

Like others in his group, he maintained that he had no Nazi sympathies, only a certain nostalgia for his lost youth and a sadness that the 'Greater Germany' of 1937 no longer existed. He was a loyal and not untypical supporter of Chancellor Kohl's Christian Democratic party, which was to reap so much advantage only months later from the prospect and then carrying through of German reunification.

Who today ventures to Kętrzyn, discreetly tucked away amidst woods and farmland near the Polish–Soviet frontier? Certainly not the touring public who throng Warsaw's Old Town half a day's drive away. Instead busloads of Polish schoolchildren, many in scout uniforms, the girls in pigtails and ribbons, are brought by their teachers to learn of the horrors of Nazism. And, the other side of the coin, coaches and Mercedes cars bring affluent West German pensioners on a curious pilgrimage. To them a trip to East Prussia is steeped in wistful remembrance of the days when this was Germany's eastern province with its landed aristocracy, when Kętrzyn with its red brick Gothic church was called Rastenburg.

At the Wolf's Lair the Polish guides showed great patience and tolerance, feeding German fascination by detailing every corner of the vast complex. 'I expect you want to see where Martin Bormann worked – you can take good photographs there,' our guide said to two keen Germans.

For their German guests, the Polish guides laid on less thickly the ideological interpretation they had grown used to giving their own people. It was the Germans who were problematic and stubborn when they questioned the authenticity of some of the photographs of Auschwitz which line the main path through the former headquarters; or when they insisted wrongly that German soldiers shown in photographs shooting and hanging partisans were in fact wearing Russian uniforms.

For the Polish schoolchildren the visit was a tremendous day out. They clambered among the ruins when the teacher was not looking, packed excitedly into one of the soldiers' former messes converted into a cinema to watch wartime newsreel film and tucked into eggs and sausages in the small canteen in another of the surviving barrack blocks.

Only a few bricks, however, remain of the most famous building, where on 20 July 1944 Hitler, more fortunate than four of his staff, escaped being blown to pieces by a briefcase bomb left under the table by Colonel Count Claus Schenk von Stauffenberg. At 12.42 p.m. on that day the bomb which von Stauffenberg had carefully planted in the conference room before leaving to make a 'telephone call' exploded. Two generals, a colonel and a shorthand-writer were killed in the blast, but Hitler emerged with minor burns, lacerations and bruises. His hair was scorched, eardrums shattered and his trousers shredded.

For the conspirators it was an extraordinary piece of ill

fortune; one of the colonels at the briefing, searching for more leg room under the map table, had pushed von Stauffenberg's briefcase further away from Hitler, so that he was shielded from the full impact of the blast. Had the briefing been held in one of the Wolfsschanze's sealed concrete bunkers – as was often the case – instead of in the above-ground barrack room, Hitler could not have survived.

Von Stauffenberg and the other 20 July conspirators had less luck. On hearing the explosion and confident that he had eliminated the Führer, the aristocratic officer set out immediately from the small airfield at Rastenburg for Berlin to put into effect the second part of the ill-fated 'Operation Valkyrie'. But that night, the conspiracy having fallen to pieces on news that Hitler lived, von Stauffenberg was shot by firing squad in the glare of car headlamps at Berlin army headquarters in the Bendlerstrasse. And in the weeks and months that followed, some two hundred others were gruesomely sent to the gallows in Hitler's furious and bloody revenge, which included hanging a number by piano wire and having their ordeal filmed for the Führer's personal viewing.

Five years previously, on the fortieth anniversary of the failed attempt, I had attended a seminar in West Berlin on German resistance to Hitler and was given a tour of the Bendlerstrasse headquarters where the army conspirators had tried unsuccessfully to carry through 'Operation Valkyrie'. I stood on the spot up against the courtyard wall where von Stauffenberg and three other officer conspirators were summarily executed. As the shots rang out his last words were 'Long live our sacred Germany!'

Now, with the sun breaking gently through the screen of birch trees at the Wolf's Lair, I could pace what had been the floor of the conference room, all that remained, together with parts of the lower walls, of the scene of the assassination attempt which so nearly altered the course of history.

Bogdan, standing by the car finishing his sandwiches and pouring another cup of tea from his thermos flask, had been to the Wolf's Lair several times before. It left him cold; it was a German affair which was not part of Poland's heroic but tragic war story. He was much more excited by the prospect of spending the rest of the weekend with a relative in the port of Gdynia and seeing one of the Polish destroyers berthed there which had valiantly taken part in the hunting and sinking of the *Bismarck*. It had been turned into a museum recording the great chase and sea battle in the Atlantic.

It was early evening by the time we reached Sopot, having motored across the flat expanse of East Prussia, crossed the Vistula again before it disgorges into the Baltic and passed by the sprawling port of Gdańsk. Though the graceful Baltic resort of Sopot may not feature on modern tourist itineraries, it was once the Cannes of the Prussian riviera. Sailing, gaming in the casino and lazing the day away in huge wicker chairs, the typical beach furniture of the Baltic, was how the Prussians spent their time at Zoppot, as it was then spelled, before it became part of Poland in 1945. Like in Gdańsk, only a twenty-minute train ride away, the German influence is tangible. Nowhere more so than at the Grand Hotel where Bogdan dropped us, its stately portico brightly illuminated by the golden evening sun.

Imagine the Lido in Venice with its extravagantly *fin de siècle* Hotel des Bains and its beach of white sand, its rich tourists revelling in bygone elegance. Then enter the Grand Hotel in Sopot and look out from a bedroom balcony on to the mirror-like Baltic, the seemingly static ships dotting the horizon, the long, slender pier extending into the bay, the ribbon of white beach. The difference is that this Polish view is finer, the northern light clearer and the hotel infinitely cheaper.

Built at the turn of the century but with classical restraint, it has, appropriately for a marine resort, the self-contained feel of an ocean liner. Its five chimneys are like a ship's funnels, belching forth clouds of pungent-smelling black smoke every morning and evening when its great boilers are stoked with local lignite to gain a good head of steam. The boilers are remarkable in themselves, constructed and installed by the same naval engineers who were producing the formidable vessels of the imperial fleet in the Danzig shipyards. So effective are they that a turn of the outsize Wilhelmine bathroom taps brings instant scalding water. To fill the Grand Hotel's capacious baths with very hot water takes little more than a minute – a credit to old-fashioned sanitary engineering. But, as the wreaths of black smoke and soot outside signal, the cost, as usual in Poland and Eastern Europe, is environmental.

Pollution has also spoiled the white sand beaches of Sopot, leaving unwelcome evidence of oil and tar and assorted flotsam and jetsam. Sadly, the shimmering water of the Baltic would today only tempt an environmentally unconscious bather to take a dip.

If bathing is not to be recommended, a stroll along Sopot's magnificent pier, unadulterated by any amusement arcades, is some compensation. Every evening young couples and families promenade along it, enjoying the view and the invigorating sea air. These denizens of what was once West Prussia are striking for their extreme blondness and deep blue eyes.

By the time we had patrolled up and down the white-painted structure, the shadows were lengthening across the seafront and a great sunset was in store, only to be outshone by the subsequent Baltic sunrise. Comfortably installed in one of the Grand Hotel's sea-facing rooms, I did not need an alarm clock to be alerted to the impending spectacle. So strong was the northern sun as it bobbed up over the horizon that its blaze of orange light could not be restrained by the curtains. Frozen on the horizon, the ships, which seemed to have multiplied by night, were picked out sharply as black silhouettes.

After a breakfast notable for its much watered-down cherry juice and the allure of the Grand Hotel's waitresses, we strode out to the pier and raced along its length in a nicely timed bid to catch the morning boat to Gdańsk. As the small steamer's moorings were unfastened, we were allowed to jump aboard without tickets – proving quite clearly that this was Poland, not Germany.

To a gentle swell, we sortied into the bay of Gdańsk and could reciprocate the view that had been savoured from the Grand Hotel. The Baltic was not quite the placid water it had seemed from there. The final stage of the two-hour journey to Gdańsk took us past the Westerplatte, with its towering memorial to the heroic last stand put up by the Poles against the Nazi warmongers in 1939, and around the Lenin shipyard where the Solidarity trade union was born, its array of cranes like the upturned legs of a giant grasshopper.

Our boat finally slipped into a tributary of the Vistula, the Mottlau, passing one of Gdańsk's best known landmarks, the Kran Tor (Crane Gate), a bulky dark red brick and wood structure which was used for the loading and unloading of vessels and dates back to the fifteenth century. We disembarked by the bridge which leads to the city's famous Long Market and its prettily gabled merchants' houses. Pulverized during the war, the old centre of Gdańsk has been restored as carefully and well as Warsaw's Stare Miasto. With its splendid Hanseatic architecture, Gdańsk is a highly attractive city, belying its heavily industrial image. Some of its ornate guild houses rival those of the Grande Place in Brussels, but benefit from a more open setting. The most famous of the commercial buildings is the Corn Exchange (Artushof, or Junkers' Hall), which was built in medieval times to serve as a meeting place for the merchants of the city. It contains a single large hall of noble proportions, its ceiling supported by four massive granite columns and its walls profusely decorated with paintings and carving. Nearby stands a late Renaissance building of exceptional beauty, the Steffens Haus, rich yet chaste in its ornament of gilded stone carving and statuary. The front is narrow, but it rises to a height of four lofty storeys. The façade is a mass of windows, while before the high-pitched roof is a stone gallery surmounted by four full-length allegorical figures.

Suitably for a city so closely bound to the sea, a grand statue of Neptune, trident raised, crowns a fountain in front of the Corn Exchange; in the summer of 1989 its iron railings were draped with a banner bearing the exhortation, 'Vote Solidarity.' The city was understandably proud of being the birthplace of Solidarity and of its reforming role in East European politics. Small children would dart up and down the street trying to sell for precious German marks Solidarity badges or pictures of Lech Walesa, the stubborn and proud shipyard electrician who had become Poland's best known face and was destined to become its president.

Positioned near the fountain, among the street vendors selling hand-spun white candyfloss and sachets of bright yellow lemonade, stood an old man supported by his stick, patiently hoping to earn a few zlotys by inducing passers-by to stand on his bathroom scales. The amber traders enjoyed more success, particularly with the hordes of elderly German tourists who return out of nostalgia for the pre-war days when the city was called Danzig and 95 per cent of its inhabitants were German. The local amber, for which the area is renowned, varies between the clear, transparent and rather bright, which is cheaper, and the more subtle and expensive creamy or honey-coloured fossilized resin.

The slender, 270-foot-high tower of the town hall, first put up in the fourteenth century but remodelled two hundred years later, marks the corner where the Long Market leads directly into the Lang Gasse, the principal business street and formerly a favourite residential quarter. This in turn leads to the Long

Street Gate, erected in 1612, behind which rises forbiddingly the squarely built Stockturm, dating from 1346 and 1508 and once the city prison with a notorious torture chamber.

Behind the town hall is the finest of Gdańsk's churches, St Mary's, built between 1343 and 1502, whose ten slender turrets and massive unfinished main tower soar above the more modest buildings in the streets around. It is a beautiful, dignified three-aisle structure of large proportions. Among its treasures are an ancient astronomical clock and a painting of the Last Judgement by Hans Memling, which so appealed to Napoleon that he included it in the loot he dispatched to Paris. Nearby hangs a small shrivelled hand, displayed as a curious and macabre warning. It is said to have been raised by a child against his parent.

The surrounding streets are full of picturesque old houses, faithfully restored and reconstructed, exquisite in form, decoration and colour; they have handsome façades, tall, pointed gables, often ornamented with stone figures, and high-pitched roofs of red tile. A peculiarity of many of the houses is the veranda on the ground floor, facing the street and approached by a short flight of steps. Where the stairs have railings, generally delicately wrought, the lower ends of these often rest on huge stone balls or other ornamental masonry.

Making our way to Gdańsk's distinctly Wilhelmine red brick railway station for the short train ride to Sopot, we passed the post office, where a gallant Polish stand against the Nazis is commemorated by a flamboyant stainless-steel monument showing a huge flying angel handing a rifle to a crumpled, wounded hero. A hundred yards further on, hard by the entrance to the Lenin shipyard, is the towering, tapering cross memorial to those killed in the strike of 1970, a place of pilgrimage and inspiration during Poland's long struggle for political freedom.

For finally in 1989, after more than forty years of communist rule across Eastern Europe, it was the Polish revolutionary flame, this time allowed to flicker by a reform-minded leader in the Kremlin, which at long last set alight the dried-out communist fabric on the continent. Late in 1981 the Warsaw government, under impossible pressure from hard-liners in Moscow and East Berlin, had been forced to stifle it, but by the end of the decade this was no longer either feasible or necessary. The dominoes were to fall fast: Poland, Hungary, East Germany, Czechoslovakia, Bulgaria, the Baltic states, ending finally and less peacefully with Romania. Solidarity, the popular workers' movement that had started in the Gdańsk shipyards and been banned under martial law, had turned the tables in a way only its greatest dreamers would have imagined possible.

Part 3

IN THE WAKE OF THE PEACEFUL REVOLUTION

9 East Berlin without the Wall

The most dramatic moment in recent German history seemed to occur almost as an accident, as an afterthought. That evening – 9 November 1989 – Günter Schabowski, the Politburo member and former party newspaper editor who had been appointed the senior spokesman of the newly reshuffled communist government, appeared soon after 6 p.m. to brief journalists on the central committee's latest decisions. At 6.57, as questions were petering out and the proceedings were drawing to a tedious close, he was handed a scrap of paper from the committee meeting. He read it out in a matter-of-fact sort of way before its meaning – to him and the journalists – slowly sank in: East Germany was opening its western borders to its citizens. This unanticipated postscript, so clumsily presented, meant sensationally that after twenty-eight years and almost three months of cruel division, the Berlin Wall had suddenly become redundant. East Germans were free to cross to the West and would no longer be shot or arrested for trying to do so.

Only a few weeks earlier Erich Honecker, who as the Politburo member responsible for security had the 'anti-fascist barrier' erected on 13 August 1961, predicted that the Wall would remain 'for another hundred years'. It was as idle and stupid a boast as Hitler's promise of 'a thousand-year Reich'. It was also an example of the extraordinary absence of realism and lack of toleration which East Germany's Stalinist regime shared with its Nazi predecessor.

In East Berlin the mood of the past few weeks had been electric. Following months of simmering discontent, protests had broken out and were savagely suppressed by baton-flailing police on the evening of East Germany's fortieth anniversary celebrations on 7 October when, with the Soviet leader present in the city, demonstrators had pleaded, 'Gorby help us!'

During the next five days the increasingly helpless authorities made over a thousand arrests, but the protest movement had become an unstoppable avalanche which on 18 October finally swept away the uncompromising Erich Honecker, a Stalinist to the end. The people were hardly reassured by his successor, the unprepossessing Egon Krenz, who for so long had lingered sycophantically in Honecker's shadow as his 'crown prince' and who despite his horse-like smile – 'Grinning Egon', they quickly called him – had a zero credibility rating. But in a desperate and ultimately futile bid to salvage the rapidly sinking communist ship, political change now came thick, fast and daily. Historians will label this period as one of 'reform communism'.

The decision to open the Berlin Wall was the greatest reform so far and was inevitably the spark which detonated an immediate explosion of enthusiasm that was to reverberate across the world. The Aktuelle Kamera television news at 7.30 carried Schabowski's obtusely worded statement and East Germans instantly realized its significance. Those who could made straight for the Brandenburg Gate, which in its 200-year-long existence had always been the focal point of Berlin's history. Others decided to test reality at their nearest border crossing point and to their amazement were allowed to pass. It was true. To Berliners it was the miracle they had so long lived in hope of.

Hundreds, and as the night wore on thousands, gathered before the Pariser Platz in front of the Brandenburg Gate, the sanctum from which they had been kept at bay for more than twenty-eight years. When it became clear that neither the long-feared Volkspolizei nor border guards would stop them, a few climbed over the street barrier; everyone followed. 'This was my first taste of freedom,' an East Berlin girl in her twenties told me. 'To be able to walk freely where we were always forbidden.'

'We were drunk without drinking,' her companion added. 'Drunk with liberty.'

Earlier my telephone had rung and an acquaintance who had succeeded in fleeing from East Germany when the Wall went up just cried and cried. 'I can't believe it, I can't, I can't,' she sobbed with joy. 'Are we dreaming? Or have we finally woken from a nightmare?'

Offering no through access ever since it was sealed off by the Wall, the Brandenburg Gate was not the best place to cross to the West. But as the impromptu party began to swell, it hardly mattered. West Berliners scaled the Wall and massed on its top, reciting a chant which was to become a mantra of the revolution: 'Die Mauer muss weg!' (The Wall must go!) They hauled some of those on the eastern side up and over into the West, while others dropped in on the East from the western side. They mingled joyously, dancing, singing, hugging and weeping around the gate, the distinctive form of which had become the symbol not only of the division of Berlin but also of Germany.

The Volkspolizei and border guards looked on, as bewildered as anyone. Their concession to history was to ignore regulations by taking their caps off, or jauntily tipping them back, and lighting up cigarettes while still on duty. 'Thank you for this wonderful night,' one incredulous Berliner said to an officer.

As word spread that everything was possible, more revellers arrived bearing bottles of eastern 'Rotkäppchen' Sekt, the sweet German champagne without which no celebration in the East was complete.

A solitary dark green and white police car toured up and

down Unter den Linden using its megaphone to issue an unprecedented instruction calling on people to use the recognized crossing points: 'Citizens of the GDR, please use the crossings set aside for exits!' For once in their ordered lives, the people of East Berlin chose to ignore instructions.

Those that went to bed awoke the next morning to find that it was not all a dream. It was Friday, they should be at their workplace. There they traded news avidly; everyone had a story. They made plans to 'test the West', as the cigarette hoardings invited in English, for themselves as soon as their shifts were over. Others took time off to break the ice straight away. When they came off the S-bahn trains, drove their battered, two-stroke Trabant cars through the border crossings or simply walked across, they continued to pinch themselves in disbelief. Stepping out of a packed carriage at West Berlin's Zoo station, a middle-aged woman pointed out to her husband the 'broken tooth' spire of the ruined Kaiser Wilhelm Memorial Church: 'Look! I never thought we would see it like this.' A young West Berlin policeman was on the platform to offer directions and give advice.

Everywhere the mood was good-humoured and often emotional. At the Invalidenstrasse crossing West Berliners greeted those from the East with flowers and cheers. Flying over the Bornholmerstrasse I could see a scrum of East Berliners massing eagerly, like ants around a cube of sugar, to cross over its bridge. Royal Military Police responsible for the border along the British sector maintained their patrols and Army Air Corps helicopters hovered overhead monitoring the remarkable proceedings.

Traffic jams paralysed the centre of West Berlin as convoys of Trabants, Wartburgs and Ladas explored unfamiliar territory. How incongruous they looked, mingling with West Berlin's Mercedes limousines, BMWs and Volkswagens, but every driver had a beaming smile. Many parked indiscriminately, only to be towed away by West Berlin police who promised that the eastern cars could be reclaimed without charge. Nobody could be petty on such a day.

In the Wilmersdorferstrasse, West Berlin's Oxford Street, I came across a group of East German workers still in their blue overalls buying doughnuts and western newspapers 'to prove we've been here!' They had just come off their early morning shift at an East Berlin factory.

'Berlin was no longer a divided city as hundreds of thousands of East Berliners streamed to the West, unhindered for the first time since the Wall was put up over twenty-eight years ago,' I wrote in a report for *The Guardian*. 'Most crossed just for the experience of a freedom they had been denied so long and simply looked at shop windows, stopped at cafés on the fashionable Kurfürstendamm street, or visited friends.'

But the priorities of some were surprising and strangely German. One scrupulously honest East Berliner made straight for the library in West Berlin where in August 1961, on the eve of the Wall going up, he had borrowed two volumes: Thomas Mann's *Death in Venice* and Friedrich Wilhelm Foerster's *The Jewish Question*. He was not asked for, and would have had the greatest difficulty in paying, the fine of 5,100 marks he had incurred on the overdue return of the books.

Back in the eastern part of the city, sullen faces had overnight learned how to smile. Life had become more bearable, the people were no longer prisoners in their own land. I shared a lift in the Grand Hotel with one of its smartly turned-out, white-hatted chefs, who was gaily whistling and grinning. 'I just can't believe it. I have already been over once early this morning and I'm going again as soon as I finish work. Just for a beer and to walk around.'

Meanwhile, as East Berliners were hurrying from work that afternoon, West Berlin witnessed its most historic rally since President Kennedy's visit in 1963 when he declared, 'Ich bin ein Berliner.'

Standing outside the same Schöneberg Rathaus, the seat of West Berlin's government, Chancellor Helmut Kohl told the more than twenty thousand people massed there, 'Long live a free German Fatherland, a free united Europe.' The chancellor, who interrupted a visit to Poland to be in Berlin 'at this historic moment for the city and Germany', then called on the crowd to sing the national anthem.

'We are and will remain one nation. Step by small step we will find our way to a common solution,' he went on, hardly realizing that those steps would lead less than eleven months later to his becoming the first chancellor of a united Germany since Adolf Hitler.

Hans-Dietrich Genscher, the untiring foreign minister who despite political change and recurring heart trouble had held the post for the past fifteen years, moved to the microphone. East Berlin was opening up five new crossings in the Berlin Wall, he reported, beginning that night with the Glienicke Bridge, notorious as the scene of spy swaps during the long years of the Cold War. New border crossings would be broken through the Wall and others which had been blocked up would be opened. The dramatic developments in Berlin were, he said, part of 'a break-out of European freedom' that had begun in the Soviet Union, had spread to Hungary and Poland and was now happening in Germany. He was probably shrewd enough to sense that it would extend further to Czechoslovakia, Bulgaria and Romania, but for all his acumen he could not have predicted the speed of the process which was largely to run its course by Christmas.

The teeming crowd of Berliners, a number of whom had crossed from the East, reserved their warmest welcome for Willy Brandt, the former social democrat leader, chancellor and governing mayor of West Berlin during the time of crisis when the Wall went up. 'Berlin will live and the Berlin Wall will come down,' he said now to wild cheers. It was for him a moment of great triumph, but he was not inclined to trumpet it. He found it hard enough to choke back the tears of joy. 'This is a beautiful day at the end of a long way. But we are not yet at the end of that way, a whole lot remains to be done.'

Some time later, after further reflection, Brandt described the momentous events of those days as 'the deepest change in our part of the world since the end of the war'. And he admitted, 'I could hardly hold back my tears.'

Stefan Heym, East Germany's leading novelist, saw the opening of the Berlin Wall as 'a new chapter in the history of this city and country which had been written by the people'. The meeting of so many hundred thousand East and West Berliners was 'a very great moment, such as one witnesses once in a lifetime'.

That first weekend of free travel continued as it started with an exuberant to and fro flow of East Germans westwards and back. It was, as Chancellor Kohl said later, 'a great celebration of reunion by the German people'. On the Saturday more than 800,000 crossed over from the East into West Berlin alone. On Sunday more than a million thronged to the western half of the city, many through the latest gap to be opened in the concrete wall at the Potsdamer Platz, the Piccadilly Circus of old Berlin. East German army mechanical diggers and bull-dozers had worked through the night to cut away two large sections of wall, reopening a passage through the heart of pre-war Berlin. At 5.35 a.m. the first piece of wall came down to resounding cheers from East and West Berliners on either side. By 8 a.m. the work was complete and West Berlin's governing mayor, Walter Momper, battled through the crowd to meet his suitably named East Berlin counterpart, Erhard Krack. They shook hands in what for almost thirty years had been a no man's land populated only by rabbits nibbling the grass that had overgrown the web of redundant tram lines, and border guards patrolling menacingly, their Kalashnikov rifles at the ready. 'This is an historic day because the hub of transport was here, the heart of old Berlin which will now beat again,' Momper declared.

Many of the East Germans who had been waiting patiently in the early morning chill for the breach to be made at the Potsdamer Platz went straight across to the Philharmonie concert hall opposite, the home of the Berlin Philharmonic Orchestra. There they were invited to a specially arranged Sunday morning Beethoven concert, conducted by the Argentinian-born Israeli conductor and pianist Daniel Barenboim. He was in Berlin recording Mozart's *Così fan tutte* with the orchestra and they decided to waive all fees for the informal but deeply felt and appreciated performances of the First Piano Concerto and Seventh Symphony, which they had last performed together at the end of October. 'What happened in Berlin on 9 November was not a political act but an unforgettable human event. Its significance was not therefore limited to Germany but was of interest to the whole world, for people here were no longer prepared to live with and in fear,' Barenboim noted afterwards.

East Germans arriving on the western side of the Potsdamer Platz by foot, bicycle or in their putt-putting Trabant cars were greeted with bunches of flowers, newspapers and West Berlin street plans. They were allowed through with a minimum of formalities, as the suddenly friendly East German border guards, trays strapped around their necks, stamped identity papers on the spot. I saw one emotionally sapped young guard in camouflage uniform coming off duty clutching three pink carnations he had been handed.

Many headed straight for the Kurfürstendamm, with its fashionable shops and cafés, for their first real encounter with capitalism. A curious sight near the Zoo station was the queues that formed outside the brash sex shops and cinemas.

They were not made up of single men in search of excitement, but of complete East German families – husbands, wives and small children – together tasting once forbidden fruit. The contrast between their own grey, too sober environment and the neon-lit excess of West Berlin was compelling.

They returned bearing bags of bananas and other tropical fruit, coffee, chocolate, false fingernails, nail polishes and cosmetics and, most strangely, trays of tinned beer. It was not so much the beer they thirsted for – their own was perfectly good – but the newfangledness to them of the beer can. For many it was the most thrilling weekend in their lifetime. But not all were bowled over; one ten-year-old East Berlin boy coming home with his family was asked for his first impression of the West. He paused before replying, 'It's rather crowded there.'

Back in a cosily smoked-out pub on the corner of East Berlin's Husemannstrasse, where good beer could be had at a fraction of the western price, Thomas and Ulrich were discussing their first trip to the West over glasses of Saxon white wine and low-quality East German cigarettes. 'It was exciting, fascinating to have a glimpse. I want to go again when things have quietened down a bit,' said Thomas, a 25-year-old mechanic. Ulrich, who until recently had served as a border guard, wished to see the leafy, residential suburb of Frohnau, across the Wall from the Pankow district where he lived. 'Ever since I was a small boy I wanted to know what the houses and streets on the other side looked like.' The Wall went up three years before he was born.

Together they had also explored Kreuzberg, one of West Berlin's most run-down areas, where many foreign immigrants live and work. They felt it would be an interesting comparison with the traditionally working-class Prenzlauer Berg district, with its dilapidated houses favoured by artists and intellectuals, which they knew so well and where they were now drinking.

At the end of the table sat an old man who looked much more than his seventy years. Except for during the war, he had never left Berlin; he was, in his words, 'baptized with water from the river Spree'. He had survived a war spent fighting in Poland, France and North Africa. He had been at Tobruk. Returning to Berlin on leave, he saw his two-year-old son killed in one of the first big British air raids. Like most Berliners, he had known considerable suffering and hardship and was as unenthusiastic about communism in Germany – 'a forty-year-long swindle by the East German Communist Party' – as about the war years. But he smiled gently at what was happening now, thought for a moment or two longer and then raised his beer glass: 'Perhaps I will after all live to see some positive change.'

Three weeks later there was a strange convergence between the scenes enacted on stage in one of East Berlin's most celebrated opera productions and the revolution unfolding on the streets. Revenge on the politically unscrupulous was being demanded – whether the kings and dukes of operetta or East Germany's discredited Communist Party leaders. For twenty-six years the cast of Walter Felsenstein's classic production of Offenbach's *Bluebeard* had on the stage of the Komische Oper called for freedom and an end to corruption and deceit in high places. Now suddenly, almost as instantly as in the most far-fetched of operas, it was being achieved with the remarkable people's revolution which was sweeping away the crooked Stalinist regime that had ruled East Germany for forty years.

Jacques Offenbach's *Bluebeard*, originally created as a savage satire on the slippery morals of France's second empire, was an immediate success when Felsenstein first staged his inspired production in September 1963, just over two years after the hated Wall went up. To an eager East Berlin public finally able to drop inhibitions and give vociferous vent to its appreciation of Bluebeard's sharp satirical barbs and mockery of authority, it had become the most politically relevant opera in the repertory. On the very night that it was given a landmark 350th performance to a predictably packed house, communist leader Egon Krenz was booed and catcalled from office only two streets away. 'Egon and Co. – Go!' the people clamoured.

When Count Oskar, the king's minister, declared in the operetta, 'One can't entrust an idiot with the fate of millions', the theatre erupted in unprecedented applause, which redoubled when he added, 'Now is the time for human rights.' The role of the manic, power-hungry King Bobèche, played in every performance since the production's première by Werner Enders, had developed further since the company had brought *Bluebeard* to Covent Garden during the summer. The king had become even more detached from reality and markedly more senile, bearing a stronger resemblance to the disgraced former East German leader Erich Honecker, now under house arrest. 'Exactly because I never knew where the path would take me, I came to lead others,' the king declaimed.

And reflecting the circle of Honecker cronies whose catalogue of corruption was daily being exposed, the king's minister explained, 'In order to get on, you have to bow to authority, never fail to agree and above all NOTE WHERE THE WIND IS BLOWING.'

But in Offenbach as in the streets of East Germany, the people call their corrupt leaders, the megalomaniac King Bobèche and the lustful Duke Bluebeard, to account. 'The people rule, the people march, according to old tradition,' the chorus sang with fresh gusto and theatre-goers applauded with a new eagerness and optimism. It was, after all, something they were witnessing daily in their own towns and cities, far removed from Offenbach's French setting.

At the end of the operetta, Duke Bluebeard's six wives, whom he had thought murdered, and the five courtiers the king believed executed, return for revenge. However, when they storm the court and expose their leaders' misdemeanours, they do not know what to do next. Like the people of East Germany, they have achieved in double time more than they thought possible. 'But we must have an ending,' implored Count Oskar, 'for the sake of our public.' Felsenstein's finale is a happy one and the audience went home trusting that theirs would be too.

At the end of the company's summer season at the Royal Opera House, Covent Garden, the East German national anthem was played and a heckler shouted from the amphitheatre, 'What about the Wall?' A few short months later the unbelievable had happened, the Wall had become a monstrous relic of the past and East Germans had gained freedoms they had long thought unattainable.

In musical and theatrical terms the Komische Oper, set up by Felsenstein in 1947 in the Behrenstrasse's former Metropol theatre, which had been damaged in the air raids, was soon to establish itself as East Berlin's and one of Europe's premier opera houses. Its brilliantly designed blue neon sign in the Friedrichstrasse was to become a beacon of artistic hope and consolation for many. Although the theatre's bomb-shattered façade was given a typically uncompromising modern look in 1966, the warm red plush and gilded stucco interior, replete with handsome, firm-breasted nude women, muscular male figures and putti disporting themselves, is characteristic of a theatre originally built in 1892 as the Theater unter den Linden by the prolific Central European opera house designers, Helmer and Fellner.

Under Felsenstein the Komische Oper took advantage of the modestly scaled theatre to create productions of great immediacy which were notable for their well-rehearsed ensemble work and high all-round standards. Following his death in 1975, the company's reputation was maintained by Harry Kupfer, a producer of often daring originality; he encouraged young singers such as the counter-tenor Jochen Kowalski, who with his distinctively timbred voice and sleek looks quickly became a star with a teenage following to match any pop singer.

Kowalski had been among the leading East German artists called to perform at the Palace of the Republic on 7 October for the fortieth anniversary celebrations. 'We saw the demonstrators outside as we arrived. It made us feel profoundly uncomfortable and unhappy, for we shared their feelings. To justify things to ourselves we said to one another that we were singing for Gorbachev. But he left early, leaving us performing for Ceaușescu and the other fogies sitting there. It was catastrophic. I forgot the words; they stuck in my throat,' he recalled later.

'Then on October 19 we had a chance to stage our own demonstration in the Church of the Redeemer, one of the Berlin churches in the forefront of the popular revolt. It made us feel much better for we were also part of the revolution.'

One of the few Berlin theatre buildings to have survived the war almost unscathed was the Theater am Schiffbauerdamm. Performances were already resumed there in 1945–6 and in 1954 it became the home of Bertolt Brecht's Berliner Ensemble, founded on the same day in 1949 as East Germany itself. Combining intimacy of scale with an extravagantly flamboyant neo-rococo interior, it is the most Parisian in style of Berlin's theatres. It was built by Heinrich Seeling in 1892 as the Neues Theater, and enjoyed a golden period from 1903 to 1905 under Max Reinhardt.

During the 1989 revolution it maintained its definitive Brecht productions, but also entered the fray with the popular cabaret duo of Mensching and Wenzel. Their portrayal of the first bloodless revolution in German history, carried through, they sang, to the beat of the spluttering Trabant, was underlined by a disturbing streak of pessimism and cynicism. 'You are a typical East German because you want everything at once' and 'I have been able to do my Christmas shopping because of the revolution' were acidic though accurate observations which ran counter to the euphoria that still prevailed, but which anticipated doubts that were later to set in. Shattering illusions was, after all, in the best tradition of the Berlin cabaret.

Years of communist propaganda and indoctrination were also being rapidly swept aside during these hectic days of reform. At the Museum of German History, housed in Schlüter's magnificent Arsenal building on Unter den Linden, the section 'Socialist Fatherland GDR', which had uncritically documented forty years of communist rule, was already shut off in November. Officials would only say that the display had been closed 'for reworking until further notice'.

The museum was founded in 1952 to present an interpretation of German history from a Marxist point of view. Its exhibits ranged from prehistoric to present times, with a strong section on the period of Prussian rule, including Frederick the Great's frock coat, and a fine collection of arms and uniforms which suitably reflected the building's earlier use. At the height of the revolution I saw a clearly perplexed teacher lead her class past everything remotely modern and settle much more safely for an afternoon of prehistory. Ideology was irrelevant among the fossils and flint-stones.

A wooden and glass partition was erected ending modern East German history in 1949, the year of the founding of the communist state. The next section up to 1961, when the Wall was put up as an 'anti-fascist barrier', according to the old communist thinking but in reality to stop the daily mass emigration westwards of East Germany's citizens, could only be dimly sighted beyond the partition. Until Honecker was toppled on 18 October this had been the heart of the museum's display. The following April, after East Germany's first free elections, it was replaced by an exhibition of some of the posters and banners calling for democratic reform which were held aloft during the massive street protests that brought down the hard-line communist regime. After a million demonstrators rallied in the Alexanderplatz on 4 November in response to a call by artists' associations, a lorry-load of placards and banners was retrieved. More were saved from major demonstrations in other cities, notably Leipzig. Photographs of the Alexanderplatz demonstration were also displayed in an exhibition in front of the Berliner Ensemble's crush bar.

Following more than forty years of enforced division, East and West Berlin's twenty-nine state-run museums prepared to club together to revive the city's reputation as the cultural capital of Central Europe. As East and West Germany united, the often absurd separation of museum collections brought about by post-war politics, ideological differences and the Berlin Wall could at last be rectified. Museum directors in the two halves of a now whole city were finally faced with the exciting prospect and challenge of cooperation instead of rivalry and friction. Their first task was to fill the gaps in their collections left by the post-war division.

As the Allied bombing of Berlin intensified, its museum collections were scattered all over the Reich for safe-keeping. The subsequent partition of defeated Germany left many works of art stranded in the wrong sector, and under communist rule East German catalogues would refer to many missing items as 'illegally held in West Berlin'. Now the fifteen state-run museums in East Berlin and the fourteen in the western half of the city could pool their resources and complete their collections.

Berlin's best known symbol, the Brandenburg Gate, was also to change its appearance with the revolution. The Goddess of Victory who rides the chariot above the triumphal arch was to be given back the Prussian Iron Cross and eagle that used to adorn her staff. The communist authorities had stripped the insignia, which they considered 'symbolic of Prussian–German militarism', from the 'Triumph of Peace' quadriga when a fresh cast of the sculpture was installed in 1958. 'Since the soldiers of the victorious Red Army hoisted the flag of socialism above the Brandenburg Gate, it no longer is a monument to chauvinistic excesses and Prussian glory,' they had declared then.

The colossal sculpture was completed in 1793 by Johann Gottfried Schadow to crown the great Doric-columned arch designed by Carl Gotthard Langhans and opened in August 1791 – 170 years before it was sealed off by the Berlin Wall. In 1806 Napoleon – 'the horse thief of Berlin' – infuriated Berliners by taking the quadriga to Paris as booty. But in 1814 the victorious troops of Frederick William III led by Marshal Blücher brought the horse-drawn chariot and goddess back in triumph, transported in six wagons pulled by thirty-two horses, and the Iron Cross designed by Karl Friedrich Schinkel was incorporated in the laurel wreath at the top of her staff.

Told about the planned restoration of the insignia, Prince Louis Ferdinand of Prussia, the senior member of the Hohenzollern family that ruled Germany until the abolition of the monarchy in 1918, expressed his satisfaction: 'I am happy. The Iron Cross and eagle recall Prussian tradition.' As for the revolution, he added, 'I am following developments in East Germany with great interest. Sometimes the whole thing seems like a miracle. I hope that the peaceful movement of liberation which we now see will be crowned with success and end with reunification in peace and freedom.'

The Brandenburg Gate was to feature twice more as the centre of attention during those eventful days. Late on 21 December, bulldozers, mechanical diggers and pneumatic drills arrived as army sappers and border guards began the arduous job of breaching the Wall at two points to the right and left of the gate, in time for festivities marking its official opening the following day. The Wall had been deliberately built extra solidly at this focal point and the soldiers, under the glare of their own arc lights and those of television teams from all over the world, worked through the night to accomplish their task. Excited spectators were kept back on the eastern side in front of the Pariser Platz, and only the Press were allowed through to witness at close hand this latest and most symbolic step towards German unification. On the western side the more intrepid sightseers climbed up into the surrounding trees for a commanding view over the Wall. A Christmas tree, lit up with a garland of brightly coloured light-bulbs, stood opposite, adding a suitably seasonal note to the proceedings. As the troops progressed painfully slowly with a thirty-foot-wide gap they were cutting near the Reichstag, I left the pack of reporters and photographers to walk alone back and forth through the great arch, disturbed only by the brightness of the nearby lights, the bone-shaking shudder of drills and the steady chipping of the 'wall-peckers', who with hammer and chisel were securing their own bits of wall and history. I was able to appreciate the fine neo-classical reliefs, which since 1961 only the border guards on duty could admire. It was a memorable moment of solitude spent during the gate's last few hours of isolation.

The next morning saw Unter den Linden bedecked with streamers and bunting for the party that was to mark the formal opening of the Brandenburg Gate. Coloured balloons hung from the lime trees. Stalls were set up selling Berliner Pilsner at 63 East German pfennigs a beaker and grilled steaks at only 1.90 marks – these unrealistically low prices were not destined to survive capitalism's harsh laws. Families arrived for a fête which mixed the excitement of the funfair with political expression. A red, black and gold German flag was overwritten with the words, 'We are one family.' A banner referring to the French president's visit, which had just drawn to a close, advised: 'Mitterrand have courage! The reunification of Germans will do peace in Europe good!' And another, mindful of the bloodshed accompanying the unfolding Romanian revolution, noted: 'You celebrate while Romania bleeds!'

Tens of thousands of people and steady rain accompanied the opening ceremony carried out by Chancellor Kohl and Hans Modrow, the East German prime minister, who walked together shoulder to shoulder to the gate through a sea of undulating flags, banners and umbrellas before each releasing a dove as a symbol of peace. The East German leader, a lean, ascetic figure of some integrity whose reform communism could not in the end keep pace with the political change demanded, drew boos and whistles when he said the Berlin Wall was built to keep the peace in Europe. 'It was,' he added, 'meant to benefit people, though in fact it hurt them very much.' The Brandenburg Gate should, he went on, now become a 'gateway of peace' through which 'the burning smell of war must never again waft'.

But neither such sobering words nor the pouring rain could dampen the enthusiasm of Berliners. 'Helmut! Helmut!' they shouted from the East as Chancellor Kohl declared that this was the 'most important hour' of his life. 'We'll be together again,' the eager crowd bellowed on the eastern side.

In the scrum that followed many were too impatient to pass through the two congested crossings that had been cut in the Wall and simply clambered over it. Those battling across on the western side were entertained by the band of the Royal Welch Fusiliers, resplendent in scarlet tunics and bearskins and accompanied by their regimental goat mascot. They played a medley of popular songs, including the highly appropriate 'Berliner Luft'. Although representatives of the four wartime Allies ultimately responsible for the city were present, the Royal Welch Fusiliers, one of the infantry battalions attached to the Berlin garrison, had a special claim since the western side of the gate formed part of the British sector.

As the huge wave of East Berliners flooded westwards to the Reichstag and beyond, hordes of westerners – with no visa fees to pay and wallets bulging with Deutsche Marks – descended on Unter den Linden and the historic centre of the former and future German capital. 'It's like celebrating Christmas and New Year at once,' said one elated West Berliner clutching a half-empty bottle of Sekt.

Christmas passed more quietly; families who had been divided for twenty-eight years were finally together again, able to reflect on the extraordinary changes they had been through in the past few weeks.

But the New Year and decade were to be seen in with the greatest exuberance yet at the obvious place for a party attracting hundreds of thousands of Berliners: the Brandenburg Gate. As at any good New Year's celebration, the champagne or, more generally, Sekt flowed and there was an extravagant display of fireworks. But in one of the first signs that the revolution had lost its innocence, there was also unpleasantness. Young people had managed to climb up scaffolding on to the top of Langhans's dignified arch with its six pairs of Doric columns. Some senselessly decided to vandalize the Goddess of Victory, her chariot and horses, carving their names and initials in the copper, breaking her staff and plundering its wreath of laurels. Such a desecration by its youth was an ill and unwanted omen for the new, nascent Germany.

10 Potsdam, Summer Residence of the Kings of Prussia

Berlin's celebrated Brandenburg Gate was not the only triumphal arch by that name to witness East Germany's revolution. For in the heart of Potsdam, the garrison town which Frederick the Great so tastefully transformed into a Prussian Versailles, stands another, far from undistinguished if much less known Brandenburg Gate. And in a confrontation that went all but unnoticed in the shadow of the dramatic developments in Berlin, riot police battled there with young demonstrators and made dozens of arrests on the night of East Germany's fortieth and final anniversary. Before being beaten back, the protesters had gathered in the Klement-Gottwald-Strasse (the Brandenburger Strasse of pre-communist days), Potsdam's main shopping street abutting on to the Platz der Nationen and the classical gate which Georg Christian Unger had designed as a Roman triumphal arch in 1770.

Potsdam, which had gained a dazzling reputation as the summer residence of Frederick the Great and subsequent Hohenzollerns, and in the aftermath of the Second World War as the meeting place of the victorious powers, was understandably reluctant to be bypassed by history. As a former Prussian royal residence and above all as the seat of deliberations on the post-war European order, now about to break up in a series of sudden revolutions sweeping across Eastern Europe, there was a special symbolism to be tapped in Potsdam's historic streets, before its Brandenburg Gate.

There had also been considerable – and intended – symbol-

198

ism in Hitler's visit to Potsdam on 21 March 1933 to shake hands with the ageing President Hindenburg over the bones of Frederick the Great and his father Frederick William I, the 'Soldier King', in the Garrison Church and so seal an unhealthy alliance between the Hohenzollerns and upstart Nazis, binding Prussian tradition with Nazi ideology.

Punishment came on the night of 14 April 1945, when British bombers razed large areas of the city, though not the park of Sans Souci and its palaces, in a raid which was intended to knock the stuffing once and for all out of Prussian militarism. 'Potsdam is wiped out,' the BBC reported following the attack. Soon afterwards, as the Red Army's tanks and artillery closed in on the parks and buildings that remained unscathed – Frederick the Great's extravagantly rococo Neues Palais (New Palace) had been turned into a military hospital – a Russian commander of some sensitivity ordered them to be spared. 'He chose to forget, if not forgive, what we had done to Russia's historic cities,' recalled a woman pensioner who had cowered in her cellar during those fateful days.

Although Potsdam, originally a Slavic settlement, is mentioned as early as 993 in a deed of Otto III, where it appears as the colourful-sounding Poztupimi, and is referred to in 1317 as Postamp, in 1323 as Pozstamp and then several times again as Postamp until 1416 when Pottstamm was favoured, what had begun as a modest fishing settlement by the Havel lakes was really put on the map by Frederick William I of Prussia (1688–1740), the eccentric and obnoxious father of Frederick the Great who collected soldiers as a more enlightened monarch would have accumulated works of art. He was delighted to be rid of a set of priceless oriental vases that he exchanged with Augustus the Strong of Saxony for a regiment of dragoons. But his greatest pride was the brigade of giant grenadiers he formed, the 'Lange Kerls' (Tall Lads), as they came to be popularly known. He swapped with the tsar a gold ship he had inherited from his art-loving father, Frederick I, for 150 oversize Russian soldiers. Beyond more usual diplomatic duties, Frederick William's ambassadors and agents scattered across Europe were charged with seeking suitable recruits for dispatch to Potsdam, by inducement or force. The Prussian ambassador in London picked up an Irishman who topped seven feet and was given a bounty of nearly thirteen hundred pounds sterling, considerably more than the envoy's salary. Otherwise foreign monarchs were invited to offer their tallest subjects as gifts to the king of Prussia. Two towering portraits of prize grenadiers used to hang in East Berlin's Museum of German History: James Kirkland, from Ireland, six feet eight inches tall, rosy cheeked and rather innocuous looking, portrayed in 1720, and, of much more forbidding appearance, Schwerid Redvanoff from Moscow. The skeleton also exists of Jonas Heinrichsohn, a smith's son from Norway, who stood over six feet nine and was presented to Frederick William by the king of Denmark. Already as crown prince he had collected 600 giants for his Guard regiment, which, on his accession in 1713, he took to Potsdam and steadily built up until by the time of his death in 1740 it numbered 3,700 men. The 'Rothe Leibbataillon Grenadiers' wore blue and red uniforms and mitre-like grenadier caps emblazoned with the Prussian eagle and the motto 'Suum cuique', which only served to accentuate their remarkable height further. They were never tried in battle and, after being called upon to provide a guard of honour for Frederick William's funeral cortège, were disbanded by his more realistic son, Frederick the Great.

While the grenadiers had to be over six feet two inches tall, Frederick William himself measured a mere five feet two. Immoderate in his eating habits, in drinking and smoking, and afflicted with gout, the king weighed more than 275 pounds and presented an unhealthy spectacle. It therefore came as no surprise, and few tears were shed, when his overtaxed body gave out at the modest age of fifty-one. He had been notoriously irascible, making himself thoroughly unpleasant to both his court and family and especially to his son Frederick, whose interest in music and literature he considered unmanly.

Yet the young Frederick, the inventor of the blitzkrieg, was to prove himself more than a collector of soldiers. He may have taken his flute and portable clavichord on his ceaseless campaigns and, in his reflective moments, composed verse, sometimes indifferent, sometimes commendable, but he was the truest son of Mars the Hohenzollerns produced: the greatest tactician of his generation. Though he was hard and vindictive, petty and mean, the people yet learned to admire him and his policies of military conquest. The Germans, more than any other European race, have always looked up to strength, authority and martial achievement. The 'Alte Fritz' (Old Fred), as Frederick the Great almost affectionately came to be called, may have bled Prussia white with his taxes and conscription, but in the end he brought military success and turned this most upstart of European nations into a superpower. In one of his more engaging and self-effacing asides, Frederick once quipped that Prussia's coat of arms should more appropriately be an ape rather than an eagle, 'as it was only imitating a great power'.

With his father it had been a very different story: the people dispersed when they saw the corpulent king approach. On one occasion he chased a Jew who was making himself scarce. 'Why are you running away?' the monarch asked.

'Because I'm afraid,' the Jew replied.

'You must love me, you rogue!' Frederick William answered, beating him viciously with his stick.

At the same time Frederick William's precious army – too valuable to risk in battle – was subject to a martial rigour, encompassing torture and capital punishment, that made Prussian discipline proverbial for generations afterwards.

Nothing delighted this king more than to see his battalions wheel round the Potsdam parade grounds with a precision gained at the pain of the whip. As Lord Macaulay wrote: 'These troops were disciplined in such a manner, that placed beside them, the household regiments of Versailles and St James's would have appeared an awkward squad' (*Frederic the Great*).

Under Frederick William I, Potsdam's area more than tripled and the number of its inhabitants swelled to eleven thousand, of whom up to nine thousand were soldiers, giving it a garrison role it was to maintain under the later Hohenzollerns, through the confused years of the Weimar Republic, the period of Nazi rule and then, with crack Soviet regiments filling its barracks, under communism.

The 'Soldier King' ended up in a copper coffin in the Garrison Church he had built in the west of the city. Despite having wished for a simpler funeral, Frederick the Great followed him there on his death in 1786 when he was placed in a tin coffin alongside his father's in a vault under the chancel. Not so many years later Napoleon stood before Frederick's tomb and remarked with some reason, 'If that man were still alive, I would not be here.' The coffins were still in place when the Nazis and Hohenzollerns sealed their dangerous pact in the Garrison Church in March 1933. Ten years later the growing threat of Allied air raids led to the bodies being moved to a bunker at the Luftwaffe's heavily protected Wildpark headquarters, and then in February 1945, with Hitler's Third Reich on the brink of final collapse, they were moved together with the coffins of Hindenburg and his wife to the safety of a salt mine at Bernterode in the Harz mountains.

The macabre odyssey was not yet over. In the summer of that year as American troops handed the area over to the Russians, they took the bodies with them westwards to Marburg on the Lahn, where the following August they were interred in the Church of St Elizabeth. Six years later, at the instigation of the Hohenzollern family, the kings were moved again, secretly but with the approval of both church and state, to the Hohenzollern seat at Hechingen near Stuttgart. The coffins were opened for inspection, revealing Frederick the Great's corpse to be well preserved, before being laid to rest for a third time in September 1952 in the castle chapel. There, according to Prince Louis Ferdinand of Prussia, the head of the family and grandson of the last German Kaiser, the royal bodies were to remain until such time as 'Germany was reunited in peace and freedom', when they could return finally to Potsdam.

Less than a year after the East German revolution this condition was fulfilled but, since the war-damaged Garrison Church had been blown up by the communist authorities in 1968, new resting-places had to be chosen. Frederick William I, the family decided, should be interred in the mausoleum by the Friedenskirche (Peace Church), which the architect Friedrich Ludwig Persius, a talented pupil of Schinkel, had modelled on an early Roman basilica (San Clemente in Rome) and which was completed in the park of Sans Souci in 1850. There the 'Soldier King' was to lie next to the marble tombs of Frederick III, who, terminally ill, ruled for only ninety-nine days in 1888, and his English wife, the empress Victoria. This left the way clear for the granting of Frederick the Great's last wish: to be buried in front of his beloved Sans Souci palace.

In his will, dated 11 January 1752, the warrior king wrote: 'I have lived as a philosopher and I wish to be buried as such, without pomp or the slightest ceremony. Let me be taken by the light of a lantern with no cortège to Sans Souci and be interred simply on the right-hand side of the upper terrace in a vault which I have had built.' It was here, above the terraced vines he had planted and the capricious jet of the great fountain, that Frederick buried his beloved greyhounds and it was with them that he wanted to rest. The spot could be surveyed from his Sans Souci study-bedroom a short distance away. There, in an armchair covered in pale green silk – still in place – its fabric partially ripped by the greyhounds and stained by Frederick's final blood-letting, the remarkable monarch, his body exhausted by a life overfilled with activity, gave up the ghost at twenty past two on the morning of 17 August 1786. The hour is recorded on the clock he kept in the neighbouring concert room. He was aged seventy-four.

Forty-two years earlier Frederick had ordered a terraced vineyard to be laid out on the slope of the Wüster Berg and provided a sketch for his architect Georg Wenzeslaus von Knobelsdorff to draw up plans for an intimate, one-storeyed summer palace to be called Sans Souci. The situation, modest scale and exquisite rococo decoration, as well as the palace's name, underlined its character as a summer residence – 'free from care' – away from the routine and ceremony of the Berlin court Frederick so disliked. Its foundations were laid in April 1745 and the building finished in little over a year; a celebratory banquet was given by Frederick for its inauguration on 1 May 1747.

The long garden front was engagingly enlivened with thirty-six caryatids of Bacchantes by the sculptor Friedrich Christian Glume that vividly reflected the vineyard motif, while a fine cupola open at its top to the sky – mindful of Rome's much greater scaled Pantheon – divided the front masterfully, surmounting the marble room where Frederick used to hold his *Tafelrunden* (round table) dinners, occasions for his brilliant male guests to display their rapier wit and score points with erudition. The back of the palace had a coolly elegant classical colonnade of double Corinthian columns, casting an arc around the court-of-honour. Through its gate could be sighted on the skyline the Ruinenberg (Ruin Hill), a strange medley of specially designed and romantically evocative Roman and Gothic ruins set among woods.

Comprising barely a dozen rooms, five for guests of whom the most notable was Voltaire, simultaneously flattered and taunted by Frederick during their three volatile years together (1750–53), it quickly became the king's favourite residence and he spent more than his summers there, carrying on government, composing and playing the flute, writing verse, drawing pictures and architectural designs and recovering from the rigours of military campaigns. For forty years Sans Souci was Frederick's home and source of inspiration. Count Francesco Algarotti, the king's valued friend and a member of the Sans Souci *Tafelrunde*, had predicted: 'Potsdam will become a school of the art of building, just as it is an academy of the art of war.'

Six days after Sans Souci's opening Frederick welcomed to the old Potsdam Stadtschloss, the baroque palace begun in 1662 which survived until 1945, the redoubtable Johann Sebastian Bach. Frederick's interest in music compelled him to meet the cantor of the Thomaskirche, Leipzig, whose complex compositions had caused such a stir in the musical world, even if the tastes of the king, who had a penchant for Italian opera, were rather more conservative and secular. Bach's second son, Carl Philipp Emanuel, had already been in Frederick's service for the past nine years, directing the court orchestra from the harpsichord, a thankless chore – the king never cared for his compositions – that he performed for almost thirty years until he took over from his godfather, Telemann, as director of music in Hamburg.

'Gentlemen, the old Bach has arrived!' Frederick exclaimed on the great composer's entry. King and composer had an animated session together, with Bach moving from one instrument to another, organ, pianoforte, clavichord and harpsichord, testing the royal collection with his improvisations. The meeting between 'the famous Kapellmeister from Leipzig' and the king was recorded in the Berlin newspapers, which reported that the composer had arrived at the evening hour devoted to chamber music in the palace and that His Majesty had himself played a theme of his own for Bach to improvise in a fugue upon the pianoforte. This would have been one of the new Silbermann 'forte e pianos' which Frederick was so keen on that he had acquired fifteen of them. According to Bach's first biographer, Johann Nikolaus Forkel, who had the story from another Bach son, Friedemann, who accompanied his father on the visit, the king took Bach from one room to another to try out all the new pianofortes. Frederick is said to have been so impressed with Bach's improvisation that the next evening he asked him to improvise a fugue in six voices; a challenge Bach initially declined, choosing instead a theme of his own. But back in Leipzig he returned to the royal theme and composed a six-voice ricercar (defined as 'a fugue worked out with art'), the high point of the 'Musical Offering' which he had published with a dedication to Frederick. The king's interest in Bach was, however, to prove fleeting and there is no record of the composer receiving any reward, as was the custom, or indeed any thanks for the 'Musical Offering'. But like Goethe's Bohemian meeting with Beethoven, it was one of history's more intriguing encounters, even if in the end the 'Philosopher of Sans Souci' failed to grasp the real depth of Bach's music. Bach was to die three years later. Frederick continued to compose for his own pleasure and performance. He also wrote libretti, until distracted by war, for Graun's operas. The wretched state of his teeth finally forced him to give up the flute in 1779 and at the same time he ceased going to the opera.

The Seven Years War (1756–63) left Prussia almost ruined but triumphant, and Frederick determined to prove to the world that he still had enough thalers in his coffers to indulge in extravagance. He ordered the creation of what he himself called a 'fanfaronade': the Neues Palais. Work on this great palace, which had been planned in 1755 but put into abeyance with the onset of war, began in 1763 at the western end of the Sans Souci park, at the bottom of a long tree-lined principal avenue, and continued for six years. The result was a theatrically massive, three-storeyed construction some 250 yards long, with 322 windows and adorned by 230 pilasters and 428 sandstone statues. The palace was divided into three wings and topped in the centre by a dome, on the lantern of which the Three Graces held aloft Prussia's royal crown. On the top of the smaller domes to the side of the bombastic façade were rampant and very obviously recently victorious Prussian eagles. The back of the building was equally splendid; the court-of-honour was completed opposite by two elaborate buildings with handsome porticos and great curving staircases linked by a colonnade, a triumphal arch at its centre. The work of Carl von Gontard, these were the domestic offices or Communs (after the French *pour les communs*, for the servants), housing the courtiers, servants and the kitchen.

While the more perfect and tasteful Sans Souci was intended for his own use and that of his most immediate circle, Frederick meant his new palace for relatives and other guests. He only reserved a few of its two hundred rooms for himself. With this great pink and white, brick and sandstone architectural wedding cake and the other creations – an Orangery (later converted into the New Chambers), a picture gallery, Chinese Tea-house, Belvedere, a Dragon House for the head gardener and two temples – that were to embellish the park of Sans Souci, Frederick had proved, at a cost of some 10.5 million thalers, that Prussia could match France, that Potsdam could rival Versailles in the magnificence and style expected of a king who through a fine grasp of European politics and military initiative had so greatly enhanced his power and the importance of his kingdom. Being a man who privately scorned pomp and circumstance, Frederick yet ensured that Potsdam and Sans Souci retained an intimacy which made them infinitely more lovable and light-hearted than the cold creations of France's 'Sun King'.

Frederick's long reign was followed by a lull in building for some fifty years until the art-loving Frederick William IV extended the park and commissioned a series of buildings of quality and restrained elegance, decidedly Italianate in style, from Schinkel and his pupils.

Such an inheritance was hard for communism to digest and expensive for it to maintain. But when in East Germany's final decade the country's Marxist historians reassessed the rule of Frederick the Great and his equestrian statue returned to its former position on Berlin's Unter den Linden in a visible sign of rehabilitation, attention turned to neglected but still imposing Potsdam. The palace of Sans Souci itself was rightly the first of its treasures to receive the attention of the restorers, who carried out their task with the greatest tact and taste. Work was very slowly extended to other buildings and when the revolution unfolded it found teams of bewildered Poles cladding the back of the Neues Palais in scaffolding. A blue sign hanging on the spear-like railings by one of the elaborate rococo sentry boxes declared mysteriously, 'Sans Souci Restoration. PPPK2 Poznań'. The Polish artisans who had earned such a reputation painstakingly re-creating Warsaw's Old Town were being employed to reconstruct Prussia's finest buildings.

But the area around the Neues Palais still presented a melancholy spectacle; weathered sandstone statues which had been removed from the palace and park were assembled and temporarily fenced off, as in a builder's morgue, in front of the dilapidated Communs buildings. At close quarters they were a shocking sight, crumbling, their faces and limbs worn away and blackened by acid rain fed by years of burning lignite for domestic and industrial fuel. On the terrace facing the park, cluster of weary nymphs retired from decorative duties were grouped at random, waiting to be taken away for restoration. Once stately wrought-iron gas lamps, now buckled, bent and rusty, stood guard over them, the palace's exterior today less atmospherically illuminated by electric lights encased in glass and plastic. Cigarette stubs littering the paths showed how long Baedeker's 1878 caveat to visitors that 'smoking in the royal gardens is prohibited' had been forgotten. The park itself remained desolately romantic, unkempt but splendid. Communism in Eastern Europe was never conducive to refined, grand-scale gardening. Only Goethe's modest though lovely back garden in Weimar, on to which he looked from his bedroom and study, was maintained with the care and attention originally given it.

Before the revolution Potsdam and its palaces were attracting two million visitors a year; inevitably visa restrictions meant that most of them were from the East Bloc. Situated south-west of Berlin, a circuitous route was needed to approach it from the eastern half of the divided city. More direct access from West Berlin was barred by the Wall. Yet one of Germany's pioneering rail routes was opened from Berlin to Potsdam in 1838 and forty years later the twenty-six-kilometre train trip, according to Baedeker, took thirty to thirty-nine minutes – considerably quicker than the roundabout route under communism – with tickets costing from 1.05 to 2.10 marks, depending on class.

During communist rule, if only for ideological reasons, at least as great an attraction as Potsdam's eighteenth-century glories proved to be its mock English Tudor Cecilienhof. Stalin, Truman and Churchill and, following his electoral defeat, Attlee, met there in the summer of 1945 to draw up the Potsdam Agreement that sealed Germany's post-war division.

At the beginning of the century the imperial family's aping of things British went as far as the Kaiser's commissioning this unremarkable stockbroker-belt country house as a wedding present for his eldest son, Crown Prince Wilhelm. It was begun in 1912 and completed four years after by the undistinguished architect Paul Schultze-Naumburg, who later became a committed Nazi. Having studied the work of Lutyens and scoured the Home Counties for ideas, he ended up producing a half-timbered building devoid of any originality and unworthy of Potsdam's distinguished architectural heritage. Nevertheless, the Nazis loved it and at the crown prince's invitation officers would come regularly for parties. Unlike the older and more elegant royal residences, it had the advantage of being highly functional and so made a suitable setting for the Potsdam Conference and later for one of East Germany's most luxurious hotels. The dark oak panelled, red-curtained conference room and its round table around which the Allied delegations sat have been preserved, along with the former imperial study occupied by Stalin, the sitting- and smoking-room given to Truman and the library allocated to Churchill. And in an unsubtle and not exactly authentic tribute, the hotel restaurant even embarked on Russian, American and British meals.

The revolution did not immediately open the floodgates to western tourists, who for several months still needed visas and were required as before to pay a punishing daily exchange. But when the relaxation came, Potsdam was immediately invaded by visitors, particularly from West Berlin, who could now approach it directly for the first time since the Cold War had cut them off. 'I used to think this was East Germany's greatest cultural asset, but when I finally stood before Sans Souci I realized this was not just theirs, but mine too. Part of our common German heritage,' a thrilled West German woman told me after her maiden visit there.

Not a few visitors left disappointed after being denied a

place on one of the limited number of guided tours of the palace of Sans Souci, the only means of entering Knobelsdorff's masterpiece. Potsdam, capable of handling busloads of well-regimented, respectful and polite East Bloc visitors, was unprepared for the onslaught of modern mass tourism which was, however, quickly expected to provide urgently needed funds to carry on the restoration and reconstruction of its historic buildings, some still abandoned since the war. The first year without the Wall saw the number of Potsdam's visitors more than double to an impossible five million. With some irony the precipitate fall of communism had truly opened this former royal retreat to the people.

Gone were the golden-brown days of late autumn or, under a becoming blanket of snow, those in winter when one could stroll the length of the park undisturbed and without great difficulty imagine meeting the ghosts of Frederick the Great, his greyhounds or the sharp-tongued Voltaire. Frederick, one feels, surveying the scene now from the top terrace of Sans Souci, where finally he has found the resting-place of his choice, would hardly tolerate such an invasion of privacy. He had, after all, come to Potsdam to escape from his capital, Berlin.

11 Dresden, Erstwhile Florence of the Elbe

Just as at every old German Christmas fair, the brass band had been playing lustily, mostly carols and chorales, while the audience warmed their hands around beakers of mulled wine and scoffed piping-hot batter doughnuts. But this was no ordinary December in Dresden. There was a tangible air of excitement; buildings were bedecked with the green and white colours of Saxony rather than the red flags of communism. The crowd at the top end of the Altmarkt facing the monstrous Culture Palace, a soulless socialist creation of the late 1960s, was buzzing with anticipation, stifling its impatience. The brass band re-formed, shuffling into a double line, and just as the shining black Mercedes limousine glided to a halt before the glass-fronted building, the musicians blared out the most suitable item in their well-tried repertoire: 'See, the conqu'ring hero comes!' Handel's memorable tune rang out not for Judas Maccabaeus but for Helmut Kohl, the physically towering West German chancellor, who unexpectedly, though with characteristic determination, was to reunite modern Germany. At that moment nothing was more inappropriate or outdated than the huge wall-painting that adorned the 'palace' on its west side, on the Schlosstrasse, the work of one, best forgotten, G. Bondzin entitled *The Progress of the Red Flag*.

Still drunk from their unbelievable overthrow of a hard-line communist regime and craving for capitalism, the crowd chorused confidently, 'Reds out! Russians out! Down with the Communist Party!' And when they sighted the ungainly figure of Kohl, raising clenched fists above his balding head like a triumphant boxer, they chanted enthusiastically, 'Helmut! Helmut!'

In his shadow the bent but dignified figure of Hans Modrow, the interim prime minister who before the revolution had proved himself a reform-minded communist chief of Dresden and been cast as a possible East German Gorbachev, wilted into insignificance. 'Helmut und Hans machen Deutschland wieder Ganz!' (Helmut and Hans make Germany one again!) declared a modestly poetic banner with a pertinent pre-Christmas message. Inside the cavernous concrete complex the two leaders faced the world's Press, hardly realizing the pace of developments which had propelled them there. Kohl, so often bluff and tactless, was quietly confident and restrained. Modrow, drawing his spectacles from their battered metal case, presented a picture of old-fashioned integrity, reminiscent of the long-serving divinity beak reluctantly elevated to the headmastership as a result of a scandal, or death. 'I see the chance that we can continue our own independent existence,' he said, failing utterly to grasp how completely East Germans wanted to forget their recent past and join post-haste the prosperous West.

But at this first East–West German summit meeting since the revolution – an important early milestone on the road to unity, however quickly it was passed – the two leaders agreed on the ultimate symbolic step: the pre-Christmas opening of the Brandenburg Gate. This was the real Christmas offering, not only to Berliners but to all Germans, and its symbolism was to inspire the world. German unity, which was formally fêted the following October, was really achieved and properly celebrated that wet afternoon in Berlin, three days after the go-ahead had been given in Dresden.

Coming away from the Press conference and the impromptu television interviews that followed, Chancellor Kohl left the back of the Culture Palace and, cutting a path with difficulty through the eager crowd, strode towards the Neumarkt and certainly the most momentous rally he had ever addressed. There in front of the British-bombed ruins of the Frauenkirche (Church of Our Lady), Dresden's most potent symbol, and before the lonely statue of Luther, Kohl mounted a simple podium. No opera producer could have set such a dramatic, so theatrical a backdrop and stage: the evening darkness was pierced and highlighted by bright white arc lights. As the crowd, swelled by men and women returning from work, ebbed and flowed in expectation, and red, black and gold German flags (the communist hammer and divider cut out of many) swirled among the throng, Kohl might have been playing Wagner's hero Rienzi before the people of Rome. Dresden, after all, had been the composer's base – when he was court conductor – for six years until his revolutionary activities forced him to flee in 1849. And Chancellor Kohl's bulk, if not his height, always suggested the opera singer. 'Liebe Landsleute!' (Dear countrymen!) he began to tumultuous applause. 'First I should like to give a word of recognition for this peaceful revolution in East Germany – the first in German history ... We know how difficult the way in the future is likely to prove but together we will make it,' his aria opened promisingly.

'In this historic moment of unity our nation should show understanding for the fears of our neighbours. We will take them seriously. Self-determination is the right of all people in this world, including the Germans, but it only makes sense when one does not lose sight of the concerns of others. We live in a century which has seen the special responsibility of Germans for some terrible things ... Peace must now always spring from German soil,' he continued. And, after invoking applause for the *perestroika* of President Gorbachev, the achievements of Solidarity in Poland and the reforms carried through in Hungary, all of which had inspired the German revolution, he concluded with some emotion, 'God bless our German Fatherland!' It was the performance of a lifetime. A politician hardly blessed with the gift of oratory whose success was based rather on dogged determination and a good dose of the common touch, Kohl had risen to the occasion: the first opportunity given a West German chancellor to address his eastern compatriots directly. Germany was no longer dividable and he was destined to lead it.

The next morning, in between appointments and with Dresden back at work, the chancellor's black Mercedes drew up outside the Georgentor, between the wonderfully elegant, now restored Catholic Hofkirche (Court Church), its balustrades guarded by an army of stone saints, and the ghostly shell of the still gutted castle. He stepped out into the empty street and, joined by a few aides, bewildered bodyguards and guided by a pair of city officials, strolled up the worn steps through the rusty, half-broken iron gate on to the once celebrated Brühl Terrace (Brühlsche Terrasse), built for Frederick Augustus II's powerful prime minister, Count Heinrich von Brühl, and famed for its view of the Elbe. Before he could survey the mighty river from this tree-lined vantage point, a bearded man in his early sixties approached the group and, shaking the hand of Chancellor Kohl's labour minister, commented, 'What wonderful times!'

From that once perfect terrace Chancellor Kohl looked on to a desolate, sad city. Dresden, despite its marvellous situation straddling one of Europe's great rivers, for all its former magnificence – indeed because of its lost glories – was the most haunted of German cities. The ghosts of the scores of thousands who perished in the fearful air raids of 13/14 February 1945 still stalked the blackened ruins of the city, which on account of its architectural beauties had been known as the 'Elbflorenz' (Florence of the Elbe). More than forty years on, the buildings that remained ruined and the regularly unearthed human skeletons told a grim tale. The horror of that night when the Royal Air Force twice descended on a city which up to then the Allies had spared and as a result was crammed with refugees from all over the collapsing Reich, followed by the merciless American raid the next morning had been too vivid a trauma to be erased over the years. The fire-storm was so furious that its heat suffocated those who were not instantly carbonized and caused buildings which had withstood the cannon of Frederick the Great and Napoleon to crumble and melt. Some 12,000 houses were destroyed, but the death toll for that night and morning of destruction – Germany's Hiroshima – has proved impossible to quantify exactly; estimates range from 35,000 to 300,000.

Memories live on. The morning the West German chancellor arrived in Dresden bringing the hope of unity, I was talking to a white-haired old woman at the end of the nobly proportioned Augustus-Brücke (ridiculously renamed after Georgij Dimitroff by the communists) in front of the Catholic Hofkirche, the very spot where Kohl was to alight the next day. Returning from the baker with a bag heavy with still warm Christmas cakes, she was eager to point out the relics of her city's Augustan age and to remind me that Elector Frederick Augustus I, better known as Augustus the Strong, reputedly fathered 352 children – almost one for every day of the year ('Of course by many women!' she was quick to add, smiling broadly). According to less reliable accounts, 'the man of sin', as Carlyle called him, had a thousand children. He earned his name for impressing a mistress by snapping a horseshoe in two and then offering her a bag of gold, more than enough to make her tumble into his arms. He would also entertain his dinner guests by crushing silver goblets in his hand. This remarkable head of the Wettin family, who in 1697 converted to Catholicism to take the Polish crown as Augustus II, is also said to have imbibed lion's milk.

But it was the war and that dreadful night which were still most vividly branded on the pensioner's mind. Before us on the Georgentor was painted a wartime inscription which would have added realism to any Hollywood war film: 'Brücken Kommandant' (Bridge Commander). Undeterred by my being British, she dipped into her bag to find a cake to offer and began to describe her own tragedy. On the afternoon of 13 February 1945 – 'It was Carnival Tuesday' (Shrove Tuesday) – she prepared sandwiches for her fiancé, who was on duty that night with an anti-aircraft 'flak' unit. 'We were in good spirits, it was carnival time, we thought the war was ending and we could soon get married in happier times. Shortly after six we set out. His unit was positioned over there on the river bank. We walked across this bridge – I remember he held my hand – kissed goodbye and agreed when to meet the next day, Ash Wednesday. I hurried off to catch the tram to spend the night with my mother just outside the city. As I was going to bed we heard the endless drone of the approaching aircraft, the wail of the sirens, the bursts of our flak gunners, and then came the great explosions. Looking out, we could see how the centre of the city was a mass of orange fire, an inferno. Like so many others, Hans had no chance. It was terrible. Every day when I walk here I think of him and our short-lived happiness.'

Another Dresdener, Therese Angeloff, recalled, 'We lived on the Schlosstrasse, by the Altmarkt, and here everything was burning furiously. We ran through the flames. The asphalt was like liquid lava. My heels kept getting stuck.'

One description recounted how the following morning, among the many corpses in the Plauenscher Platz near the station, an ambulance stood in the square apparently unscathed, the driver and his colleague sitting on the front seats motionless, like dolls, dead.

Helga Schütz remembered a lorry parked outside the Brühl

Terrace which had been loaded with paintings from the picture gallery, and next to it three Red Cross vans which had brought children from a Breslau hospital. In the hail of phosphorous bombs the Red Cross vehicles were quickly burned out and the lorry took a direct hit, destroying some two hundred old masters, including paintings by Parmigianino, Giorgione, Caravaggio, Cranach, Brueghel and Van Dyck. But in the arches under the terrace some two hundred people – adults and children, Dresdeners and evacuees – who had sought refuge by the river survived.

Nearby, the Frauenkirche, with its great and ambitious 300-foot-high sandstone cupola that George Bähr built with such difficulty and which was only completed in 1743, five years after his death, started to burn in the second British air raid that began after midnight. Hermann Weinert, who was the church's inspector, recorded how its windows and doors were blown open by the explosions outside and the oak chairs in the nave and the benches in the gallery simultaneously and furiously went up in flames. The main water hydrants under the altar had already been cut in the first air raid and the lack of oxygen made any attempt to use smaller extinguishers useless. As burning debris began falling, fire-fighting efforts were concentrated on the last remaining exit door so that those who had taken shelter in the church and in its cellar could escape. As the last of a dozen water barrels was expended, the church had to be abandoned and, hand in hand, the exhausted men, women and children were led over the burning asphalt to the Brühl Terrace. The famous cupola, from which the young Goethe had surveyed the destruction wrought on Dresden by Frederick the Great's army* and which Canaletto depicted in

---

* 'From the cupola of the Frauenkirche I saw the sorrowful devastation sown between the city's ordered streets' (Goethe, *Autobiographische Schriften*; author's translation).

his views of the city, finally collapsed at 10.15 a.m. on 15 February 1945, having for hours been subjected to temperatures of up to two thousand degrees. Scientific research shows that sandstone can be expected to withstand a maximum temperature of one thousand degrees.

Along with Dresden's principal Protestant church had perished its marvellous organ, the work of the master organ builder Gottfried Silbermann. At a cost of eight thousand thalers Silbermann completed this, his thirty-ninth organ, on 22 November 1736 and ten days later Johann Sebastian Bach, who was in Dresden because of his appointment as a composer to the court of Saxony, spent two hours improvising on the wonderful instrument. He praised its tone, though he differed with Silbermann over the correct 'musical temperature' for an organ; Bach preferred the north German organ type and Silbermann the French. It had been planned that Bach and his French rival Marchand should compete at the instrument before Frederick Augustus II, but after the Frenchman, hidden in the choir loft, sneaked a preview of the great master at practice he disappeared in great haste. When sought the next day he was nowhere to be found.

In 1944, a few months before the celebrated organ's destruction, the Frauenkirche organist, Hanns Ander-Donath, gave a Bach recital which was relayed on German radio. This was later transferred to disc, so that the unique sound of the Frauenkirche's Silbermann has survived its loss in the relentless flames that consumed Dresden's most famous church.

All these years the Frauenkirche has been left ruined as a memorial to the dead of that night. More than any other symbol in grey, communist-ruled East Germany, its stark ruins came to be associated with opposition to the regime. In the early 1980s members of East Germany's Protestant church backed peace movement, which was to play such a pivotal role in the revolution at the end of the decade, began a tradition of gathering every 13 February in front of the broken arches and rubble, candles in hand, to mark the anniversary of Dresden's destruction. The unofficial peace demonstrations attracted young people from all over the country and were quickly frowned upon by the communist authorities, who feared broader protest. They began a tradition that ended in the massive street rallies in Leipzig, Dresden and then East Berlin, which were finally to topple the corrupt, unbending regime of Erich Honecker in October 1989. So concerned were some communists at the possible repercussions of the annual Frauenkirche demonstration and vigil that they proposed clearing the ruins completely. But in the end the shattered remains were saved by the revolution, and a committee of leading Dresdeners, headed by the trumpet virtuoso Ludwig Güttler, was formed to coordinate the massive task of rebuilding the church as a symbol of both a reborn Dresden and a reunited Germany. Plans were drawn up for the colossal undertaking at a provisional cost of 168 million marks.

The Catholic Hofkirche, like the royal residence it served and to which it was linked by a passageway, was completely gutted in the fire-storm, but was none the less luckier than the Frauenkirche in several respects. It too was the proud possessor of a Silbermann organ which was ordered in 1750 for the not inconsiderable sum of twenty thousand thalers and finished in 1755, eighteen months after the celebrated organ builder's death. The instrument, on which Mozart played in 1789 and which he described as 'exceedingly beautiful', was dismantled in 1944 and put away safely in the St Marienstern monastery a few months before the devastating air raids. As a result it was the only one of Dresden's Silbermann organs to survive the conflagration. The church itself, a light, exuberant baroque building begun in 1739 to the plans of the Italian Gaetano Chiaveri and completed in 1755, was not beyond reconstruction. This was duly started in the 1950s and successfully concluded thirty years later.

But Dresden was attracting only a fraction of the sums which the communist regime was belatedly spending on rebuilding and restoring its more visible, war-scarred 'capital', East Berlin. Whole bomb-ruined streets in the Saxon metropolis, once famed for their baroque buildings – particularly the Pragerstrasse leading down from the station – had already been razed and transformed into characterless concrete boxes of offices and flats in the 1960s. As if in revenge for the architectural brutality of socialism, the Pragerstrasse was to be a flashpoint of the revolution. When early that October some 7,600 East German refugees who had been cooped up in the palatial West German embassy in Prague were allowed out and transported in sealed trains through East Germany to the West, they travelled through Dresden station. Their passage was tumultuous. Baton-flailing riot police battled during the night to keep back the thousands of demonstrators welling up the Pragerstrasse in a bid to reach the trains and try and jump aboard or just wave them on. A little over 140 years after Richard Wagner and the architect Gottfried Semper joined Dresdeners at the barricades, the Pragerstrasse was again a revolutionary address.

The city's greatest architectural jewel, the Zwinger, built between 1711 and 1728 by Matthaeus Daniel Pöppelmann as an orangery for Augustus the Strong's more exotic shrubs and plants – previously he had entrusted their winter accommodation to a merchant named Apel in Leipzig – and then to house the royal collections, was devastated in the air raids. This supreme example of Saxon baroque, of incomparable lightness and elegance, makes even the chapel of King's College, Cambridge, and its court seem ponderous by comparison. It is breathtakingly festive architecture, extraordinary in its originality. Journeys to Rome, Vienna and especially Versailles had left Pöppelmann brimming over with ideas of his own. His chief collaborator was the sculptor Balthasar Permoser, who, working in local sandstone, created figures of wonderful vitality. Pöppelmann adorned the gate of the magnificent south-west gallery with a massive crown of Poland, while Permoser referred to his royal patron by placing atop the Wall Pavilion, the Zwinger's highest point, his only signed figure: the 'Hercules Saxonicus', a depiction of the antique hero bearing the globe upon his shoulders that was meant as an apotheosis of Augustus the Strong.

In the mid eighteenth century Frederick the Great's Berlin would have seemed hopelessly provincial set against Dresden, which no doubt explains his delight in sacking and pillaging the Saxon capital. But what, I wonder, did the pilots and crew of RAF Bomber Command think when, clearly illuminated by phosphorous flares and fire, they disgorged their bomb loads on and around the Zwinger, this least military and most aesthetically pleasing of targets? In fact Pöppelmann's plans for the Zwinger had from the outset incurred the opposition of Augustus the Strong's generals and military advisers, who argued that its generous spread between the castle and river and extension beyond the city wall would weaken Dresden's defences. But Augustus was sufficiently impressed by Pöppelmann to override such objections.

One can perhaps equate the bombing of the Frauenkirche with the Luftwaffe's miraculously averted destruction of St Paul's; or the burning of the Hofkirche, the Kreuzkirche (Church of the Cross) and other Dresden churches with the wanton damage inflicted on Wren's masterpieces in the City of London; even the gutting of Dresden's Renaissance castle can be put against the German bombs dropped on Buckingham Palace. But the Zwinger? London has nothing like it, nor in the worst days of the Blitz did it experience anything like Dresden's nightmare on 13/14 February 1945.

Slowly, painstakingly the shattered Zwinger has been pieced together in the post-war years, like a jigsaw with so many missing bits. The main exterior reconstruction was completed by 1964, but restoration continues as the devastation of war is now added to by the insidious eating away of the sandstone by acid rain, a damaging by-product of Dresden's lignite-fuelled industry. Among the restorers were predictably the ubiquitous Poles, this time appropriately working on a building which was the pride of a king of Poland, and a style with which they were familiar. Augustus the Strong had after all exported to Warsaw the Saxon baroque he had perfected at home.

Pöppelmann never completed the fourth, Elbe-facing side of the Zwinger as he had hoped. Funds were exhausted and Augustus was distracted by other building projects. The elaborate wooden architecture and tribunes which had been raised on the Zwinger's river side for the marriage celebrations of the prince elector and the archduchess Maria Josepha of Austria in 1719 were dismantled and replaced in 1722 by a simple screen of wood. It fell to Gottfried Semper 125 years later to close the gap with his High Renaissance style picture gallery building, a satisfactory and highly competent solution, though lacking the light touch of Augustus the Strong's great architect.

Dresden was long famous for its picture collection, built up by Augustus the Strong and expanded gloriously by his son Frederick Augustus II (who became Augustus III of Poland) following his accession in 1733. After the end of the war with Sweden, Augustus the Strong, making use of his ambassadors, agents and scores of dealers to scour Italy, France and the Low Countries, acquired several hundred paintings, among them Mantegna's *Holy Family*, Giorgione's intensely erotic *Sleeping Venus* (better known as the *Dresden Venus* and a particular favourite of the lascivious monarch) and also works by Titian and other Italian and Dutch masters. But the greatest coups were brought off by his son, whose passion for collecting exceeded even Augustus's. Through the offices of the same

Count Algarotti whom Frederick the Great so admired, important pictures by Palma Vecchio and Holbein, together with Liotard's popular *Chocolate Girl*, were acquired, and then for 100,000 ducats the cream of the duke of Modena's collection came to Dresden in 1746; it included four paintings by Correggio and works by Andrea del Sarto, Titian, Rubens and Velazquez. The imperial gallery in Prague yielded important pictures in 1742, 1743 and 1749 and Paris provided masterpieces by Vermeer, Rembrandt and Rubens, as well as the marvellous set of Poussins which became the heart of Dresden's rich French collection. In 1754 lengthy negotiations were crowned by the purchase for 20,000 ducats of one of the most perfect pictures of the late Renaissance, Raphael's *Sistine Madonna*. Contact had been made some time before with the Church of San Sisto in Piacenza, which owned the great Madonna, but early attempts to buy the picture came to nothing. Finally the efforts of Ludovico Bianconi, an Italian doctor at the Dresden court, resulted in the monks of San Sisto agreeing to sell the work provided they were furnished with a copy to hang in its place. The *Sistine Madonna* immediately became the centrepiece of the royal collection – the king is said to have moved his throne for it – and confirmed Dresden as one of Europe's foremost artistic centres, its gallery the peer of the Uffizi or Louvre. What distinguished it then, as now, was the quality of the paintings and their superb condition, the result of impeccable provenance and taste; they were given a distinctive hallmark by the splendid, uniform rococo frames of 1746 into which they were placed, each emblazoned with a regal AR for Augustus Rex.

In 1834, aged thirty-one, Semper had been appointed professor of architecture at Dresden's Royal Academy of Arts and was soon commissioned to build an opera house to match the great theatres of Milan, Rome, Paris and Berlin, using the space between the Zwinger and the Elbe. His first opera house was built between 1837 and 1841 and established his reputation well beyond Saxony, from which, like Wagner, he had to flee hurriedly on account of involvement in the abortive May 1849 revolution. Years of exile followed, in England, Zürich and Vienna, where he was responsible, among much else, for the Burgtheater. Semper was still *persona non grata* in Saxony when twenty years later the Dresden opera house was gutted by fire. But the people and parliament demanded the architect's return and the government finally relented, commissioning a new theatre that was constructed under the supervision of his son Manfred and opened in 1878 with Goethe's *Torquato Tasso* and Weber's *Jubel* overture. Built in the same neo-Renaissance style as the picture gallery with which he had completed the Zwinger, it complemented it well and created a square, the Theaterplatz, of spacious harmony, the whole overseen by a bronze quadriga crowning the theatre front depicting Dionysus and Ariadne in a panther-drawn chariot. Its rich interior and exceptional acoustics quickly gave it a reputation as one of Europe's outstanding opera houses. While Semper's original opera house had seen first performances of Wagner's *Rienzi, Flying Dutchman* and *Tannhäuser*, the second witnessed a series of premières of works by Richard Strauss, notably *Salome* in 1905, *Elektra* in 1909 and *Der Rosenkavalier* – staged by Max Reinhardt – two years later. A succession of distinguished chief conductors maintained a tradition which the burning down of the opera house in the fearsome air raid failed to break.

While Heinrich Schütz, who directed the court orchestra from 1617, can claim with *Daphne* to have composed the first German opera in Dresden in 1627, Carl Maria von Weber, appointed chief conductor in 1817, founded the German romantic tradition in opera with his *Der Freischütz* of 1821. Richard Wagner, made court conductor in 1843, went further until, with a warrant out for his arrest, he was forced to flee to Zürich in 1849.

The musical roll of honour was later to include Ernst von Schuch, who for a forty-two-year reign presided over the Saxon State Orchestra and conducted the early Strauss premières, and that most sensitive of musicians, Fritz Busch, who was music director for eleven years until he was hounded from the post in 1933 when the Nazis came to power. The Austrian Karl Böhm filled the gap left by Busch and remained in Dresden – 'artistically the best and most significant years of my life' – until 1942. 'The Dresden strings, more than all the other instruments, had a very special sound, partly due to the old Italian instruments which are communally owned by the orchestra, but mainly, I think, attributable to the proximity of Czechoslovakia, which seems to me to be the spiritual home of good string players,' he was to note later.

The 81-year-old Richard Strauss was in the midst of writing his heart-rending *Metamorphosen* for twenty-three strings – a deeply spiritual swansong inspired by the total desolation wrought by war – when news came that his beloved Dresden opera house had also succumbed in the bombing, a final act of tragedy. But though the Semper opera house long remained a ruin, Joseph Keilberth, Rudolf Kempe, Franz Konwitschny and Otmar Suitner ensured in the post-war years that the Saxon city and its orchestra, renamed the Dresden State Orchestra, was still a name to conjure with in music. The reconstruction of the opera house, faithful to Semper's designs, was completed in 1984 and the following February, exactly forty years after its destruction in Dresden's fateful night, it was reopened, appropriately with performances of Weber's *Freischütz* and Strauss's *Rosenkavalier*.

And as a post-revolutionary postscript, the Dresden State Orchestra chose the highly acclaimed Italian maestro Giuseppe Sinopoli as its chief conductor for a five-year term from 1992. Musically at least, Dresden had woken from its nightmare.

Jerome K. Jerome, writing about Dresden in the early 1920s,

noted: 'There is music everywhere. In the cheap concert halls one takes one's Beethoven symphony together with one's beer and sausage' (*Dresden: Saxony's Fair Capital on the Elbe*). The opera was reasonably priced – as it was later under the communists – and 'there is no special dressing required'. Jerome also recorded an insistence on the 'garderobe', or cloakroom, which like many things under communism was preserved long after it had been abandoned in the West. No theatre or restaurant in East Germany or pre-revolutionary Eastern Europe could be entered without fulfilling the obligatory ritual of leaving one's coat at the cloakroom, even before a table had been secured. 'At the opera the ladies take their hats off. There is no arguing about it – no wondering as to whether this dame will, or that dame will not. She takes it off and leaves it in the "garderobe" before she is allowed to sit down.'

No portrait of Dresden could be complete without mention of its china. This along with so much else in Saxony had its origins in the golden age of Augustus the Strong. At the age of twenty-seven in 1709 the alchemist Johann Friedrich Böttger succeeded in winning porcelain from clay, something which up to then only the Chinese and Japanese had managed. On 23 January 1710 Augustus the Strong, already an avid collector of oriental porcelain, sanctioned the setting up of a Saxon porcelain manufactory, which opened in June on the Albrechtsburg near Meissen, fourteen miles from Dresden, and began production three months later. Having won credit as the European inventor of porcelain, Böttger directed the factory until his death in 1719. Initially Meissen porcelain was distinguished by the intertwined initials AR for Augustus Rex, as on the royal picture frames, but then in 1723 the famous hand-painted blue crossed swords which have been its hallmark ever since were introduced. After Böttger's death, Meissen blossomed under the direction of the court painter Herold and the sculptor

Johann Joachim Kändler, both of whom died in 1775 after brilliantly translating rococo designs and forms into exquisite porcelain.

During the forty years of communism Meissen became the state's biggest money-spinner, earning up to sixty million marks (twenty million pounds) annually in hard currency with 80 per cent of its wares destined for export. East Germans themselves could only acquire what was left over. The retail outlet in Meissen's historic market place, which dutifully used to display a portrait of a youthful-looking Erich Honecker near the door, offered only a meagre selection of porcelain in mostly modern patterns. Similarly, the best pieces to be found at the prestigious Meissen gallery on East Berlin's Unter den Linden were invariably labelled 'Exhibition piece; for display only'. Yet any quality china shop in West Germany, and beyond, stocked Meissen's beautiful and costly products.

Little more than six months before the revolution Meissen's managing director defected to the West while visiting a trade fair. About 100 of his former workers followed later in the year, joining the exodus of refugees westwards that precipitated political change. Many of them were highly skilled porcelain painters who were hard to replace and made up 800 of Meissen's 1,900 workforce. With only 50 new painters trained a year, the absence of those who left was felt long afterwards.

Although Meissen has always retained its pre-eminence, 'Dresden China' is not entirely a misnomer for the porcelain of high quality which continued to be manufactured there as 'Dresdner Porzellan'. During the revolution in East Berlin I passed a window daily which was graced by a handsome porcelain figure of an Irish Guards officer. Expensive as Meissen or Dresden china invariably is, I was at first content merely to admire him for several weeks. There was one detail about his uniform that was extremely curious, finely modelled and superbly painted though he was. The Dresden artist had

evidently painted him from plates dating from the 1920s showing uniforms of the Brigade of Guards and, while every other
detail, including his bearskin, was correctly Irish, his collar
tabs depicted not shamrock but the leeks of the Welsh Guards.
There was something peculiarly and appealingly German about
this oversight. In real life, dropped behind the lines, this
impostor would quickly have been found out. The day the
Brandenburg Gate was opened I finally decided to procure
him, pipping to the purchase an affluent West German who
had less of an idea of the Brigade of Guards than the Dresden
painter.

If under communism Meissen and Dresden porcelain continued to thrive thanks to capitalist tastes abroad, capitalism
was to prove overwhelming for two of Dresden's more exotic
products: marzipan and oriental cigarettes. No longer viable in
the face of western competition, the 'Elbflorenz' marzipan
works, for whose delectable products East Germans used to
queue every Christmas, closed its doors a few months after the
introduction of a market economy. And the former Yenidze
cigarette factory (a magnificent crenellated brick building designed in 1909 in the style of a mosque, complete with a multi-
coloured glass cupola and minarets) ceased its operations as
the VEB Tabakkontor and manufacturer of 'Exquisit Orient'
cigarettes. Blended from 'Macedonian and oriental tobaccos of
outstanding quality' and packaged in distinctive yellow packets
of ten, they may only have ever had a limited market, but they
were the equal of the finest products of Sullivan Powell in the
Burlington Arcade, and considerably cheaper.

In this city where he stamped his character so strongly Augustus the Strong still sits firmly astride his charger in the richly
gilded copper equestrian statue that rears above the Neustädter
Markt, on the other side of the Augustus-Brücke, once again
rightly named after the illustrious elector rather than a

Bulgarian communist. In Wiedemann's statue of 1736 Augustus surveys all before him as once he did his troops and his fair city on the Elbe. It portrays a king who, for all his human failings, came to be looked on in bleaker times as a father figure – quite suitably, considering his generous progeny – by Dresdeners grateful for a golden age when theirs could claim to be Germany's fairest city, 'the balcony of Europe', in Goethe's description. Hitler's war finished that and if Dresden's devastation was not enough, then forty years of communism was a heavy additional price.

In February 1945 the 82-year-old poet and playwright Gerhart Hauptmann looked at the shattered remains of the city and grieved: 'Whoever has forgotten how to weep will learn it again with the destruction of Dresden – this bright morning star of youth which had lit up the world.' Yet all was not lost. Forty-five long years later revolution and reunification finally furnished hope of an end to Dresden's eclipse. The period of mourning was over.

12 The Forgotten Provinces: From Ludwigslust to Weimar

Not far from where a Soviet sentry shot dead an inquisitive American army major in March 1985 lies the grave of a Russian officer killed 172 years earlier.

Major Arthur Nicholson, a liaison officer attached to the American military mission in Potsdam, was shot while trying to take photographs of secret Red Army tank sheds near the northern East German town of Ludwigslust. Major Pushkin of the Imperial Hussars, an ally in the war against Napoleon, was killed during the relief of Lauenberg in 1813. His grave lies undisturbed in the park of the late baroque residence that gave Ludwigslust its name. In the shade of tall beech trees reminiscent of his homeland, under a grey granite slab ornately inscribed in italic script, the Russian major rests alone and almost forgotten. But in these melancholy northern woods, where with only a covering of snow one could so well picture the poet Pushkin's Onegin duelling with Lensky, there is also a Russian princess who is more grandly remembered. A coolly harmonious classical mausoleum, its pediment supported by four Doric columns, was built nearby in 1806 to house the mortal remains of Crown Princess Helene Paulowna.

Ludwigslust's ducal park, so imaginatively laid out in the nineteenth century by Peter Joseph Lenné, the Bonn-born landscape gardener who was to prove a worthy German successor to England's 'Capability' Brown, is not short of surprises. Apart from the unexpected graves of a Russian princess and a gallant hussar hidden in its wooded confines, there is a less

231

cold, smaller mausoleum – as befits a duchess – more visibly situated behind the Schloss. In exquisite taste, it strongly anticipates the best of Schinkel. Two stone lions guard the entrance. Duchess Louise's name is carved plainly above, watched by a pair of sphinxes in the oculi on either side which give the building a distinctly Egyptian-classical appearance recalling Schinkel's evocative designs for *The Magic Flute*. Yet it was built by a lesser architect, one J. G. Barca, as early as 1809.

The path in front of this delicate building of almost stage-set quality leads into a landscape of lush greenness and considerable romance. Meadows give way to thickly wooded paths: the Hofdamenallee and Lindenallee. Suddenly around a corner a robustly baroque single-span stone bridge dating from 1760 bursts into view, surmounted in the centre by a massive urn with decoratively carved garlands and topped at either end by weighty sandstone balls. Underneath a most measured waterfall drops five feet as an aesthetically engineered canal proceeds as far as the eye can see in a perfect straight line through a series of pools and cascades enlivened with fountains. The whole vista is gloriously enclosed by trees of now ancient and distinguished pedigree that only allow the brightest daylight to filter fitfully through. When in the second half of the eighteenth century Duke Christian Ludwig of Mecklenburg was having Ludwigslust (literally 'Ludwig's desire') built as his seat, there was no ready supply of water so an almost twenty-mile-long canal was excavated to furnish the principal fountain in front of the castle and embellish the park.

The town had already been laid out by the architect J. J. Busch, who completed the somewhat solid Schloss with its cube-like central section in 1776. Neither the Ionic pilasters that decorate the façade nor the forty stone figures and sixteen urns that adorn the roof quite succeed in lightening the ponderous impression left by the building. A monumental affair, it has none of the vitality or elegance of Potsdam's rococo palaces, even if Ludwigslust is sometimes loosely referred to as 'the Potsdam of Schwerin'.

Like Frederick the Great, Duke Christian Ludwig had sought in an age of absolutism to emulate the extravagant architecture of France under Louis XIV. So the modest settlement of Klenow – its linguistic derivation means 'place near the acorn trees' – was transformed into something altogether grander: Ludwigslust.

Under communism the funds to maintain the former ducal residence in its proper state were not available, even though the local council moved in and the antler-bedecked hallway on the garden side was turned into a surprisingly agreeable café offering a wide range of brightly coloured and quite palatable cakes. The park's narrow canal, like every waterway in environmentally uncaring communist East Germany, had become murky with pollution, the fountains clogged up. But the silvan setting retained its magic.

Only the shortest striking distance from what was the western border, the country between Ludwigslust and Schwerin bristled with Soviet bases. Travel off the recognized transit routes was closely watched and at least discouraged when not actually prohibited for foreigners. Although under post-war agreements the wartime Allies were allowed to patrol each other's zones freely, just how sensitive an area this remained was tragically illustrated by the Nicholson incident.

The East German provinces, which for so long were off limits to outsiders except for the most compelling reasons, were nothing less than a vast Soviet garrison embracing some 500,000 soldiers and dependants, as well as a phenomenal arsenal of equipment. Entering the centre of Schwerin, Mecklenburg's principal city, involved passing through drab modern suburbs where a succession of Russian barrack complexes seemed to predominate even over the huge barren industrial housing estates.

In the old heart of Schwerin – northern enough in mood and appearance to have an affinity with some cities of the Baltic states – groups of Soviet soldiers loitered outside the commissary shop, a fine neo-classical building in the Goethestrasse, smoking and talking, their caps tilted back at awkward angles, their womenfolk distinctive in embroidered and gaudily flower-patterned headscarves. They neither laughed nor smiled and paid no attention to the German populace who studiously ignored them. They were an occupation force which during the forty years of communism had only come to be passively accepted. There was never any integration.

The cobbled street leading up the hill to the towering fourteenth-century Cathedral of St Mary and St John the Evangelist rang to the metal-heeled boots of a section of young conscripts, ruddy faced under their peaked caps. In the castle gardens, on a bench by the lapping water's edge of the Schwerin lake, an officer played with his four-year-old daughter, her blonde locks splendidly tied up in the outsize white ribbons that are obligatory for all small Russian girls.

Schwerin's castle, picturesquely placed on a small island jutting into a vast, mirror-like lake (as early as 973 the Arab merchant Ibrahim Ibn Yacub noted a castle on the spot), is for the most part an extravagant mid-nineteenth-century essay in the neo-Renaissance style, inspired by Chambord on the Loire and based on plans of Gottfried Semper carried through by Georg Adolph Demmler and Friedrich August Stüler, the pupil of Schinkel responsible for the strongly classical Berlin National Gallery. Remnants of real Renaissance work are still to be found in the castle chapel, which was built between 1560 and 1563 by J. B. Parr. Otherwise, with fifteen turrets and towers soaring from its five-cornered mass, it is hard to take seriously, being too much in the vein of Disney's Camelot.

More graceful is the baroque-designed garden to which the castle is linked on its south side. Devised by Engineer-Captain von Hammerstein in 1708 and renewed by J. Legeay in 1756, it includes limpid canals, long verdant arbours and lively sandstone figures of antique gods and the four seasons from the workshop of Balthasar Permoser, of Zwinger fame.

On the other side of Schwerin's centre is another stretch of water, the Pfaffenteich, bordered at its southern end by the extraordinary arsenal which Demmler completed in 1844 in Florentine Renaissance style. An extended crenellated building with short towers, it stands out distinctly, painted bright white like a desert fort.

But Schwerin's jewel is its lofty Gothic cathedral, a soaring red brick building completed in the early fifteenth century. A sharply spired west tower was added between 1888 and 1892, successfully making the church appear less bulky and providing a focal point for miles around. The interior is spacious and bright, well lit by tall windows. Tracery and the lines of the vaulting are unusually picked out in bright pink and green painted bands, leading the eye upwards.

Schwerin and its cathedral played their role both in East Germany's peaceful revolution and during the months of transition to democracy when one of the participants in the round-table discussions held in East Berlin could be found helping to sell postcards of the church's treasures at weekends. Its reward was to be confirmed after unification as the capital of the revived northern state of Mecklenburg-Vorpommern in preference to the Baltic port of Rostock.

Before the war, Königs Wusterhausen, south-east of Berlin, was Germany's Hilversum, famous for its broadcasting station, a name to tune in to on the radio dial. The municipal coat of arms depicts three radio masts over a segment of the globe with – more appropriately for the BBC, one would think – the British Isles in the centre. Before its radio fame, Königs Wusterhausen was best known as a hunting retreat favoured by the

Hohenzollerns, who acquired its land in the late seventeenth century. The thick-walled Renaissance hunting lodge, which under the communists was the seat of local government, dates from the mid sixteenth century but underwent substantial changes in 1717. It was especially popular as a royal hunting residence between 1866 and 1914.

In 1693 Elector Frederick III commissioned the Kreuzkirche (Church of the Cross), a modest country church which was dedicated four years later when he presented it with its bronze bells. These were sadly sacrificed to the Kaiser's war effort in 1917 when they were melted down for guns for the Western Front and made to ring a deadly peal. The organ, a gift from the Prussian king Frederick I in 1709 and built by Quise of Berlin, was more fortunate and survives. Extended in 1758, the church then had its distinctive octagonal tower added by Friedrich Albert Eytelwein in 1822. What is most remarkable today is that even Königs Wusterhausen, with fewer than twenty thousand inhabitants, and its unpretentious though distinguished Kreuzkirche were to play a part in the revolution. The wax caked thickly outside the church railings was evidence of the long candlelight protest vigils which were beyond the control of the communist authorities the moment they ceased being isolated and extended irrepressibly across the country. The gravity of the situation must have become clear to the fossilized communist leadership when the people protested not only in great industrial cities like Leipzig and Dresden but in small suburban communities like Königs Wusterhausen.

Whether as a favourite hunting retreat of the kings of Prussia or a weekend escape for East Berliners under communism, Königs Wusterhausen has long been an almost idyllic spot. Traditionally its inhabitants have been foresters and market gardeners, though many were later to work in the sprawling 'Heinrich Rau' heavy-machinery factory in neighbouring Wildau; its red brick Wilhelmine buildings, which somehow survived Allied air raids, stand as a remarkable industrial monument in the late twentieth century.

On the eve of East Germany's first free elections there was no fish on the menu of the Happy Pike (Froher Hecht) and no chef ('we are looking urgently for a cook', according to the sign in the window) at the Bear Spring (Bärenquell), which nevertheless managed to offer venison, red cabbage and dumplings, accompanied by Potsdam beer. But there was a good supply of optimism, whether expressed by the owner of a doughnut stall by the canal lock gates or one of the volunteer firemen outside the fire station, with a fine wooden tower and bright red doors, which had recently celebrated its centenary. One of their hopes was that the incessant stream of Soviet military traffic would cease to rumble day and night down the high street. 'We will be voting to get rid of this recent history and for a better future,' said a gardener working in the cemetery. Only four months later Helmut Kohl, 'chancellor apparent' of a united Germany, won agreement from Moscow that Soviet forces should leave East German territory by 1994.

Brandenburg, astride the river Havel and its lakes west of Berlin, is an East German Henley for a short time every summer when it has colourful regattas. For the rest of the year it is the grimiest and most run-down of steel producing towns. Originally a Slav fortification of considerable strategic value, it became highly prosperous as a trading centre in the Middle Ages, was an important garrison under Frederick the Great and thrived with the development of commerce and industry in the nineteenth century. But today its name is welded inseparably to steel. The city's main hall is the Stahlhalle (Steel Hall) and the local football team plays in the East German first division as Stahl Brandenburg. Its 100,000 inhabitants depend on the base metal for their livelihood.

To the once pleasing skyline, dominated by the Gothic cathedral and the two other principal churches, have been added the sixteen smokestacks of one of Eastern Germany's most old-fashioned and heavily polluting steelworks. Even Brandenburg's coat of arms has been modified to include four smoking chimneys above its walled and turreted ramparts.

The dismal decline of a settlement which Albrecht the Bear, the first margrave of Brandenburg, had finally cleared of Slavs in 1157 began with its devastation in Anglo-American air raids during the Second World War. On the doorstep of Berlin, the Nazis chose Brandenburg to put up a fierce but hopeless stand against the steadily advancing Red Army in April 1945, ensuring its further destruction. War damage is evident everywhere. 'They haven't done anything since the Russians blasted their way through in their drive to Potsdam and Berlin,' complained one woman pensioner.

The communists sought to bring Brandenburg back to life by building the biggest steel combine in the country. On the fringes of the city they put up towering blocks of anonymous flats to house the steelworkers and their families, but they allowed the historic centre to decay, its rot hastened and the health of the local people undermined by the fearful pollution caused by industry on such a scale.

'The neglect has become criminal,' sighed the old woman in the newspaper kiosk in front of the station. 'It wasn't long ago that the cornice of one of the many damaged and uncared for buildings crashed down and crushed to death two children and an adult in the main shopping street.'

Despite their dependence on it, steel was to become a dirty word to Brandenburgers. An outcry accompanied the post-revolution publication of pollution statistics which the communist authorities had kept secret for years. The figures showed that every year the steelworks had been belching 9,000 tonnes of heavy metal dust into the atmosphere, including over

4 tonnes of the toxic metal cadmium. Scientists calculated that since the giant steelworks was started up after the war, altogether 36,000 tonnes of zinc, 12,000 tonnes of lead, 5,000 tonnes of copper, 2,000 tonnes of chrome, 100 tonnes of cadmium and 60 tonnes of nickel have been deposited on what was one of Prussia's finest cities.

When it rains in Brandenburg every drop is blackening. Puddles become slimy black pools where children fear to tread. Washing is hung indoors to dry and no one bothers to clean their car.

Nobody wants the dirt, but there is a human price to cleaning up. The most effective way of cutting the alarming pollution levels meant the rapid shut-down of outdated steel furnaces and making workers redundant. 'I fear for my job, but I fear for the health of my children more,' a steelworker in his mid-thirties told me.

It was a concern appropriately expressed after the revolution by several hundred schoolchildren in a demonstration organized by the New Forum opposition group, which had helped bring down the communists but which was quickly upstaged by the bigger, well-financed western parties when it came to the ballot box. Ten days before East Germans enjoyed the right to choose their own government freely for the first time, the children brought traffic to a standstill by marching down Brandenburg's high street clutching balloons and beating drums behind a banner bearing the motto of the peaceful revolution: 'Wir sind das Volk!' (We are the people!)

Conversations with Brandenburgers were depressing in those days. The euphoria of political liberation had in its grey streets worn off more quickly than elsewhere. Within minutes of arriving at the dilapidated station and asking for directions I was put down. 'God knows what's brought you here! There's nothing but steel and – look – dirt!' a bearded mechanic replied. In his gloom he forgot to mention the fine cathedral on its own island or Brandenburg's other two main churches, the largely fourteenth-century Katharinenkirche and the older Gotthardtkirche, often closed but with an excellent cake-shop on the corner in the Mühlentorstrasse.

Horst Eilert and his wife, behind the counter, were doing a brisk trade in mouth-watering cakes of a type and at a price which would have changed little since his father set up the business before the First World War. A queue of appreciative children spending a few pfennigs pocket-money on the way back from school extended out of the small shop and around its maroon-painted front into the street. His poppy-seed cake was a delicacy.

The Cathedral of Saints Peter and Paul lies splendidly across the water on the far side of Brandenburg, its tall red brick seventeenth-century tower rising nobly over a building which though begun in 1165 is largely fourteenth century. It was renovated in the fifteenth century and again in 1834–6 under the expert supervision of Schinkel. It has its treasures, among them an exquisite pair of candle-bearing bronze angels on the altar that date from 1441, but also curiosities that recall darker moments in German history. In the crypt is a roll of honour, a page of which is turned daily, listing the names of Protestant priests murdered by the Nazis between 1933 and 1945, and on one of the Romanesque capitals in the neighbouring cloister there is an early and vicious example of anti-semitism: the 'Judensau' (Jewish pig). The sow is shown with orthodox Jewish ring locks suckling her progeny. Dating from 1230 to 1235, it can claim to be the oldest known anti-semitic depiction of its kind.

Under communism Brandenburg's cathedral was a magnet for a great number of mostly young people who questioned the system. They came for the sermons, for prayer meetings and vigils, and to hear its well-preserved late baroque organ, built by Joachim Wagner in 1723–5, which has a magnificent array of two thousand pipes and thirty-three registers. But the interest soon flagged once the communist yoke had been thrown off. A year after the revolution organ recitals which earlier had sometimes collected over seven thousand marks from audiences grateful for the distraction could only yield a miserable seventy marks from a half-empty cathedral. Eastern Germany was changing, and so were its people.

The train from East Berlin to Leipzig paused with little ado at Wittenberg; 'Lutherstadt' (Luther City), the station signs reminded travellers. A handful of passengers disembarked, two boarded and the red-lipped stationmistress, fair curls cascading from under her crimson cap, her full chest tightly restrained by her brass-buttoned blue tunic, blew her whistle.

Those who looked out of the window on the right-hand side cannot fail to have seen in the middle distance the overimposing, 'helmet'-capped tower of the castle church, a pompous late nineteenth-century embellishment. And if their eyesight was sharp enough they might just have made out the metre-high words inscribed in Gothic script in a band around the tower's crown: 'Ein' feste Burg ist unser Gott' (A mighty fortress is our God), from the chorale written by Luther, the theme tune, if there had to be one, of Protestantism.

Gloomy, sober Wittenberg, still locked in the Middle Ages, encapsulates the great reforming Protestant spirit which in the early sixteenth century swept from its newly founded university across northern Europe. Other German towns, whether Eisleben, where he was born and died, Erfurt or Eisenach, can also claim a close association with Martin Luther, but none is so haunted by him.

In its heyday from the turn of the fifteenth to the early sixteenth century Wittenberg attracted an extraordinary collection of critical and original minds, enough to make it the cradle of the Reformation. First there was the formidable elector, Frederick the Wise or 'the Fox of Saxony', founder of the university in 1502 and patron of Luther, who made it all possible. The bronze statue of his tomb in the castle church depicts a ruler who feared little and understood much. The list would go on to include Philipp Melanchthon, the sympathetic scholar and humanist who arrived at the university in 1518 as a 21-year-old professor of Greek and later took over Luther's mantle after his death in 1546. Their gravestones, also in the castle church, reveal how nearly identical their lifespan was. Luther, according to the bronze plaque on the simple sandstone tomb, 'lived sixty-three years, two months and ten days'. Melanchthon managed 'sixty-three years, two months and two days'. There was Lucas Cranach the Elder, one of Wittenberg's most prosperous burghers between 1504 and 1547 (he owned a good slice of the town's commerce, including a chemist, printing press, book and herb shops, as well as a wine bar); quite apart from his position as court painter, he was a town councillor and became mayor. His studio was taken over by his son Lucas Cranach the Younger, who was born in Wittenberg, another painter of repute and an acute visual chronicler of his times. The Who's Who of Reformation Wittenberg would also list Hans Lufft, the best known of some thirty printers active in the city at the time, who published Luther's translation of the Bible in 1534 and subsequently his complete works, and Johannes Bugenhagen, a professor, reformer and Luther's confessor. But for all its alumni, Wittenberg's character was uniquely formed by the rebellious Augustinian monk who arrived in 1508 as preacher and professor at the university. More than five hundred years after his birth Wittenberg remains overpoweringly the 'Lutherstadt' its civic subtitle proclaims.

The reformer's presence is felt from the bottom of the town at the 'Luther Oak' where in December 1520 he burned the Papal Bull that threatened his excommunication. It extends westwards down the 'Protestant Mile', which leads past the

Augusteum, the university building where Luther lived, Melanchthon's house, the Renaissance town hall and the distinctive twin-towered city church, to the castle at the far end of Wittenberg. Along this axis, either side of which the city is clustered, everything seems to be associated with Luther. A hosiery shop near the market square had an elaborate arrangement of brassières and corsetry in the window in the midst of which were displayed Luther's words, 'Nobody knows how great God is until they put their trust in him.' Only the Russian T-34 tank elevated into a war monument opposite the castle church belonged to a very different world, and so it was no surprise when a few months after the revolution it was removed by popular request to a western museum.

The original 'Luther Oak' succumbed to the siege of Wittenberg in 1813, a casualty like the great university itself of Saxony's unswerving support for Napoleon. His defeat in 1815 meant that Saxony had to cede three-fifths of its land, including Wittenberg, to Prussia, which already had six universities. So in 1816 Wittenberg's 'Leucorea' university, where Luther and Melanchthon had headed a long and illustrious list of professors, was forced to close, its buildings turned into barracks and its professors ordered to be transferred to Halle. There had been an old students' saying which reflected the university's serious academic reputation: 'Willst du dich vergnügen, geh' sonstwohin; willst du studieren, geh' nach Wittenberg' (Should you seek pleasure, go anywhere else; should you want to study, go to Wittenberg). The present oak was planted in 1830, since when it has developed noble proportions.

No distance from where Luther lived is Melanchthon's house on the main street, built in 1536 with an elaborate Renaissance gable of five arched segments, split front door and charming back garden. It is now a museum given over to the humanist who was called the 'Praeceptor Germaniae' and his times – except very curiously for two rather enjoyable top rooms where a collection of nineteenth-century dolls and toys and one of finely painted flat tin soldiers are exhibited. They are an unexpected, light-hearted distraction from ancient Greek scholarship, theology, Dürer's penetrating 1526 portrait engraving of the broken-nosed Melanchthon and the sombre stillness of the sparsely furnished study where he died. More macabre and with as little relevance is the display in the hall of the tiny shrivelled hand of the 'Giftmörderin' (poison murderess), who killed the four children of her first marriage and in 1728 was the last person to be publicly executed in Wittenberg.

Melanchthon is also to be found in the long, spacious sixteenth-century market place, where his statue stands not far from Luther's, both under handsome baldachins designed by Schinkel in a neo-Gothic mood. Above them towers the city church, St Mary's, rising authoritatively above the houses on one side of the market square. Luther often preached in the church where in 1521 communion in two kinds was first celebrated. Lucas Cranach the Elder's altarpiece of the Last Supper includes portraits on its side panels of Melanchthon and Bugenhagen at a baptism scene and of Luther preaching.

Despite its heavy-handed late nineteenth-century restoration, the castle church, which concludes Wittenberg's 'Protestant Mile', still breathes the Reformation. Schinkel had submitted much more tactful plans for the famous church where at midday on 31 October 1517 Luther so momentously nailed his ninety-five theses to the door. Prussia's most gifted architect wanted to return to the late fifteenth-century style in which it was originally built. But his ideas were not carried through and the church was later restored in a typically bombastic Wilhelmine manner. Reflecting the church–state relations of the time and the dominant spirit of Prussian militarism (every soldier's belt buckle bore the inscription 'Gott mit uns', or 'God with us'), the castle to which it was joined served suitably as a barracks until 1919.

Nobody today would be able to pin anything to the church

door which in 1858 was cast in solid bronze engraved with the full Latin text of the theses. The original indictment of papal indulgences had been 'written in plain hand', according to a contemporary chronicle, and was only intended to launch a scholarly dispute. Instead it unleashed a storm which within two years engulfed the whole of Germany in revolutionary change: the Catholic hierarchy collapsed, celibacy was abolished, monasteries were dissolved and church property seized. What began with the ninety-five theses of Wittenberg led to the tumult of the Reformation and schism.

Wittenberg's reformist tradition was not entirely forgotten during the communist years and by the time they ended with the East German revolution the incumbent of the castle church, Pastor Friedrich Schorlemmer, had played a part of some significance. Like his great predecessor, he had not been afraid to question and criticize the authorities from the pulpit. And afterwards, in the socially and economically harsh transition to capitalism that came with German unification, he remained a champion of the people or, as he preferred to be seen, 'a man of the Protestant Left'.

In the late twentieth century this is still very much Luther's city. 'We have always looked to the great reformer for inspiration, through good times and bad, weighed his words and teaching and acted accordingly,' I was told by a proud citizen in the shadow of the castle church where the old heretic lies.

Excommunicated and banished, in 1521 Luther was sent by Frederick the Wise to the safety of his castle on the Wartburg, outside Eisenach, where the reformer had spent some time during his school days. There he was able to translate the New Testament into German undisturbed under the guise of 'Junker Jörg'. His oak-panelled room remains much as it would have been when he sat for hours in front of his small desk by the flickering candlelight, quill in hand, rendering the Gospels from the Greek into the vernacular.

No fortress is more steeped in German history than the Wartburg, which has dominated the wooded slopes above Eisenach since 913. As well as being Luther's refuge between May 1521 and March 1522, in the twelfth century it was a focus of German poetry and song on account of the 'Minnesänger' (Minnesingers, or knight minstrels) with such ringingly romantic names as Walther von der Vogelweide, Wolfram von Eschenbach, Heinrich von Morungen or Herbort von Fritzlar. The Wartburg was the scene of the legendary song contest of 1206 which inspired Wagner, who stayed in the castle in 1842, to write his opera *Tannhäuser*, first performed three years later. Goethe had already lingered in the half-timbered buildings of this most medieval of fortresses in 1777.

Long the seat of the landgraves of Thuringia, the Wartburg was the most historically symbolic possession of the rulers of Saxony until they surrendered it with the abolition of the monarchy in 1918. Following the revolution in East Germany the head of the family, Prince Michael of Sachsen-Weimar-Eisenach, returned to visit the ancestral seat but laid no claim to it.

Although forever in the shadow of the Wartburg, Eisenach itself is a town of considerable character and interest. It was the birthplace of the great Johann Sebastian Bach and he is remembered in the house on the Frauenplan where he was born in 1685. It is a most superior museum where the woman who takes the entrance tickets will unexpectedly settle down every so often to play some Bach on the Silbermann spinet, a minuet on the Bohemian clavichord or a prelude on the mid-eighteenth-century Swiss chamber organ which form part of the remarkable collection of period instruments that has been assembled. At other times tape recordings of Bach's music drift through the well-arranged rooms, some with furniture of Bach's time, others with displays of books and manuscripts, and all permeated by an air of cosy scholarship and a smell of wood polish. In the best sense it was all extremely East German, even on the eve of unification. The bulk of the visitors were young people and children displaying a deep fascination for a composer whose avuncular statue outside can only have looked on approvingly. Johann Sebastian, whose father, Johann Ambrosius Bach, was the town piper, spent the first ten years of his life in Eisenach before moving to live with his brother Johann Christoph in Ohrdruf after the death of his parents.

Quite apart from Bach, Eisenach has a notable musical history. Franz Liszt conducted there and in June 1890 it witnessed the first performance of Richard Strauss's most Lisztian symphonic poem, *Death and Transfiguration.*

It can also boast a strong revolutionary tradition, the majority of its citizens siding with the peasants in their bloody revolt against the ruling princes in 1525. When the town came to be occupied by the princely armies, seventeen of the rebel leaders were summarily and gruesomely executed.

In 1869 the German Social Democratic Party, so frowned upon by Bismarck, held its inaugural conference there and drew up the 'Eisenach Programme'. When it came to the 1989 revolution the townspeople congregated in the late Gothic Georgenkirche for prayers and protest. They packed its capacious galleries and, once every inch of pew space was occupied, stood at the back before spilling out into the long market square clutching candles, their flickering flames ingeniously protected by shields of empty yoghurt cartons. In front of the deep red Renaissance town hall with its crooked seventeenth-century tower and the modestly baroque castle, which has become a museum, they demanded reform and quickly gained much more.

Eisenach's final claim to fame was the sprawling car factory that produced the Wartburg, which, being made of metal and having a four-stroke motor, was the more solid and powerful rival of the plastic fibre bodied, two-stroke Trabant that most East Germans possessed. The cluster of tall, narrow factory chimneys was as visible as Eisenach's church towers or the ancient Wartburg fortress crowning the rocky crag in the distance. One of the chimneys had the word *Frieden* (peace) painted in white along its side, and peaceful the revolution was, for the first time in German history.

On the straight, tree-lined road to Erfurt, the regional capital where Luther went to university in 1501 and was ordained six years later, lies Gotha, a ruby among the treasure of Thuringia's historic cities. The solid mass of its castle, Schloss Friedenstein, built in the mid seventeenth century as a residence for the ruling ducal family of Sachsen-Gotha, and its generous park still command the city. A curvaceous baroque terrace offers a compelling panorama of Gotha, ancient and modern. Centre stage is held by the town hall, Renaissance and red painted as in Eisenach but grander, with fine old houses, including one that belonged to Lucas Cranach, and fountains on either side. The distant backdrop of modern flats, offices and factories is less attractive but largely obscured by the splendid frontage and the daily smokescreen of lignite smog so typical of Eastern Europe.

With Germany a day or so away from formal unification a young Soviet officer from the nearby garrison was showing his visiting parents the newly imported western washing machines in a shop window while two small Gotha boys were collecting fat conkers as the wind brought them down from an aged horse-chestnut tree. A few yards away was the most evident post-revolutionary change: a caravan renting video tapes around the clock. Queen Victoria and her Sachsen-Coburg-Gotha consort, Albert, would have hardly approved.

In Luther's day a hundred church towers graced Erfurt's skyline; today there remain just over twenty, including the six spires that soar from the two great churches commanding the cathedral hill. East Germany's most ancient city was established as a bishopric in 742 through the efforts of the Anglo-Saxon missionary and martyr St Boniface, 'the Apostle of the Germans'. It was then referred to as Erphesfurt. Well placed on the Via Regia that stretched all the way from Strasbourg to Kiev, it developed as a key trading centre and thrived on the local production of the blue plant dye, woad. Some of the tall storehouses used for drying woad still exist.

But medieval prosperity was not matched in modern times. Wartime bomb damage from Allied air raids was scarcely or only slowly remedied. The river Gera and the picturesque canals linked with it, giving Erfurt something of the air of an East German Bruges, became clogged up with weeds and refuse, and stagnant. Only in recent years was the restoration of the fourteenth-century Krämerbrücke, the only bridge north of the Alps with shopkeepers' houses on either side, begun in earnest.

Generally the communists followed their usual practice of building nondescript blocks of flats on the city outskirts, derisively referred to as 'workers' lockers' by their occupants, while allowing the historic centre to decay. Even if the municipal authorities had good intentions, which is questionable, they were constrained by the marked precedence the state gave to Berlin over the provinces when it came to the reconstruction of historic buildings. Despite the chronic situation in Thuringia's largest city, it was forced to allocate to Berlin 5 per cent of its own building capacity annually. When a great jamboree was made of Berlin's 750th anniversary in 1987 Erfurters responded by attaching to the back of their Trabants stickers declaring, 'Erfurt, 1,245 years old!'

It was not the first time that Erfurt had suffered from the uppishness of Berlin and Prussia. Its great university, founded in 1392 and attended by Luther, gained a reputation during the early sixteenth century as one of Europe's foremost centres of humanist learning, but it was forced to close in 1816 for the same reason as less ancient but equally distinguished Wittenberg. Prussia had enough universities of its own and Erfurt, which had been governed by the French from 1807 to 1814, had with the defeat of Napoleon become yet another Prussian prize.

Earlier, in 1808, Erfurt was the scene of one of those extraordinary historical encounters which raise more expectations than they can ever realize, as when the child Mozart flirted with the ill-fated archduchess Marie-Antoinette, or Goethe and Beethoven walked together in the Bohemian spas. On this occasion Goethe met Napoleon on the fringes of the Congress of Princes – an interview pregnant with unanswered questions.

Erfurt is still under the spell of its long history in spite of communism's misguided attempt in the 1960s and 1970s to give it a modern aspect by cutting a swath through the old centre for the grim Yuri Gagarin ring road and the towering Kosmos Hotel, a Thuringian relative of Leipzig's gloomy Merkur. The Kosmos's only merit was to offer an unparalleled view of the city's magnificent array of church spires and the stunning cathedral hill. The most fashionable shops are still in the Anger, around which the electric trams clatter and ring, the best restaurants those in the highly decorative Renaissance houses that together with the lofty neo-Gothic town hall grace the cramped Fischmarkt.

But it is the cathedral hill which dominates, a great sweep of seventy steps leading up to the two churches from the vast square at their foot. On the left looms the noble Gothic bulk of the cathedral, on the right like a great trident the sharply defined, almost fragile spires of the Severikirche (St Severus's) pierce the sky. The mighty appearance of the cathedral is magnified by the booming of its great bell, the 'Gloriosa'.

Weighing twelve tons, with a height and diameter of over eight feet, this glorious monster in bronze was cast by the master bell-founder Gerhard Wou from Kampen on 8 July 1497. Standing outside the church door almost five hundred years later I let myself be deafened at close quarters by its decibels: it was the same resounding peal that once roused Luther to prayer. Inside the spacious cathedral he would also have known, and may even have been distracted by, the seductive maidens playing heavenly instruments who are so beautifully carved in the choir-stalls of 1350. None is more winning than the not so demure princess who sultrily turns sideways while playing her pan-pipes.

Next door in the lighter, brighter fourteenth-century Severikirche it was reassuring so soon after the feast day of St Michael to see the fearless archangel putting down most coolly a particularly unpleasant-looking horned devil in a painted alabaster relief of 1467. St Severus himself, or at least his bones, lie in a tomb surmounted by a relief dating from 1365 that portrays the fourth-century wool weaver who became bishop of Ravenna, with his wife and daughter on either side.

It was Erfurt which in 1970 so acclaimed the then Bonn chancellor, Willy Brandt, during the first summit meeting between the two divided Germanys that to avoid any further embarrassment the people of northern Güstrow were kept away from his successor, Helmut Schmidt, eleven years later. And it was run-down Erfurt which after the revolution had to face capitalism head-on with its two chief economic activities: the high-technology factories of Robotron, whose products were decidedly 'low tech' by western standards, and the production of horticultural seeds for which it had been known since the mid eighteenth century. Woad, on which Erfurt's prosperity had once been so soundly based, had long ceased to be counted on as 'blue gold'.

*

No driver I know instils greater confidence than Stephen Baxter. Had he not reached the higher realms of corporate consultancy, he could always have fallen back on this more mundane ability. A master of both the seamless gear change and precision navigation – most motorists seem able to excel only at one or the other – he yet had difficulties finding our route out of Erfurt to Weimar. The dismal Yuri Gagarin ring road took us repeatedly to the heartless industrial suburbs and corrective action brought us invariably back to the huge reassuring expanse of the cathedral square. On the third attempt, despairing that this once great city should ever release us, we disengaged from Yuri Gagarin and to our surprise quickly found the old, well-tried road to Weimar. Like the other roads we had followed in Thuringia, it was slow, narrow and lined with trees, every shade of their yellow, brown and red leaves gloriously resplendent in the autumn sun.

If one figure could and should symbolize newly regained German unity and a national identity based on culture and enlightenment rather than either military might or economic dominance, then it was Goethe. No German had ever been so amazingly diverse in his interests and talents. Even the remarkable ability of Schinkel, who was so proficient in such a range of styles of architecture, in drawing, painting and design, was limited by comparison. In a long lifetime which had bridged the Prussian absolutism of Frederick the Great and the French imperialism of Napoleon, both of which he had observed firsthand, Goethe had managed to create a German cultural consciousness within Europe. The Germans had been barbarians, and would again in modern times return to the role of the Hun, but they had on occasions, as Goethe demonstrated, been immensely civilized. No wonder then that after the 1939–45 war where Britain had the British Council flying its cultural flag abroad, West Germany employed its well-distributed Goethe Institutes to propagate its best side.

For all his travels, whether to the ancient cities of Italy or the fashionable spas of Bohemia, no place became more closely identified with Goethe than Weimar, where he spent the last fifty years of his inordinately full life.

With the days to unification slipping by, it was imperative to be there for the occasion rather than brasher Berlin, which had inimitably celebrated and anticipated the event on a rainy afternoon just over nine months earlier. Furthermore, it had been to Weimar that the National Assembly had retired to escape the pressures of Berlin when adopting a new constitution and founding a republic in 1919.

Weimar, we had been told, was hopelessly booked out, but we were determined to try our luck. The place to stay in eastern Germany's most elegant city is unquestionably the Elephant. It was there that friends of Goethe were often put up and ever since it has enjoyed a reputation as the city's premier address, even retaining its charm through communism. Far from returning a frosty response to our presumptuous inquiry about rooms at a time when German history was being made, the splendidly rotund, good-natured girl running the reception instantly gave us not only an encouraging smile but two keys. Against the odds, we had secured the Elephant's last two rooms with unexpected ease. Other guests for the occasion were the West German economics minister with his unprepossessing bodyguards and, more interestingly, Prince Michael of Sachsen-Weimar-Eisenach and his family.

Weimar, thanks to Goethe and the circle of thinkers, poets and artists Duke Carl August (Charles Augustus) attracted to this late eighteenth-century German Parnassus, is overwhelmingly classical in spirit, if not always in appearance. It has its Renaissance relics: corners of the castle and two fine houses in the market square, in one of which Lucas Cranach the Elder died in 1553. In the castle gallery there is a rich collection of Cranach's works, all, except for a coldly erotic Venus, reflecting the particularly Germanic cruelty of his age: the paintings are peppered with instruments of torture and torn flesh. But unlike Eisenach or Erfurt, Weimar's mood is hardly medieval. It does not breathe the Reformation like other cities in this corner of Germany; Luther does not loom around every corner, even though he is well portrayed in the crucifixion altarpiece painted by Cranach for the city church. Far from any fire and brimstone, there is in Weimar a feeling of comfortable security that not only endured but thrived under both the Nazis, whom it voted into office as early as 1929, and the communists who followed. Weimar is almost self-consciously civilized, genteel, cosy and correspondingly secular. Moulded by the antiquities and ideas Goethe brought back from Italy, its taste is cleanly neo-classical, matching France's 'style empire' with the best of German Biedermeier.

More than the disjointed castle, a medley of different styles, Goethe's house on the Frauenplan remains the hub of Weimar, from which, in his words, 'the gates and streets led to all the corners of the world'. An unostentatious baroque building dating from 1709, Goethe at first rented only part of it until Duke Carl August bought the whole house for him in recognition of his duties and services as a privy councillor. He needed the space for his constantly expanding collection of antiquities, works of art and scientific and rock samples. By the time of his death the inventory of the collections catalogued altogether 50,000 pieces, made up of 26,511 works of art, 18,000 geological specimens and some 5,000 objects related to his scientific studies. He redesigned the fourteen-room house himself to accommodate the collection, reserving the upstairs rooms for their exhibition and for entertaining. His private rooms were downstairs, giving out on to the delightful back garden he cultivated lovingly. There hangs on the study wall a programme of work for Herzog, his gardener, as left the day

Goethe died. But unlike so many once splendid gardens in Eastern Europe, Goethe's has continued to be well tended. The vines are still trained carefully outside his bedroom and study windows; the herb corner remains meticulously labelled.

The modest, almost spartan bedroom with its single window looking on to the garden has been left as it was when the great German died there in his chair at noon on 22 March 1832, weary, having achieved the grand age of eighty-two and witnessed an extraordinary span of European history. The only other furniture is a low footstool, his simple single bed with its faded red eiderdown and two small tables. A cord bell-pull hangs down by the bed, and a small brown rug covers little more than a yard of bare wooden floor. A patterned green hanging decorates two of the walls while the monotony of the others is only relieved by a geological chart, two barometers and a thermometer. The room connects directly with a study furnished and equipped solely for work, containing several writing desks, lecterns, a table, three Chippendale chairs, cabinets and a cupboard with shelves. Nothing but the mirror on the wall and the pleasing view of the garden through the two windows could distract from thought. The poet's private quarters were completed by his library of 6,500 volumes next door.

From this pleasant den of scholarship Goethe would escape, when not engaged in court duties, to the neighbouring inn, the White Swan (Zum weissen Schwan), for refreshment and company. 'The White Swan will greet you at all times with open wings,' Goethe wrote, and on the eve of unification, having steeped ourselves in his poetry, drawings, experiments and ideas, we followed his example and adjourned to the comfort of the hospitable Swan. The cannon-ball embedded in its outside wall remains an intriguing reminder of the town's shelling and occupation by Napoleon's troops after the battle of Jena in 1806. Schiller, with whom Goethe developed such an inspiring friendship, occupied the house next door during his first Weimar sojourn. He was later to buy the much more handsome late baroque town house on the former Esplanade in 1802 and live there for the last three years of his life.

The eve of German unification was marked in Weimar by fireworks, a Wagner opera and, as throughout East Germany, mixed emotions. By mid-afternoon workmen restoring the castle were drinking beer and raucously practising choruses of 'Deutschland! Deutschland!'

Schoolchildren anticipated the German Unity national holiday by stocking up at market stalls with penny bangers and squibs, previously unavailable even for officially sanctioned communist events. The usually sedate English park laid out in such good taste by Goethe beside the river Ilm reverberated to their repeated echo. In the market place one stallholder was trading briskly in 'Unity Sekt' bearing a label in the red, black and gold national colours. Another dealer found much less demand for his stock of German tricolour elastic braces. Several jewellers were selling alarm clocks and watches for twenty marks with the national flag and the words, in English, 'Germany, it's time.'

In the communist-named Platz der Demokratie, in front of the Fürstenhaus (now the home of the Franz Liszt College of Music) and next to the equestrian statue of Duke Carl August, so reminiscent of Rome's Marcus Aurelius, an ungainly sculpture incorporating barbed wire was suddenly unveiled: a frontier marker and crash barrier, all jumbled together and entitled *Grenze* (Border). Upsetting the square's harmony like a rather jarring piece of modern music inserted amidst a programme of Haydn symphonies, it aroused no more than fleeting curiosity among the conservative townsfolk.

The National Theatre, gaily bedecked with red and white Thuringian flags, was performing Wagner's *Tannhäuser* as its final offering before unification, though it was his *Lohengrin* which Liszt, 'conductor extraordinary' to the court of Weimar, had first directed 140 years earlier.

Outside the soberly classical building, in front of the famous double statue of Goethe and Schiller, workmen were busily erecting a stage for a live four-hour television transmission on 'Unity Day'. And inside, queuing for a seat for the opera, Lotte Hiller, aged eighty-three, said she was looking forward to reunification. 'Perhaps finally I shall be able to get a clear telephone line when I speak to my daughter in Jena – it's only a few kilometres away.'

Others saw unification as an excuse for heavy drinking and lined up outside liquor shops for trays of West German canned beer. 'Kill the Reds!' bellowed one bearded man who had begun celebrating early and was zigzagging down the Dimitroff-strasse. Groups of locally based Russian artillerymen walked nervously in the Schillerstrasse, Weimar's main shopping street.

Next to the house where Franz Liszt lived for almost twenty years, its drawing-room still draped with the same red and black curtains and dominated by his Bechstein grand piano, is a park enclosing a small Russian war cemetery, its gate surmounted by an iron hammer and sickle, now symbolic of another age. As the morning sun filtered through the yellowing leaves and caught the dew glistening on the simple gravestones, the stillness was disturbed only by a family of blackbirds busily pecking at the turf and the occasional red squirrel collecting nuts for its winter stockpile.

Monetary union three months earlier had resulted in Weimar's shops being completely restocked with western goods that many found hard to afford. But its outward appearance was little changed. The air remained heavy with the acrid smell of polluting lignite, the odour of Eastern Europe.

'We are all worried – about our jobs, about our rents, about prices, but the sooner the process is completed, the better,' said a middle-aged shopkeeper, who sold me a finely blown Thuringian glass vase. 'We asked for this, now we cannot complain.'

Though the transition for Weimar, privileged because of its rich cultural heritage, was likely to be easier than for less favoured, more industrial and run-down cities, signs of strain were already emerging.

A once popular café had closed down to make way for a Bavarian bank, prompting a forlorn sign outside with the sentiment, 'Did the 1989 revolution only mean we would lose a café and gain a bank?'

Then the tourists promised to be bothersome. 'Less than a year ago our museums were deserted and one half expected to bump into Goethe in one of the empty rooms of his house. Now we are braving a mass tourist invasion for which we are ill prepared,' complained a museum assistant. A Darmstadt publisher was financing the introduction in the house of a central heating system for the winter.

Meanwhile at the Elephant, preparations were afoot 'to dance in the new times'. Westernization was to be ensured by the presence of two Filipino girl singers with plenty of amplification.

But returning from the evening of Wagner at the opera through streets crackling with prematurely exploding fireworks, we preferred to surrender ourselves to the excellent offices of the Elephant's head waiter, who as in the opening of Thomas Mann's *Lotte in Weimar* was a most cultivated man. He placed us at a table next to Prince Michael of Sachsen-Weimar-Eisenach and his family and brought us omelettes stuffed with Russian salmon caviar accompanied by one of the last bottles of good East German wine. At five minutes to midnight he sent the wine waiter to the tables with a trayful of glasses of champagne. 'Take two, for both Germanys!'

Glasses in hand, we all trooped upstairs and out on to the

market place as the town hall's clock of Meissen porcelain struck midnight, Germany became one again and the sky and square exploded in an orgy of shattering bottles and fireworks.

The price of too wild a party risks being a wretched hangover. And so it was with German unification. October 3 dawned brightly, a clear, crisp morning full of promise greeted the street cleaners as they swept up the debris of broken bottles and glasses, of spent and charred firecrackers. The crash and clatter of the cleaning-up operation must have grated on sensibilities left frayed and fragile by the long night. Apart from the dustmen and sweepers, the streets were strangely deserted. Occasionally and at long intervals pockets of revellers, arm in arm in twos, threes or sometimes solitary, bottle still in hand, staggered into sight, giddily winding a tortuous route home.

Hangovers are inevitably disagreeable and a cause of regret. But they pass. However, the unification hangover was exceptional for its duration. Apparently no effective pick-me-up had either been devised or was available. Six months later with eastern Germany, or 'the five new states' (*Neue Länder*) as the area had come to be termed in the West, on the brink of complete bankruptcy, the gloom and despondency that came with the hangover persisted. The transition from a communist 'command economy' to capitalism was proving much more painful than East Germans had been prepared to anticipate when in their first free elections they voted so overwhelmingly to become part of the affluent West and possessors of the prized Deutsche Mark. Unemployment soared and lay-offs mounted daily as industrial and other concerns – including the state airline – were no longer deemed viable in free-market conditions and forced to close down. New investment from the West was slow in coming and well short of the desired scale. The euphoria of shedding the communist yoke began to be forgotten as a mood of bitterness swept through the neglected East, a feeling that after all the people of eastern Germany had been through they had yet been hoodwinked, even swindled by western promise.

The first president of reunited Germany, Richard von Weizsäcker, a politician with a strong sense of history who on more than one occasion previously had uttered suitably soothing and judicious words at the right moment, planned his inaugural official visit to Saxony in February 1991 to coincide with the anniversary of the terrible wartime destruction of Dresden, its capital. The situation was, he warned sternly, 'alarming', and it was 'time those in the West opened their eyes to the joint problem in the East and gave encouragement to the people there'. The East might have been rediscovered; it still had to be saved.

Select Bibliography

Angeloff, Therese, *Meine Seele hat ein Holzbein*, Munich, 1982.

Baedeker's Berlin u. Potsdam, Leipzig, 1878.

Baedeker's Nordost-Deutschland, Leipzig, 1902.

Bassett, Richard, *A Guide to Central Europe*, London, 1987.

Braun, Hermann, and Neubauer, Michael, *Goethe in Böhmen*, Hof, 1982.

Dawson, W. H., *Danzig: The Independent City-state*, London, 1922.

Farmborough, Florence, *Warsaw: Historic Capital of a State Reborn*, London, 1922.

Fontane, Theodor, *Wanderungen durch die Mark Brandenburg*, 4 vols., Berlin, 1862–82.

Goethe, Johann Wolfgang von, *Autobiographische Schriften*, Berlin edn, vol. 13, Berlin, 1960.

   Selected Verse, translated and with an introduction by David Luke, London, 1964.

Granville Baker, Lt-Col. B., *Bohemia: Hill-girt Entity of Central Europe*, London, 1923.

   From a Terrace in Prague, London, 1923.

Jerome, Jerome K., *Dresden: Saxony's Fair Capital on the Elbe*, London, 1922.

Kristek, Jan (ed.), *Mozart's 'Don Giovanni' in Prague* (essays), Prague, 1987.

Kugler, Franz, *Geschichte Friedrichs des Grossen*, illustrated by Adolph Menzel, Berlin, 1842.

Macaulay, Lord, *Frederic the Great*, Edinburgh, 1842.

Mittenzwei, Ingrid, *Friedrich II von Preussen*, Berlin, 1979.

Select Bibliography

Olivovà, Věra, *The Doomed Democracy: Czechoslovakia in a Disrupted Europe 1914–1938*, translated by George Theiner, London, 1972.

Ploetz Verlag, *Preussens Grosser König* (essays), Freiburg, 1986.

Reid, Major P. R., *The Colditz Story*, London, 1952.
Colditz: The Full Story, London, 1984.

Thiel, Rudolf, *Martin Luther: Ketzer von Gottes Gnaden*, Berlin, 1933.

Index

Index

Index

Index

Index

Index

Index

Index

Index